Tsunami of Blood

2nd Edition

HOW FEAR-MONGERING POLITICIANS, HATE-MONGERING THEOLOGIANS AND IRRESPONSIBLE PRESS ARE GUIDING US TO AN AGE OF HORRORS

SKIP CONOVER

Words Matter, LLC
Suite 130, 3 Church Circle
Annapolis, MD 21401
410-280-6685

Designed by Jocie Salveson
The Lockwood Agency, Visalia, California

Manufactured in the United States of America

Library of Congress Cataloging-in-Publication Data
Conover, Donald L.
Conover, Skip
Tsunami of Blood: How Fear Mongering Politicians, Hate Mongering Theologians, and Irresponsible Press Are Guiding Us to an Age of Horrors / Donald L. Conover

ISBN-13: 978-0-6151-3978-4

"*Words Matter*
and *Tsunami of Blood*
are like the helpless ravings of a seismologist,
who has seen a 9.5 earthquake
on his instruments, and knows there is
nothing he can do to stop
the imminent catastrophe
but shout at the dark."

Table of Contents

Foreword ... 9
Prologue ... 11
This Is What I Believe ... 13
Chapter 1: The Kaleidoscope Shifts ... 19
Chapter 2: So You Want to Be a Pundit!? ... 23
Chapter 3: Flight from Death ... 29
Chapter 4: Unstuck in Time ... 31
Chapter 5: Terror Management Theory ... 35
Chapter 6: The Glory of God ... 39
Chapter 7: Disgusted ... 43
Chapter 8: Mitt Romney's Speech to Heritage Foundation ... 47
Chapter 9: Sheldon Solomon Explains the Psychology of Suicide Bombing ... 49
Chapter 10: Respect ... 53
Chapter 11: "Sectarian" Is No Better ... 57
Chapter 12: Reality Check ... 61
Chapter 13: Abu Yousef ... 65
Chapter 14: Where Are Our Leaders? ... 67
Chapter 15: Mohammed Abbas ... 69
Chapter 16: Three Kinds of Muslims ... 71
Chapter 17: One for the "Good Guys" ... 73
Chapter 18: Contradictions ... 77
Chapter 19: Corruption ... 81
Chapter 20: Lubna Hussain ... 83
Chapter 21: "America" is Self Correcting ... 85
Chapter 22: We Can Close Gitmo ... 89
Chapter 23: Ahmadinejad Makes Monkeys of Western Press ... 91
Chapter 24: Lubna Hussain's Comment ... 93
Chapter 25: My First Meeting with Lubna Hussain ... 95

Chapter 26: CNN Compared to Hitler's Propaganda Machine 99
Chapter 27: Bad Dream, Good Dream 103
Chapter 28: Lori's 9/11 105
Chapter 29: Planting Organs 109
Chapter 30: In Memoriam: July 11, 2006 111
Chapter 31: Pyrrhic Victory 113
Chapter 32: Wrong Move 115
Chapter 33: Mohammed's Honeymoon 119
Chapter 34: Distressing News 121
Chapter 35: An Open Letter to Nick Robertson 125
Chapter 36: Recognizing Reality 127
Chapter 37: "Under God" 131
Chapter 38: Sunni v. Shia 133
Chapter 39: Very Little Time 135
Chapter 40: Tinkering with Population 137
Chapter 41: Where Are the Muslim Clerics in Iraq? 139
Chapter 42: What Is a Mosque? 141
Chapter 43: Saudi Arabia Takes the High Ground 143
Chapter 44: He's Just a Feckless Old Man in a Turban 145
Chapter 45: Losing Progressive Arabs 149
Chapter 46: It's the Stupidity Stupid 151
Chapter 47: Seven Habits of Highly Ineffective Governments 153
Chapter 48: Media Shame of the Week 157
Chapter 49: Advertisers – That's the Ticket 161
Chapter 50: America's Peril 163
Chapter 51: Letter to Advertisers 167
Chapter 52: Laws of Physics 171
Chapter 53: Media War 175
Chapter 54: The Conover Doctrine 179
Chapter 55: Leadership Shame of the Week And Corollary 23 181
Chapter 56: Fifty Questions for the Women of Iraq, Lebanon, Israel, Palestine, Iran, and Syria 185
Chapter 57: Costs and Benefits of Confrontation with Hezbollah 187
Chapter 58: The Hypocrite and The Charlatan 191
Chapter 59: Worse than a 9.5 Earthquake! 193
Chapter 60: Counterpoint Needed 195
Chapter 61: Sowing Seeds of Distrust 197
Chapter 62: Double Standard? 199
Chapter 63: We Need to Turn It Around 201
Chapter 64: News Flash: August 29, 2006 203
Chapter 65: Democracy? Who Are They Kidding? 205
Chapter 66: Economics; Human Rights; Right to Pursue Dreams 209
Chapter 67: The American Dream Is a State of Mind 213
Chapter 68: The "Butcher of Qana" on Capitol Hill 215

Chapter 69: On Separation of Church and State 217
Chapter 70: "The Rapture" Comes, but Life Goes On 219
Chapter 71: Should We Fear Iran's Nuclear Developments? 223
Chapter 72: The Power and The Glory 225
Chapter 73: Overwhelmed with Wombs 229
Chapter 74: In Memoriam September 8, 2006 231
Chapter 75: What It Takes to Win the War on Terror 233
Chapter 76: A Time for Cynicism 237
Chapter 77: The Importance of Unbiased Media 239
Chapter 78: Muslims Elected George W. Bush 241
Chapter 79: Response to a Conservative 243
Chapter 80: To God Direct 247
Chapter 81: On Monarchies and Nehru Jackets 249
Chapter 82: I Rest My Case 253
Chapter 83: Where Are the Moderate Muslims? 255
Chapter 84: Imperialist Power 257
Chapter 85: Bush as Neville Chamberlain? 261
Chapter 86: Iraqi Death Report, True or False? 263
Chapter 87: Muhammad Yunus, Beacon for Peace 265
Chapter 88: Death of My Father 267
Chapter 89: Dean Dianne Lynch 271
Chapter 90: Samar Fatany 275
Chapter 91: Moralists at Sea in a Sea of Immorality 279
Chapter 92: Withdrawal from Iraq Costs and Benefits 283
Conclusion 291
Acknowledgements 295
Bibliography 297
Index 299
About the Author 306

Foreword

Many people worldwide are concerned about the human condition, especially the multiple crises in the Middle East in general, and within the Muslim community in particular. As an American executive working in the region, Donald L. ("Skip") Conover, shares such worries, pondering current events there and their implications for the future. Like all of us, *Skip* was profoundly affected by three horrendous happenings in the opening of our new millennium – the 9/11 attacks of 2001 upon the United States; the terrorist murders in Riyadh, Saudi Arabia, in May 2003; and the London bombings of July 7, 2005, in the United Kingdom. The perpetrators were all anarchists and terrorists who happened to be Muslims bent on destroying Western power, as well as Arab leadership and values. In human civilizations, anarchy has periodically arisen among extremists aiming to destabilize society by overthrowing governments, authority, as well as the rule of law, so as to cause political disorder and social confusion. Londoners have learned to cope with many of this ilk over the centuries, experiencing a series of bombings and uprisings from many quarters.

Thus, the future author of *Tsunami of Blood* analyzed these events, worsened by America's 21st century precipitous interventions in Afghanistan and Iraq, both Muslim societies. He became incensed at the way modern media, especially CNN and Fox News, reported such happenings superficially, indiscriminately blaming the global Muslim community of some 1.3 billion people. From his extensive travels in the Middle East and friendship with many Muslims, he knew that 99% of them were moderate persons who peacefully practiced the religion of Islam. Apart from writing letters of protest, his first project to remedy the distortions and promote more balanced views was to initiate a current affairs program called *Words Matter*, which has been broadcast nationally (www.wordsmatter.tv).

Then on June 12, 2006, Skip started his on-line diary to share his own thoughts and experiences on these matters. These electronic communications became, in effect, the original edition of *Tsunami of Blood.* The blog was intended to forestall a future bloodbath between East and West, while promoting mutual understanding between Christians and Muslims. His "stream of consciousness" writings would result in reactions from thousands of readers in 115 countries. Subsequently, Conover's Internet installments (www.tsunamiofblood.com) became the basis of this second edition of his book, now in print for those of us who prefer to read a bound, hardcopy.

Conover is an astute observer of the contemporary world scene, who brings a rare perspective to a variety of related topics. Raised during formative years in Japan and educated in the United States, he served as a Marine in Vietnam, ending his military career with the rank of Lieutenant Colonel. Then Skip went on to become an international attorney and executive, as well as founder of his own company with partners in India. His extensive Middle Eastern travels have given him unique insights about the many crises in that region.

In this current version, the writer's Prologue sets forth his premises for this volume, as well as a listing of his personal beliefs. This Prologue enables readers to respond to the author's purposes and convictions in preparing this publication. In these pages, Skip's commentary covers many themes, such as: the evolution of his mindset; position on the war and chaos in Iraq; disgust with international media reporting; results of video interviews with prominent experts and authors; hijacking of Islam and distortions of the *Koran* by fundamentalist fanatics; arrogance and misunderstanding by American political "leaders"; terror management theory; Western misperceptions of the Muslims in 57 countries; how to build bridges of understanding with the Muslim world, especially in North America; diverse Muslim reactions to imperialistic interventions in their societies and the divisions within Islam; how to win the "war on terror" and prevent a "tsunami of blood"! Finally, in the Epilogue he summarizes his major points, adding his views on more recent developments in Iraq, like the emerging civil war and the inchoate execution of its dictator, Saddam Hussein.

Skip Conover has "bared his soul" in this forthright book. Readers may not always agree with him, but his input is "mind stretching"! As the author/editor of some 45 books, myself, I welcome this published text of *Tsunami of Blood*, and hope readers will share my enthusiasm. Both the electronic and published versions of this work demonstrate how one person can indeed impact, and maybe, even change our world!

Philip R. Harris, Ph.D., La Jolla, California, 2006
Co-author and co-editor of the *Managing Cultural Differences Series*
(www.books@elsevier.com/management)

Prologue

These days, I am seeing the World "as if through a glass, and darkly." For a year, I was arguing for complete withdrawal from Iraq, as the only way to end the United States being blamed by both sides for the mess. The kaleidoscope of my liberal arts education and experiences has changed, once more, and not for the reasons the Administration espouses publicly. I am now of the opinion that reduction of hostilities and/or American departure from Iraq will be the beginning of 25 very bad years.

Here's the premise of *Tsunami of Blood*:

1. Iraq is prologue; the real problems will come post a reduction of hostilities in Iraq. As a military man, the best training I can give my men and women, short of actual combat, is a "live fire exercise." When we took Afghanistan away from *Al Qaeda*, and attacked Iraq, we provided Osama bin Laden with his dream scenario; a reason to recruit Muslim young men (to get the infidels out of Muslim lands) and a "live fire exercise," to train his "army." When things settle out in Iraq, even a nervous truce, this "army" will have nothing to do. Many of them are Saudis (about 50%), Jordanians, Syrians, Egyptians, etc. They will be going home.

2. There is a very dangerous demographic developing in the Kingdom of Saudi Arabia, and other populous and volatile parts of the Arab World. For the purposes of this introduction, I will limit this discussion to Saudi Arabia, but the same applies in many other places. Approximately 22% of the Saudi population is between 15 and 23, about 3.5 million people, and half of those are men. What happens to all of that testosterone when there are no movies, few sports teams, little needed education, few jobs (about 22% unemployment in a country that has 6 million guest workers), very little access to women (even to share a coke), and no other real outlets for the inevitable frustrations? In my view, this is a crisis waiting to happen.

3. Now let's envision a reduction of hostilities in Iraq causing the surviving junkyard dog fighters to go home—in *The Washington Post* of June 11, 2006, there's an article entitled "Smoke of Iraq War 'Drifting Over Lebanon': In Political and Social Life, Returned Fighters Inspire Climate of Militancy."

4. For a catalyst, let's mix the demographic and the junkyard dog fighters, coming home from Iraq, with the probable targeting *Fortune* magazine recently published in an article (April 11, 2006), which said that the fall of the Saudi Royal Family would cause oil prices to go to $262 per barrel, nearly 4 times the highest to date. *Al Qaeda* already knew this, so I am not blaming *Fortune* for a diarrhea-of-the-pen sin.

5. If the Saudi Royal Family falls, what do our politicians do? ..... And this only considers the issue of Saudi Arabia. Yikes!

Like a *tsunami* at sea, the potential of these issues, all mixed together, is still invisible, but carries tremendous power. I'll readily acknowledge that I may be totally wrong, as many will accuse, but I am writing because I feel I'm one of the few Americans who sees that something might be amiss on the far side of Iraq. I hope I'm wrong!

This book is about the origins and experiences I've had since the London bombings of July 7, 2005, in creating *Words Matter*, a current affairs television program and radio network, and their accompanying web sites, www.wordsmatterradio.net and www.wordsmatter.tv. I fear *Words Matter* and *Tsunami of Blood* are like the helpless ravings of a seismologist, who has seen a 9.5 earthquake on his instruments, and knows there is nothing he can do to stop the imminent catastrophe but shout at the dark.

This Is What I Believe

December 1, 2006

In reading a book of opinion, like *Tsunami of Blood*, it is quite natural that you would want to know where the author stands on a variety of issues. These are my beliefs, which are relevant to the understanding of this book:

1. I believe that The United States of America, with all of its faults and problems, has the best system of government and the best economic system, of all of the countries in the World. The results speak for themselves.

2. I believe all media outlets should recognize that we must help Muslims disassociate their religion from criminal behavior by murderers and thugs. Just because a political party calls itself Islamic, and wraps its leaders in the symbols of Islam, does not make it Islamic. To the extent that media outlets continue to allow this confusion to exist, they play into the hands of the gangsters, who are making our World so treacherous today!

3. I believe that theologians must recognize and acknowledge that God has made everything on our fragile planet. God has dictated that we will worship in different manners. Who are mortals to claim that one way that God has dictated is less valid than another way?

4. I believe that God speaks to all human beings every day. Unfortunately, most of us fail to listen!

5. I believe in the Wisdom of the average man and woman.

6. I believe that we should start all negotiations with those things we have in common, rather than with those things we view differently. All human beings want the right to a decent life, with a standard of living commensurate with our

willingness to work hard; we want the right to raise a family, and see our children and grandchildren prosper; and we want the right to grow old, and be respected in our later years.

7. I believe that politicians who use fear to manipulate their people should be invited to joins the ranks of the retired. Let us face our problems full on and pragmatically, without being stampeded to one view or another.

8. I believe that the leaders of both Israel and Palestine are reprehensible for not having found a way for their people to live in peace over the last 100 years. Within the past few days, I have heard pundits urging the USA to send a "high powered delegation," to find a solution to the problems there. But isn't that what Joseph Sisko and Henry Kissinger were doing with their "shuttle diplomacy" post-1967. Have we (human beings) learned nothing in the past 40 years?

9. I believe that Islam is a valid World View, which supports the spiritual needs of approximately 1.3 Billion human beings.

10. I believe that politicians in many countries impoverish their people, by failing to open their eyes to what works and what does not work economically, and the results for the standards of living of their people prove my point. One of my favorite pet peeves is the idea that there must be 51% or greater local ownership of an investment, in order to accept investment from abroad. This discourages investment from abroad! Why would a company invest all of its intellectual capital and money into an operation from which it can take only 49% percent of the profits, or less? Any business executive worth her salt can do better than that in almost anything in the USA. So why should they take their know how to the developing country?

    Japan is an example of a country, which made the change, and benefited from it hugely. About 1970, Japan began allowing 100% investments from abroad. Let me give an example of what that meant economically, in just one small case, where I was directly involved. I created an American subsidiary in Japan in 1979, 100% owned by the USA parent. Over the next 5 years we built a $10 million annual business, we employed 100 Japanese citizens, and, in its first five years, my company never took any money out of Japan. Instead, it continued to reinvest. I was the only American, who earned anything from that venture, during that period. Since I lived in Japan, most of my earnings were also spent in Japan, thereby further enhancing the Japanese economy. How is that bad?

    In the United States, we accept foreign investment from almost anyone. Indeed, The People's Republic of China owns a very large proportion of our United States Treasury bonds.

11. I believe that Diversity is The Glory of God, and that the Diversity we have

accepted in North America, now The United States of America, is the fundamental factor, above all others, which makes the American economy the driving force of the World economy. It gives us a far higher standard of living than any other country with a population larger than 10 million people. We temper (strengthen) our economy by adopting every good idea from the best and the brightest of all societies (they export their brains to the USA, because of their own inept economic policies, which do not provide sufficient opportunity for their smartest citizens), and, over time, we pound all bad ideas out of the system. The only countries with higher per capita GDPs, and there are 5 of them, are less than 2% the size of the United States, and most have some special circumstance, which gives them their position. Here are the 2003 per capita GDP standings of some major countries, for comparison of the performance of their economic systems:

#6United States	$41,800	
#14 Canada	$34,000	(The next country with over 10 million people.)
#34 Qatar	$27,400	
#43 Bahrain	$23,000	
#56 Kuwait	$19,200	
#72 Oman	$13,200	
#75 Saudi Arabia	$12,800	
#117 China	$ 6,800	
#160 India	$ 3,300	

12. I believe that we must bridge the gap between the bubble of the Muslim World and the bubble of the Western World. As my *Words Matter* project has been demonstrating, over the past year, people throughout the World believe in peace and mutual respect in almost the same manner. We must find ways for all of our citizens to understand that.

13. I believe that the Muslim community throughout the World must become much more successful in getting its message of Peace heard. It seems to me that many Muslim Americans are reticent, because their families became American very recently. But this reticence leaves the stage to murderers and gangsters, who shout loud enough to drown out the decent Muslims in the World—greater than 99% of all Muslims are not being heard.

14. I believe that the greatest resource any country has is its people. To the extent that countries allow women to be ignored and marginalized, they freely squander ½ of the value of their human capital, any country's greatest and only renewable natural resource. In my experience, women have at least as much brain power as men, which has nothing whatever to do with their sexual equipment. I believe that women should have absolutely equal rights to those of men in society at large. Where would we be without Madame Curie, Susan B. Anthony, and Madelleine

Albright? Where would Islam be without A'isha, Barakah, and Nasibah bint Ka'b? God has dictated that women must bear children, so they carry an extra burden in the family, which puts them in a disadvantaged position vis-à-vis men in competing in society. But, who are mortals to say that their disadvantage should be any greater than what God has given them?

15. I believe in fighting murderers and gangsters, through the courts, if possible, but through our combined strength, if necessary.

16. I believe in compassion, tempered by wisdom. When I find a centipede in my house, I normally help it to walk onto a piece of paper, and then deliver it to the outside of my house. BUT, last winter my mother was overwhelmed in her home by field mice, which were getting into all foodstuffs in the house. It was not possible to help them out of the house. Indeed, my sister had attempted to use "live traps," which allowed the trapping and removing of the field mice, without killing them. Unfortunately, they continuously found their way back into the house, creating a health hazard. I went to the hardware store and bought 10 mouse traps; the deadly kind. I killed 18 mice in 2 days, thereby restoring normal standards of human existence to my mother's home.

17. I believe that Hezbollah is a criminal organization. On October 23, 1983, they exploded what was then called the largest non-nuclear explosion in the history of the World, killing 241 United States Marines and Sailors, who were peace keepers, trying to make it possible for the airport in Beirut to operate, in the face of various Lebanese killing one another. I do not think the fig leaf of having some members in the Lebanese Cabinet changes their stripes. On July 14, 2006, I heard Prime Minister Fouad Siniora of Lebanon, in an interview with CNN, say that the Lebanese government allowed Hezbollah to continue to operate on Lebanon's southern border "as a reminder." I have no objection to a reminder, as long as it is a peaceful reminder. I favor letting the members of Hezbollah live in peace, not forgetting but regretfully accepting that nothing will restore the lives of those 241 Marines and Sailors, and so many others, and this is the only way to put down the weapons and establish peace. BUT, if Hezbollah cannot operate in a peaceful and appropriately diplomatic manner, respecting the Rule of Law, then I believe that the mousetraps should be used until the job is done. I do not condone what Israel has done in the summer of 2006. There are good and bad people and behaviors on all sides, but I believe that the World community can have zero tolerance for gangster behavior. Canada would never allow the United States to condone a criminal gang operating along the northern border of Maine, making incursions into Canada. If the United States would not clean up such a mess, Canada would certainly defend itself and its citizens.

When Debbi and I lived on Capitol Hill, only 14 blocks from The United States Capitol, there was a group of dealers operating a drug house only 4 doors from us.

The street was always crowded with addicts, coming to get their fixes. There were multiple occasions when the FBI tried to raid the house, but informants within the police department, always caused the raids to come up dry. These people thought they were above the law entirely. They stopped paying their electric bill, so their electricity was stopped. The same happened to their water and sewer service. The smell became unbearable. The neighbor next door to the drug house called the Health Department, which found human feces in the bathtub, and bricked the doors and windows of that house that very day. The traffic on our street dropped in half instantly.

In his CNN interview, Prime Minister Siniora was saying that, if only the Israelis would stop their attack, and withdraw from a certain peace of real estate, the reason for Hezbollah's behavior would be gone, and they could begin to operate as a normal political party. I am sorry to say that since Hezbollah is still behaving as gangsters, 23 years after the attack on the Marine Barracks in Beirut, I find his argument difficult to swallow. I believe that if Lebanon expects to be treated as a nation state, with all of the rights, privileges, and obligations thereof, it must control gangster elements, within its own territory, never giving a free pass to such miscreants.

18. I believe that the United States was foolish to allow terrorist training camps to operate around the World. In the 1992 movie, *Patriot Games*, a scene takes place within CIA headquarters, in which one of over one hundred terrorist training camps acknowledged to be operating in North Africa was wiped out in a "black" raid. It was common knowledge, at that time, that such camps were operating in many countries. The United States did next to nothing to change that fact, perhaps because, without the 9/11 attack, there was not enough political will in Washington to solve the problem. Once 9/11 occurred, however, we can never again be so foolish (indeed no government can be so foolish) as to think that it is OK to allow gangster training camps, where illegal activity is the intention, in any part of the World, regardless of how remote. This is not the Boy Scouts!

19. I believe that there is enough blame to go around. I believe that the United States is at fault for the problems in the Middle East. I believe that Israel is at fault for the problems in the Middle East. I believe that the Palestinian government is at fault for the problems in the Middle East. I believe that the government of Lebanon has shirked its obligation to secure its own borders, and prevent a criminal gang from operating within its territory, to the detriment of its neighbor, Israel. I believe more blame could be passed on to other scapegoats. I believe it is time for nation states to do what nation states do, and solve their differences diplomatically. If Palestine wants to be a nation state, its government should behave responsibly, and prove it. Hezbollah is not a nation state, so it should stand down, and assume the role of concerned, but peace loving citizens of Lebanon.

20. I believe that the United States is reprehensible for eviscerating the United Nations. When I was twelve, I visited the UN in New York with my grandfather. I remember what high hopes we had that such an organization could bring World Peace, and solve the problems of famine and disease. As I review the record of American votes at and payments to the UN, over 60 years, however, I am not proud of how the United States has met its own responsibilities. The vote of July 13, 2006 at the Security Council was no exception! This does not fulfill the hope that my grandparents had; nor the hope that my parents had; nor the hope that I had as a boy. What can our leaders possibly be thinking? I expect United States diplomacy to be an example for the World; not a monkey wrench to be dropped into the Hopes of the World. As of 2001, the United States owed the United Nations $2.3 Billion. President Bush spends more than that every 12 hours in Iraq. Couldn't we just stutter step for half a day, and pay the debt? I know there is more to it than that. Misguided politicians are using the debt as some sort of lever to make the UN buckle to some American point of view. I believe we should lead by example, rather than exercise the powers of a deadbeat!

Words Matter, LLC

By Donald L. ("Skip") Conover,
Author and Publisher
December 1, 2006

Chapter 1

The Kaleidoscope Shifts

High above the Saudi desert, flying from Doha, Qatar to Jeddah, Saudi Arabia, dozing perhaps, I had no idea that my life was about to change forever. Over three years of crisscrossing the Middle East had not prepared me for the impact of my dark vision of the future, which led to the writing of this book. Indeed, during that blissful trip, the horrors of terrorism seemed far away in time and space.

"Have you heard the news about London?" were the first words out of my colleague's mouth, after my hour long wait to pass immigration and customs in Jeddah. You would think that an airport, which handles more than two million people within a few days, during the annual *Haj* to Makkah, would be able to push a few sleepy businessmen and off season pilgrims through in a few minutes. But no, like so many things in the Kingdom of Saudi Arabia, unintended consequences abound. Here one of the World's newest fleets of airplanes bakes in the desert sun, far from any terminal, cover, or air conditioning. Here aged pilgrims must struggle down ladders to buses, because the terminal is too small to accommodate even a single airplane. These observations have weight, because this book is, in part, about the failure of one of the World's richest countries to accept the need to modernize quickly, in both infrastructure and attitude.

"No, I haven't," I replied.

"There have been several bombings in London. Many people have been killed," he informed. My mind immediately flashed to an image of two of my best friends, who, on September 11, 2001, were on the same airplane bound to Atlanta. One was stranded there for three days, and had to take a 20-hour bus ride to his final destination in Lafayette, Louisiana. The other found no rental cars available, so he hired a truck to drive back to his home, an evolution of over 24 hours. I wondered what I would be doing to finish my travels in the Middle East, and return home. In the ride to The Jeddah Hilton, my friend filled me in on the details as we knew them.

"Islamic terrorists have blown up three subway trains and a bus in London! Officials believe suicide bombers were used to carry out the attack." This was the gist of what the CNN commentator was saying, when I arrived at my room. I felt I had received two punches in the solar plexus. The first came from the carnage of the attack itself, of course, with all of its senseless destruction. But, it was the second that changed the direction of my life.

"Islamic terrorist," "Islamic extremist," and "ethnic Pakistani" were terms, which caused me to respond viscerally. I had not practiced law for 27 years, but the law of slander came immediately to mind. "How can these CNN reporters be saying these things?" I immediately wondered.

Over the past twelve years, I have traveled in 10 Muslim countries. I have always seen Muslim countries as peaceful places, where the populations are more family-oriented than we have time for in our frenetic modern cultures in the West. This perspective has always allowed me to differentiate between the terrorists of 9/11, and the Muslims I run into in my everyday life. In my personal self-deception, had the luxury of knowing that Muslim countries are quiet places, which respect the family and where the inhabitants respect one another. While I still think this is true, in places where Islam is practiced in a traditional and moderate way, regardless of the specific version of Islam, my views have changed as I have peeled back the layers of the onion, and seen what is beneath the placid surface.

On that first day, July 7, 2005, the initial shock dissipated quickly. My colleague and I needed to discuss business, and the terrorism seemed far away. We turned off the television and had our conversation, not bothering ourselves further with the unfortunate crisis faced by our modern World.

When I returned to my television, CNN's drumbeat was just coming into high gear. Everything was "Islamic terrorist" or "Islamic extremist," and their valuable air was nearly filled with the anguish and sounds of horror. I began to become alarmed by their use of these defamatory terms. There are approximately 1.3 billion Muslims in the World, and very few of them are terrorists or inclined toward senseless violence.

"Don't they know that they are attacking all Muslims everywhere?" I asked myself.

There was little I could do to change the situation then, so I continued my travels. I remained eleven more days in the Middle East, in Oman and Saudi Arabia. Throughout this period, CNN's drumbeat of "Islamic terrorists" and "Islamic extremists" did not change, and stories on the topic seemed to fill more than 90% of their air time. I was becoming alarmed at how that drumbeat must be affecting the more than 300 million Muslim young people around the World. And it was not CNN alone. The BBC, *Al Jazeera*, NBC, and many others were all following CNN's lead, with no consideration of the consequences.

As a business executive, I am painfully aware of the value of one minute of television air time. Even one minute on national television, which we call "PR" (public relations), can cost tens of thousands of dollars. When our global mainstream news media gave the majority of their air time to terrorism, during the weeks following London, they were giving billions of dollars worth of free PR to the terrorists!

As a military man, I know that one important piece of intelligence is damage assessment, after an attack. The media made this requirement easy. Days of anguished faces on the tube, meant that the West had been damaged very severely in London. The images of the "brave" terrorists marching aboard the train at Luten Station, backpacks on their backs, looking like they were going off to Boy Scout camp, inevitably lionized these murderers more than any suicide bomber handler could possibly have hoped. Our media gave terrorism a recruiting poster and training films worth tens of millions of dollars.

Lest you be misled, I do not question the media's right to publish. Indeed, for decades I have been a vociferous promoter of the 1st Amendment Rights, which are among the critical elements which make life in the United States unique. But that does not mean that I must sit silent, if I disagree with the content of our media. Indeed, it is those very rights, which give me the right to criticize their content, particularly when I regard it as dangerous to our way of life.

Chapter 2

So You Want to Be a Pundit!?

Everyone is afraid, in our World situation. There is an important part of my story that cannot be told here, out of deference to a friend. If it someday can be told, it may well be part of an important revision of this book, but at this point in time, "Mum" is the word. The painfully edited version of this chapter, which follows, contains only excerpts of an e-mail exchange, but they are important to give a sense of my thinking, as I departed from Riyadh, on July 17, 2005. .... I was totally disgusted with the international news coverage of the London bombings, which continued in its steady drumbeat—100s of millions of dollars worth of free PR for terrorism; and anguish at the results, as expressed on the faces of the commentators. If Osama bin Laden still lives, he must have been filled with joy! The last thing I did, before leaving my hotel in Riyadh, on my homeward journey, was write an e-mail to a friend. We corresponded throughout my journey home. The following is a severely edited version of the exchange:

Skip Conover wrote:

Dear xxx,

..... I am really very troubled by the way the London story has been handled, particularly by CNN, which is giving the wrong side more free television time than most corporations could hope to buy in a century. This is becoming a cause celebre for me. I have been sitting in the Muslim world for all of the time since the London bombings, and I am frankly appalled by CNN's coverage in particular, and other networks in general. I blame CNN, because the others are simply following their lead. In my opinion, it is time to "turn the ship." I have come to the conclusion that the issues I worry about cannot wait for me to launch them at my Kalmbach Distinguished Alumnus Lecture in the fall. I'm sitting here in Riyadh, about to return to the USA (on Monday afternoon) after 1 month of travel in the Muslim world, including all of the time since the London bombings. I thought that perhaps, by writing to you, I could

suggest ..... The following is an excerpt of my Kalmbach lecture, which contains ideas I had intended to launch when I give my speech in the fall. While these ideas may be overcome by events, if ... I launch them now, I don't think the World can wait that long. Here is what I was planning to say, as part of my lecture in the fall:

Quote: .....

Which leads me to the issue of misperceptions all of us hold about the Middle East. Thanks to that self congratulatory mother of all war mongering media outlets, CNN, all of us are misinformed about the Middle East and the Muslim World. Because they lead with the Baghdad bombing story every half hour, unless there is a bombing story closer to home, many of our countrymen think that all Arabs live in mud huts, in abject poverty, and carry AK47s or worse. The result is that by-and-large CNN is making an entire generation of Americans miss the biggest economic boom for this quarter century.

Our news media needs to add some perspective to their reporting. There were more Americans killed on the highways of Michigan in 2004, than Americans killed in Iraq. Where are the stories decrying the laxity of American drunk driving laws? When 107 people were killed in a train accident in Pakistan, 1 week after the London bombings, the story barely got a map and a telephone interview, and no comments on Pakistan's railway regulations. CNN was back to the drumbeat of the London investigation. What could these so called Media Giants possibly be thinking? I am genuinely sorrowful for the losses in London. I am genuinely sorrowful for the losses in Pakistan, not to mention the 21 people killed in a bus accident in Ethiopia and the >100 miners killed in China during the same week. What CNN is doing is playing right into the hands of the terrorists! By blowing the London incidents out of all proportion, across the World, they are giving the terrorists the free publicity they do not deserve, encouraging more of the World's 300 million young Muslims to join in the glory of whatever they think their cause is.

And I do blame CNN as the main culprit in this problem, because all of the other networks, to include Al Jazeera and Al Arabia, simply follow their lead like lemmings, creating more and more PR for the wrong side! While I respect CNN's accomplishments in the past, they are just being lazy journalists now, by flocking around these terrorist and bombing stories, rather than focusing on a few stories that do nothing but encourage the very behavior about which they are so outraged!

***It is said that sanity and insanity are two sides of the same piece of paper.** What CNN must do is give these events as little play as possible, certainly no more than they merit among the many sorrows of this World, and soldier on, "business as usual, like all of the courageous New Yorkers and Londoners."*

They need to focus on other, at least equally important stories: the decline in American educational standards; the AIDS epidemic in Africa and India; the decline of respect for American values in the rest of the World; the missed economic opportunities in the Middle East. There are plenty of subjects for important stories, without providing free advertising for the terrorists.

UNQUOTE:

If this point of view rings a bell with you, let's .....

Best regards, Skip Conover

By the time I arrived in Dubai, I had a positive response. To which I responded as follows, before boarding my flight to Gatwick:

Dear xxx,

Many thanks! ... I'm in Dubai International now, and will not be home until 6:00 p.m. Monday. ... By the way, I have been thinking that this story comes under the category of the parable of "The King's New Clothes." ... It is about how people can hold an illusion, in this case CNN continuing with its self-congratulatory nature, until someone finally calls them on it. Then the illusion drops away, and the situation is seen by everyone for what it is. Let's talk later in the week.

Best regards, Skip

By the time I arrived in Gatwick, I had a further response, which is deleted. ...By this time I was pleased that my idea, ... , had been well received. Once on my flight across the Atlantic, I wrote the following e-mail, which was the origin of the name of my project, http://www.wordsmatter.tv/.

From: Skip Conover
Sent: Monday, July 18, 2005 2:41 PM
To: xxx
Subject: Words Matter!

Dear xxx,

...

... to make a difference for the Muslim community with respect to terrorism, ... take on the World's largest media networks. It is they that are proliferating the incorrect vision of Islam! It is they that are defaming Muslims in general! For example:

Let us insist, hence forward, that CNN and the other major networks (including Al Jazeera and Al Arabia) stop using the terms "Islamic Terrorists" and "Islamic Extremists." These two phrases are incredibly incendiary, and are NOT appropriately *descriptive. I have traveled very extensively in the Muslim World, including India (31 visits--the second largest Muslim country in the World, after Indonesia), Pakistan (10 visits), Saudi Arabia (16 visits), UAE (too many to count), Qatar (10 visits), Oman, Bahrain, Kuwait, Lebanon, Indonesia, Malaysia, AND I have never heard a single one of my Muslim friends or acquaintances say that these terrorists represent Islam in any form. So the descriptor "Islamic," is by definition incorrect, and needs to be discontinued immediately. Just because these murderers *call themselves* Islamic this or that, does not mean that the media must accept that they are.*

*That just gives them a handle to persuade impressionable young people. ... stop such defamation of a ... religion, not to mention the peaceful national origins of many American and British *citizens*. "Extremists" suggest that there could be a wing of Islam that could reasonably accept such a philosophy in a civilized World ... NOT! "Terrorists" glamorizes these people, suggesting that they might trying to proselityze a reasonable political philosophy within humanity, and that these people are just fighting for that philosophy ... NOT again!*

Let's just call these people "MURDERERS" and be done with it. Let us make certain that every one of the 300 million Muslim youths understand that what these people are doing is MURDER, a crime, and there is NO room in heaven for such people. To the extent that the bad people have hijacked Islam, it is the Muslims who will need to take it back. In reading USA Today, on my flight across the Atlantic (so it might be the European edition), I find a report on P. 4A, which comments on British Home Secretary Charles Clarke going to parliament today to propose security measures that would ban [among other things] "..... glorifying or indirectly inciting terror attacks." In my view, that would ban much of CNN's coverage in the past 11 days. I would personally be against such legislation, because if there are ideas I believe in above all others, they are contained in the First Amendment of the US Constitution, which include freedom of the press. BUT, that does not mean that I condone CNN's outrageous and inexcusable coverage of the London bombings, which I do believe glorifies and indirectly incites terror attacks. I simply believe that it is up to the free market to call them on it, and correct there behavior. It is not appropriate for it to be legislated by government, or we will very soon fall down the slippery slope toward becoming police states.

So, it is up to [us] to "police" [them] by calling them on their ridiculous coverage, and set the record straight about Islam, and about the millions of Americans and British who happen to be Muslim. I guess I should note that I was looking at the International edition of CNN for the past 30 days, so the coverage in the USA might have been somewhat different. The problem is, it is the audiences outside of the USA and UK that are most worrisome. The Wall Street Journal Europe today, P. A10, is referring to the perpetrators of international terrorism as "ethnic Pakistanis," rather than the British citizens they are. If I were Pakistani, I would be absolutely outraged, because they are smearing the entire nation, without identifying who these fringe elements really are--and as it is, I am outraged enough. One thing is clear: American and British Muslims must stop thinking of themselves as second class citizens. As a Caucasian American of Dutch, Swedish, British, and German heritage (my 4 grandparents), I can tell you that the reason I spent 23 years actively in the U.S. Marine Corps was to defend the fact that United States citizens come from every "ethnic" nationality on the planet. It has been a very long time since members of my family thought of themselves as anything but American. The strength of our country (and I think the UK as well), and the reason we are the envy of the civilized World, even today, is that we take the best ideas of every culture. With more than 500 different national and cultural groups, when good ideas emerge, we adopt them; when bad ideas emerge from one group, the other 499+ ethnic/national groups pound them down. As a result, we as a country, the United States of America (and I think the UK), represent the best of the best on the planet ... and that INCLUDES the Muslims! ... These are some of the values I believe ..... These are the values I think ... regardless of..... As I said in an earlier e-mail, in my opinion, CNN has just reverted to very lazy and sloppy journalism, and they need to be called on it..... I am nearly out of power on my laptop, now, somewhere over the North Atlantic, so I guess I'll stop, and save enough to send this to you when I reach Newark. ...

Best regards, Skip

[An important part of the story is omitted here, for very good reason.]

Chapter 3
Flight from Death

The Thought Police, and the paranoia they engender, have forced me to omit much of what occurred between July 18, 2005 and September 24, 2005. Suffice it to say that a friend taught me that I would need two "3CCD" broadcast grade video cameras, if I wanted to do at least a semi-professional job with *Words Matter*. He pointed out that as recently as 3 years ago, these cameras were selling in the range of $5-7 thousand, but that by then there was at least one model that was as low as $1 thousand, the Panasonic GS400. He also recommended wireless microphones as the best way to go. I had originally hoped I could limit the investment to one camera, but he argued that the sound would be imperfect, and the interview would look strange, if I did not record both the interviewee and me simultaneously. By the last week of September, 2005, I was well and truly launched on my project.

My wife, Debbi, practices Tibetan Buddhism quite actively. I am more of a Buddhist dilettante. We do not regard Buddhism as a religion, *per se,* but rather as a philosophy. Buddhism espouses no god, no heaven, no hell, no saints, no sinners, no apostles, no prophets, no right, no wrong, and no sins. It is a set of approximately 80,000 teachings about life in general, and human life in particular, passed through generations of teachers over the last 2,500 years, and refers back to the beginning of time as we know it. There is a joke that Japanese become Buddhist when they approach death, because Buddhism does offer a useful psychological technology for dealing with one's own death. Indeed, many of the *Sangha* activities in the United States (and many other countries) are dedicated to training care givers on dealing with the dying, and the dying on facing their own death. This has little to do with this story, except for what happened next.

I believe in serendipity. One Saturday, in late September, I was browsing in our local Sun Coast video store, when I came upon a DVD entitled *Flight from Death: The Quest for Immortality*. My eyes were drawn to it because the image on the cover was that of a grave site, with a carved weeping angel sitting on top of a crypt. I am sure this cover caused many thousands of these DVDs not to be sold, but for a dilettante Buddhist, married to a serious Buddhist, interested in death and dying, it seemed as exciting and useful as any adventure epic. The cover said that it had won 8 film festival awards, so I picked it up, plunked down my plastic, and happily took it home as a small gift to Debbi.

The DVD sat on top of our TV for about a week. The following Saturday, I walked Shadow and Karma, our two standard Collies, as I do nearly every morning I am at home. When I came back into the driveway, Debbi was on our front deck. "Hon, you have to watch this DVD," she said excitedly.

"I will," I said, assuming that I would get to this uplifting topic of death, sometime in the next year or so.

Debbi knows me well. "No, hon, you need to watch it now! You're going to be surprised! It's right on the point of your project!"

I was skeptical, but after my shower, on a Saturday morning, I began to watch *Flight from Death.*

Chapter 4
Unstuck in Time

Like Kurt Vonnegut's protagonist, Billy Pilgrim, writing a memoir of something like this is a recipe for becoming "unstuck in time," as Vonnegut described that in *Slaughterhouse-Five.* Since I began writing this book, and showing it to my friends, I have that sense, especially since many of my friends consider it likely that I will experience Pilgrim's fate.

Being unstuck in time, I find that sometimes it may make sense to jump ahead in the story, even to the present moment, in order to provide context, while at the same time ruining the chronology, of course. I leave it to my editors, of my still unidentified publisher, to decide what goes and what stays, and in what order.

I wrote a novel online in 1993, which was read by over 100,000 people, but it is par for my course to be a pioneer, as in, "You can tell the pioneers by the arrows in their chest." This experience is better! That was before the commercial Internet really got going. Who could have imagined then the possibility of giving 40 million iPod and Nano users access to an audio book of my serialized work, as it is being written. I never would have imagined making my office look like a recording studio, but so it has become.

Like my 1993 experience, my writing is making me sit bolt upright in bed, at between 05:00 and 06:00. I regard that as good, because it means my subconscious is getting through my transcendent function. More on that later, or in another book: the comment is here for thems knows. Whisper who dares!

Two insights I've had about Iraq are worth mention early on, especially for my readers in Northern Virginia, and certain District of Columbia environs:

The Role of Islam

The solution to Iraq will not come with guns and boots on the street. The answer will come through Islam, not in spite of it. I do not believe that the behaviors of the terrorists and insurgents represent Islam in its moderate and pure form. I believe that 99.9% of all Muslims live peaceful and family oriented lives. To the extent that there is criticism for the behaviors of men toward women in Islam, I wonder whether the proportion is more or less similar to behaviors of men throughout the World. We only gave women the vote in the United States in 1916, after all, so we American men can hardly claim the moral high ground here. Many types of sexual abuse at home, and in the office, still exist in the United States in huge numbers. The difference, perhaps, is that we have relatively reliable statistics about such things; and we have laws to prevent them. When Muslim countries begin to keep reliable statistics on such abuses, they will naturally move toward the same types of proscriptions of behavior, which Americans and Europeans have found necessary over the past 50 years.

In my 2006 interviews, I have consistently asked my Muslim interviewees whether there is anything fundamentally in the difference between how Islam is followed by its Sunni and Shia followers, which would justify these two groups killing one another. The answer, like the answer for Irish Catholics and Protestants, is "Absolutely not!" It is for this reason that I decry use of the term "Sectarian," to describe the fighting in Iraq. It is tribal; it is a Hatfields and McCoys style feud; it is *Al Qaeda* finally making its way into Iraq for training, because Afghanistan is no longer available to it as a training base; but it is not based on religion. The sooner we Americans get it through our thick skulls that we need to differentiate between what is political and what is religious, the sooner we will allow a solution. To the extent that our media constantly keeps trying to tie terrorism and the tragedy of Iraq into a religious struggle, they perpetuate the same, because impressionable young people can actually believe such nonsense. Yes, there are assuredly problems and differences within Islam. But these are for the Muslims to resolve, in a peaceful way. 1.3 billion Muslims means that, like Hitler's Nazi regime, the "final solution" cannot ever be reached by violence, because if one embarks on such an exercise, the World outcry will at some point overwhelm the process. The very idea of the United States being worried about Iran having nuclear weapons is ludicrous! It's just something our politicians are using to scare us. The truth is that if anyone ever pops another nuclear weapon in anger, just one ballistic missile submarine (and we have many), would pound the leadership, which espoused such an attack, into a black hole, sending hundreds of thousands of their countrymen with them. This would not be good for their PR.

I am often told that Islam is a good and peaceful religion. I believe this. It is necessary, without a doubt, that Islamic scholars and leaders throughout the World begin to consider how they might communicate in a civil manner, and resolve their differences peacefully.

To the extent that politicians are using Islam as their excuse for continuing the bloodshed, they must be shown up like the rats they are. Like rats in a dark corner, true Muslims must shine a bright light upon them, and expose their venality. That done, no good Muslim will stand for their continuation in positions of power.

But there's the rub! It is not for me to say. These facts seem obvious, and yet, only Muslims can clean up the house of Islam. Only Muslims can take back their religion from the miscreants, who have hijacked it to their nefarious ends. Since I have been listening, I have heard many Muslims take the position that Islam is a moderate, peaceful, and fair religion. King Abdullah, of Saudi Arabia, convened a meeting of leaders of all 57 Muslim nations in Makkah last December, and all bought in on the "Makkah Declaration," which said exactly that. I was personally thrilled to read the news coverage of that event in foreign newspapers, as it was barely covered in the Western press. But, as someone close to me once said often, "Actions speak louder than words." Conferences and symposia about the issues are great beginnings, but they are useless if nothing happens. It is not for me to say whether anything is really happening, as I am not Muslim.

The Role of Women

Women must take a larger role in Muslim societies. For many good reasons of culture, location on the planet, and stages of development, women have been disenfranchised in many parts of the Muslim World. As I understand it, this is not dictated by true Islam, but it has been forged into the religion as it exists in some countries today. The whining and wetting of their sisters in the West cannot help Muslim women. Women in the West have, with great sacrifice, taken back their role in society, especially over the past 150 years. I do not deny that winning rights and freedoms, such as our women enjoy in the United States, can only come from sacrifice. But, it is a truth that no one can make a change of this magnitude from outside. The change must come from within.

How does a conflict like Iraq get solved? How did the conflict in Ireland get solved, though it festered for more than 400 years? How do feuds, like the apocryphal American example of the Hatfields and McCoys get resolved? They get resolved when the community decides that it will live in peace. As long as people are carrying AK47s, and condoning violence, as long as it happens to the other group, there will be no end. After the first year, there is no "even" in a feud, because no one knows what "even" is. No one can tally the losses on either side, and say that there can be an end, because "we are even." The members of each society must simply decide that they will raise their children in peace, and settle their differences through peaceful means. Only when that happens will there be an end to Iraq. It sounds stupidly simplistic, but at the base, it is so.

I have joked that many parts of the Middle East represent the unfortunate results of a several millennia experiment on what happens when you have testosterone uncivilized by estrogen. The wonderful thing about women is that every family started with at least one, and most households have at least one, even today. And, even in Iraq, if Muslim women accept that the sacrifice for gaining their rights must be their's, and begin insisting that there be peace, it will be so. Women have their ways!

To those men who claim that women are the weaker sex, and must be protected, I say, "Why don't you try to have a baby, brother, and we'll see who's the strongest? Why don't you try living with you, in the ways you require, and we'll understand which is the strongest sex?" The way these societies have developed, from an evolutionary point of view, is understandable. There is no need to be embarrassed about that. But the way to avoid the title of this book, is to recognize that it is time to evolve further.

Chapter 5
Terror Management Theory

I am most grateful to Patrick Shen and Greg Bennick, who produced *Flight from Death: The Quest for Immortality*. I never knew them before that trip to Sun Coast, and still have not physically met them, though I hope to rectify that soon. Their movie provided both a direction for my *Words Matter* project, as well as a pointer toward the leaders of the research into the thought of Ernest Becker, much of which is now described, in abbreviated form, as Terror Management Theory ("TMT").

Professor of Psychology Sheldon Solomon, at Skidmore College, is one of the principal investigators of this research. I interviewed Sheldon, and his colleague, Jeff Greenberg, Professor of Psychology at the University of Arizona, Tucson, shortly after seeing the documentary for the first time. Here's how Sheldon defined TMT in our interview:

"Sheldon:

> Terror management theory was originally derived from the ideas of Ernest Becker, who, in the 1970's, wrote a series of books in which he claimed that the uniquely human awareness of death has a great deal to do with just about everything that human beings do day to day. His argument is that people are the only creatures that are smart enough to recognize that we're here, and if you know that you're here, you also realize that you won't always be around. On top of that, we realize that we will die someday, and that our deaths can occur at any time, for reasons that we could never anticipate or control. We also recognize that we're animals and that, whether we like it or not, we're no more significant than lizards or potatoes.
>
> According to Becker, all these realizations would give rise to potentially debilitating terror, but for the fact that human beings, rather cleverly, although not necessarily consciously, solved this existential dilemma by the creation and

maintenance of what anthropologists today call "culture." Becker's point was that human beings construct cultural Worldviews, beliefs that we share with other people in our groups, that essentially give us a sense that we are individuals of value in a world of meaning. When we have those beliefs, when we confidently subscribe to a belief that we have meaning and value, that in turn gives us a sense that we can live forever, either literally in the context of different religions, that provide the hope for an afterlife, or symbolically, just the idea that tangible representations of our culture will remain nevertheless.

Skip:

You're calling it 'Terror Management Theory.' Were you calling it that before 9/11?

Sheldon:

Yes, absolutely."

More of Sheldon's interview is available at www.wordsmatter.tv and www.wordsmatterradio.net. Sheldon went on to say that, because our culture protects our psyches from the fear of death, if someone challenges our worldview or culture, then we often feel the need to defend that worldview in a variety of ways. If we are desperate enough, we may even be willing to kill others, who do not subscribe to our worldview, which explains quite elegantly most of the wars in the history of man. Sheldon asserts that approximately 175 million people were killed in the Twentieth Century alone, because of one group trying to change another group's worldview by means of violence.

When you think about it, applied to the current tribulations of our fragile planet, we can see that much of what is happening regarding life in the Middle East, and with terrorism, is directly related to these ideas.

While I do not relish being compared to a lizard or potato, I do have to ruefully admit that my death is inevitable, and that, at the most base level, I am a stomach, fitted with teeth, who leaves great quantities of waste in the World, while consuming only other living things, in their herds, flocks, schools, gardens and orchards. I speak only for myself! All of this notwithstanding, I do feel a strong attachment to a supreme being, who we call God and Muslims call *Allah*, so I found Sheldon's comment rather troubling, and likely unacceptable and disparaging toward holy figures in many parts of the World.

Sheldon corrected me immediately. He said that Becker, himself, was a very religious man, and that psychology only drops one off at the doorstep of religion.

I infer from Sheldon's comment that, as all of God's children know, there are some points that cannot now, nor ever will be, explained by science. It is at this point that religion provides us with faith about the absolutes. But just as religions are modalities for great good, they can also be modalities for great evil. All religions have been on both sides of this equation, from time to time. It seems to me that it is in the making of that distinction, on that holy/unholy teeter totter, where the future of humanity hangs in the balance.

Chapter 6
The Glory of God

"What one factor, above all others, makes the United States of America the strongest country in the World?" This is one of two questions, which I have had the presence of mind to ask every interviewee on tape. By presenting it here, I may be reducing its "zinger effect," of putting my interviewees slightly off balance, but in terms of the objective of writing *Tsunami of Blood*, it is the right thing to do.

We live in two bubbles: the Western World and the Muslim World. Very few Americans, prior to 9/11, knew anything at all about the Muslim World, regardless of their ethnic or social background. A recent poll indicated that more than 60% of Americans could not locate Saudi Arabia on a map; a tribute to the eating out of our public education system by our vaunted politicians, over the past 50 years.

While a few financially well off Muslims, who still live in the 57 "Muslim" countries of the World, may have traveled or studied in North America or Europe, very few less fortunate Muslims know more about the West than they can glean from their television set. It is an appalling truth that *Bay Watch* is the most popular television program in the World (or at least it was the last time I checked). You can go to the poorest village in India, which has only one television set, and find 50-200 people gathered around the village's one device and watching Pamela Anderson run down the beach in her bathing suit. I shudder to think what that audience takes from the experience. They must think we are all vacuous to the max. But, if it gives them pleasure to fantasize about a life most can never experience, I am all for it.

Like generations of different ethnic and national groups before them, today's Muslim communities in the United States remain insular. Since the vast majority of American Muslims only came to the United States in the past 50 years, this is quite normal. It is the experience of every other group. It is often true that national groups continue to speak their native language at home in the first generation in North America, but by the third generation you cannot differentiate their speaking habits from those of my daughters, who represent the 16th generation of the Dutch descended parts of my family, some of whom are mentioned in Russell Shorto's *Island at the Center of the World: The Epic Story of Dutch Manhattan and the Forgotten Colony that Shaped America.*

When I ask my question I get *angst* from my interviewee, most often. Few have actually thought about what makes America strong. I get responses from Ph.D.s which can only be regarded as stammering. So, why do I ask it? I ask it because I think it important to demonstrate to my audience how alike we are. Muslims in the United States regard themselves as under siege by the rest of us. They feel their ethnic and religious values are in question. This is largely true, but I want to point out that this is a normal phase of coming to America, which has happened to all Americans. It is a phase which passes.

The other question I ask all interviewees is, "How did your family come to North America?" It is a truth that every human being in North and South America is descended from someone who emigrated, to find a better life, less than 13,000 years ago. One does not leave one's home, to live in a far off place, unless it is to improve one's living situation in some way. So, the point of my question is to demonstrate, subliminally, that we have all been through the same struggles, and the same process of immigration and acceptance in "The New World."

In the case of my first Dutch ancestor (1/8120 of my blood line, for the record), Wolfert Gerritsen Van Couwenhoven, when he was about 40 years old (in an age when that was the average life expectancy), he moved his wife and three sons to Manhattan, becoming one of the first 200 settlers of that Dutch colony. He and his wife, in their lifetimes, were among the founders and first residents of Manhattan, Brooklyn, Albany, and Rensalear. They traveled to Manhattan as indentured farmers (under a contract very similar to those signed by "guest workers" in many parts of the World today). Farm life in Holland had been too difficult for them, because religious zealots (in this case the Spanish Monarchy) had made their lives miserable. They were escaping the 80 Years War, in which the Spanish came to Holland every summer to try to convert the Dutch to Catholicism, at the tip of a sword, and the Dutch every summer flooded their country, to chase the Spanish away for another season. Wolfert's second son was murdered by (so called) native Americans, whose motives were probably very similar to today's American "rednecks." As in, "Why should we let that scum in, so that they can ruin what we have already built here?" But America was then, and is now, a big place, with lots of opportunity, so the native Americans moved west, in order to avoid the conflicts which did ensue, and my family fought for their place on the North American continent, just as every immigrant family before and since has done. The only difference, in experience, between them and today's American Muslims, is that their experience is long forgotten, as Russell Shorto so eloquently pointed out.

In thinking of the plight of American Muslims, last summer, I had the epiphany that *the strength of America comes from its Diversity*. We have so many national, religious and ethnic groups, in North America, that our country has experienced a process of tempering, like making steel. Impurities of the human condition are forced out over time.

I put it in terms of ideas. Whenever a good idea surfaces, from whatever ethnic group, all of the other groups accept it immediately. Since it is global, my favorite example is Starbuck's. I often work in a hospital in Riyadh, Saudi Arabia, where there are four Starbuck's coffee shops within the building. So this proves that when an idea is good, not only do all Americans adopt it, but everyone adopts it.

When an idea is launched from one group, which is bad, however, all of the other groups pound it out of the system. This is, at best, a messy and noisy process, and at worst can be a very bloody process. My example for a bad idea is slavery. For nearly 250 years, slavery was practiced in North America. Finally, we fought our Civil War over the issue, killing tens of thousands of men and women. In 1863, it was abolished by Abraham Lincoln in the Emancipation Proclamation. We still suffer in this strongest country in the World from the fallout of that bad idea. We have racial hatreds, and poor black minorities still. But the messy and noisy change is on, and things have improved dramatically in my lifetime. In 1957, the Governor of Virginia closed all of the schools in the State to avoid integrating. I experienced that because I missed a semester of my 7th grade year, until my parents were able to move my family to Pennsylvania. Today, that ugly episode of American history seems far behind us, and, in the last decade, I have only met one person, to whom I mentioned it, who even knew it ever happened. But it did; and it happened to Americans!

So yes, it is absolutely true that the United States is not perfect. It is now, and ever will be, a work in progress. Our Founding Fathers could not possibly have imagined what it would become when they put their signatures to the Declaration of Independence, risking execution for treason, and proclaimed "that all men are created equal. They are endowed by their creator with certain inalienable rights. That among these are life, liberty and the pursuit of happiness." Many of them were slave owners, but they knew the system would somehow have to change, much as many of today's leaders live, knowing that their systems are unjust, and that women and men of conviction and courage will change them violently (as we Americans have done), if they are not changed by their leaders in a responsible and ethical manner. This is inevitable. Our Founding Fathers put their names, their lives, and their fortunes on the line for principles, the long term effect of which even they could not have imagined. But, the 230 year tempering process, of good ideas adopted and bad ideas hammered out of the system, which really started with the first colonists, in 1607, has created the strongest (if not the greatest) country on the planet.

Over the past year, I have mused on my idea that *diversity* is the reason for the strength of the United States many times. It occurred to me that when I meet an American in my business life, or any other nationality for that matter, of a different race, ethnic or religious background, I rejoice, because I know that they will bring a new perspective to the business problems we face together, and make our company stronger. I know that many of my countrymen have not consciously thought about the strength of the United States in this way, and would not agree, but perhaps it will become a mantra across our land, and make us better for it.

On one occasion, much later in my story, I referred to *diversity* as The Glory of God. It occurred to me that God made us all, regardless of skin tone or religion we follow. Indeed, God created *all* religions, did S/he not? I have raised this point in several interviews and conversations with Muslims, both in the United States and abroad, and they have all agreed on this point. And so I will assert that it is true for the whole World we live in, that *Diversity is the Glory of God*, and when everyone in the World accepts and believes that truth, all of our children will live in peace everywhere.

Chapter 7
Disgusted

Debbi worries that this book will be controversial among many groups, and therefore contain a certain danger between its covers.

"I'm disgusted!" I respond with vigor.

"If you're disgusted, then you should say why," is her rejoinder.

By now you know that the leak in the dike of the repression of my disgust was irresponsible media coverage surrounding the London bombing incident of July 7, 2005. I felt that the mainstream media were giving terrorism more free PR (useful for recruiting) than I could buy for my company in a century. Furthermore, I felt that the media were intentionally inflaming the news. The later Mohammed cartoon controversy is another case in point, where a relatively small incident, which could have been resolved reasonably, was whipped up into such turmoil that hundreds of people were killed worldwide. In my opinion, many of those deaths can be laid at the feet of the mainstream media. But that is a story for a later part of this narrative, so I will leave it for now.

I'm disgusted with a President, whose mantra is "stay the course" until "final victory," and yet fails to define what he means by those generalities. What happens after Iraq settles down, Mr. President? That's what I want to know! As I pointed out in the Introduction of this book, I think the demographics suggest that we are in for a lot of trouble. Am I the only one who can see this problem?

I'm disgusted with federal and state governments, and politicians of both parties, who have allowed the American public education system to decline to such a degree that most of my countrymen are so ignorant, that they are satisfied with such a lame mantra from our President.

I am disgusted with an Administration, which is so bull headed that it will not participate in diplomacy in a reasonably patient manner, thereby causing a shameful decline of American prestige around the World. This is the same Administration, which fails to enforce the law of our land. In 1996, Congress passed the Health Insurance Portability and Accountability Act ("HIPAA"). In 2003, HIPAA became effective to protect the privacy of the medical records of all Americans. On June 5, 2006, *The Washington Post* reported that of 19,420 grievances filed, none (that is zero) had resulted in fines, and that of the 319 criminal cases referred to the Justice Department, only 2 have led to prosecution. One of these involved the theft of credit card information, which surely would have been protected under other statutes, and one involved the theft of an FBI agent's records (to their credit, the Administration takes care of its own, at least some of the time).

I am disgusted with fundamentalist religious authorities everywhere, whose sophistry leads to more and more international hatreds, while proposing no viable solutions. For the purpose of providing examples, I'll stick with the Christian fundamentalists here, but as for other religions, everyone knows who you are anyway.

I once attended a relatively moderate Christian fundamentalist service. The scripture for the day was Acts 19:23-41. The events in that passage involve the mission of the Apostle Paul, who was regularly preaching among the Ephesians about early Christianity. He had been quite successful in his mission, and as he converted many Ephesians, he turned them away from worshipping Diana, the Greek goddess of the hunt, which in turn caused them to buy fewer statues and images of Diana. One Demetrius, a silversmith, was incensed, because Paul's preaching was cutting into his business, so he gathered a crowd of other unhappy artisans, and was in the process of attacking Paul, when the Roman clerk (a local magistrate, perhaps) intervened. The clerk pointed out that Paul had neither robbed a temple, nor had he blasphemed Diana. He was simply preaching his religion. The clerk insisted that if Demetrius had a valid complaint, he needed to take it up through the legal system, and not resolve it through violence. The result of Paul's approach, of not blaspheming the Greek gods and goddesses, is that Christianity is one of the major religions of the World today, while the Greek gods and goddesses are worshipped by no one in the World, except in a secular and commercial sense. This was the message of the sermon that day.

But my complaint came later, in the very same service, when the very same minister, during a time when the congregation is asked to assume an attitude of prayer, which I would argue amounts to opening one's subconscious to God, blasphemed Islam twice. I was irate, and immediately so. I very nearly spoke up in protest before departing the sanctuary and making a scene. For social reasons, I did not, but immediately carried on a several hour debate on the matter with several members of the congregation. I was urged to write to the minister, expressing my complaint, which I did. There ensued a 3-month long correspondence, in which sophistry abounded. Finally, the minister pointed out, correctly, that I was not a member of his congregation, and he had important matters to deal with to support "his flock." The debate ended, but the lesson to me about the sophistry of certain members of our Christian clergy endures.

By the same token, many fundamentalist preachers insist on the infallibility of the Bible, and yet there can be no debate that many of the dictates of the Bible have been overcome by events, and cannot be acceptable in the modern World. My favorite book to demonstrate this point is Deuteronomy, which, in Chapter 13, calls for the killing of missionaries and those converted, by stoning. Ironically, it is the fundamentalists, who do most of the missionary work in Christianity, and since Deuteronomy predated Christianity, it can be argued that they would be included within the definition of missionary in this case. I am sure they do not teach this passage when they are proselytizing.

Later on, in Chapter 21, Deuteronomy allows that if one is in battle, and takes a female captive, he may take her home as his wife, but if he does not like her, he can just let her go (Deuteronomy 21:11-14). The American Uniform Code of Military Justice would take a dim view of this kind of behavior among our Armed Forces today, regardless of an individual's religious persuasion. Later, Deuteronomy 22:13-21 provides that, if a man hates his wife, he can get rid of her by claiming she was not a virgin at the time of marriage, and require her father to provide the proof of her virginity, in the form of a bloody sheet used on the wedding night. If the father cannot produce such evidence, Deuteronomy provides that the woman should be stoned to death. Oh please!

It seems to me that it is high time that our media, our politicians, and our religious leaders behave in a responsible manner, and craft solutions for the World we live in today, rather than holding us hostage to a World our tyrannical ancestors inhabited thousands of years ago. We have many politicians and religious leaders, who claim that God speaks to them today. If S/He does, and I am not disputing the point, then it seems to me that S/He can be providing us with answers for today, correcting the flawed records, which come down to us from yesteryear. What does God tell us TODAY? All of us learn from our mistakes; surely God does! In fact, the record tells us S/He does, in so many words.

Chapter 8
Mitt Romney's Speech to Heritage Foundation

Massachusetts Governor Mitt Romney, in my opinion, is one of the most dangerous politicians in the United States. He is attractive, he is articulate, he has an excellent track record, and his rhetoric can make giving up our 1st Amendment Rights, for which our Founding Fathers pledged their wealth and their lives, and for which millions of Americans have fought over centuries, sound like we just need to be prepared. The most dangerous fact about him is that he is clearly, to me, running for President of the United States.

By mid-September, 2005, I was already down the road of defending the American Muslim community against generic and unreasonable attacks. I continue to feel that such attacks are very dangerous, because they deny our own system of government, and the values by which the majority of Americans live their lives, and, in their unreasonableness, they promote, among impressionable young people around the World, the kinds of hatred, which can lead to a tsunami of blood.

My outrage rose to the boiling point, when I heard Governor Romney's speech to the Heritage Foundation, which he delivered on September 14, 2005. Unfortunately, if you listen to his insidious rhetoric, he sounds very reasonable. But, in my opinion, his innuendo is unmistakable. I infer that he does not believe that Muslim Americans are as trustworthy as Americans of any other ethnic or religious group.

You can make your own judgment about what he said. You can download Governor Romney's speech, and decide for yourself, from the Heritage Foundation site, http://www.heritage.org/Press/Events/ev091405b.cfm. The phrases to which I object began at 23 minutes and 3 seconds into his speech, when he was talking about domestic intelligence. Here's what he said:

"What do I mean by domestic intelligence and counterterrorism? Of course there's foreign intelligence ... I'm not going to [talk about] that. Domestic intelligence: I'm talking about monitoring people who come here from foreign countries that are terrorist sponsored countries. Individuals that may have been taught at places where terrorist training is going on. Tracking students, visitors. We have 120 colleges and universities in Massachusetts, roughly. How many individuals are coming to our state and going to those institutions who have come from terrorist sponsoring states? Do we know where they are? Are we tracking them? *How about people who are in settings, mosques for instance, that may be teaching doctrines of hate and terror.* Are we monitoring that? Are we wiretapping? Are we following what's going on? Are we seeing who's coming in? Who's coming out? Are we eavesdropping; carrying out surveillance on those individuals that are coming from places that have sponsored domestic terror? And by the way, whose job is it to do that? Should I do that as a Governor? I've got those colleges and universities. Should my state police develop an intelligence unit that's monitoring people that are coming in? We're an international port; Boston has a lot of flights coming in. Should we be checking people who are coming from places of concern and following them, finding out where they go? Checking their hotels? Seeing who they meet at their hotels?"

To Governor Romney's credit, he said that his research suggested that these are matters for the federal government, and that we must rely on the eyes and ears of our citizens to report suspicious activity. Regretfully, his reference to mosques seems to rule out Muslim American citizens as likely to have an interest in reporting suspicious activity.

News reports about this speech indicated that several Muslim groups had approached Governor Romney to apologize for his comment, and the way it was said, implying that Muslim Americans would not have an interest in the homeland security of the United States. The same reports indicated that Governor Romney declined to retract or apologize for the comments about mosques.

In my opinion, this speech stated clearly Mr. Romney's attitude about our Freedoms, and our system of government. It denies that the citizenship process of the United States, which has served the country over years, can be trusted. I infer from his remarks that he believes we cannot trust certain groups to be Americans, here specifically the Muslims, even after successfully completing the process of citizenship.

I will state publicly that, in my opinion, Romney's rhetoric does not represent the country I believe the United States is. I believe his insidious comments reflect the early rhetoric of totalitarian states. Aldous Huxley's *Brave New World* and George Orwell's *1984*, with its references to "big brother" and the "thought police," come immediately to mind. The great thing is that the strength of the United States is that I, as another American citizen, am free to rub Governor Romney's nose in his remarks for the rest of his career. Speaking for myself, I will work for the rest of my life to see that Governor Romney, and those who support this rhetoric, will never again hold public office in the United States of America.

Chapter 9

Sheldon Solomon Explains the Psychology of Suicide Bombing

Flight from Death profoundly influenced the direction of the *Words Matter* project. One of the critical points to be considered is, "What in human nature allows and/or causes a person to become a suicide bomber?" Is it some sort of mind control, by a talented handler, or is there something in religion, that is the driving force? The truth seems to be that the tendency, to kill oneself for one's beliefs, is hard wired into the human psyche.

Watching the DVD, that September morning, as Debbi had insisted, immediately canalized my thinking, through the elegance and simplicity of its argument. The basic idea is that in psychological terms, each of us wants to make a difference during our lifetime. We all want to be a "hero" in some large or small way. This heroism can be manifested through raising children, leaving works of art or poetry, by philanthropy, or by leaving large piles of money to our heirs. There is no limit to the number of possibilities. Knowing that we will die is terrifying to all of us, but it is hard wired in the human being that, if we know that our lives counted in the "great ledger book" of the species, we can somehow face our death with more equanimity. Though dying is never easy. As W.C. Fields had engraved on his tombstone, "I'd rather be in Philadelphia."

Since Sheldon Solomon is the hero of this chapter, at least, the fact that I have written about him here could be seen as one plus mark on the great ledger book of humanity. His colleagues, Jeff Greenberg and Tom Pyszczynski were no less important to the research, because this team of researchers has held itself together, through thick and thin, for decades, adding depth to the insights of Ernest Becker (*Denial of Death* and *Escape from Evil*) through over 300 field studies in social psychology. Meanwhile, Dr. Neil Elgee has nurtured Becker's memory and vision through The Ernest Becker Foundation.

When you watch the DVD, you will recognize Sheldon as that articulate academic in the colorful tie died T-shirt. His voice and demeanor are so mesmerizing that one is immediately drawn into his topic.

Greg Bennick and Patrick Shen were kind enough to put subtitles in the documentary, identifying who the speakers were. From this, I learned that Sheldon was at Skidmore College, only a 2.5 hour drive from my ancestral home, which I visit regularly. Since it was apparent that Terror Management Theory ("TMT") was such a crucial element of my project, I immediately wanted to speak with one of the highlighted experts in the DVD. Sheldon was the closest, so I decided to begin with him.

Our first interview was a disaster! Sheldon was his naturally gracious and articulate self, giving me a 2-hour private lesson in TMT, which has proven invaluable throughout the project. But, since it was my first major interview, there were some issues. It has come as a surprise to me that major colleges and universities do not seem to have adequate venues for conducting private interviews, which have nothing to do with their mainstream business of educating their students. Skidmore is no exception, so we set up the cameras in Sheldon's faculty office. Like so many faculty offices, and my office is no exception, Sheldon's, after decades of producing intellectual literature, can only be described as a "black hole." Indeed, that is the affectionate and official name Debbi has assigned to my *sanctum sanctorum*, so I know the genre. (This book is being written on my dining room table). Once we cleared a few square inches of debris, so that we could set up my tripods, we began, with me not realizing that the top of an open cardboard box, at the level of my head, appeared to be sticking in my ear throughout the entire interview. Worse was the sound. My cheap $100 wireless microphones interacted with the fluorescent lighting to produce a steady hum throughout the tapes, which have proven to be unusable. Fortunately, Sheldon gave me the benefit of the doubt, and agreed to do everything all over again a month later. The interview, which appears at www.wordsmatter.tv , is the product of that second interview, on November 11, 2005. As you can see, the venue we could find for our non-Skidmore activity was still lacking in polished pundit finesse, but, by that point, I was happy to take what I could get. For anyone reading this and considering becoming a maker of documentary films of any type, I recommend you use *Sennheiser's* wireless microphones, at about $500 each. They allow you to electronically determine whether you have radio frequency interference before you begin. But I digress!

The big issue to be addressed was, "How can it be that *Al Qaeda*, and other terrorist organizations, find it so easy to recruit suicide bombers, at least from a TMT point of view?" The answer seems to be that most of the people who become suicide bombers have led hopeless and frustrating lives. In the case of the toxic demographic, which I mentioned in the Introduction, many young men in the Muslim World are extremely repressed. This has nothing whatsoever to do with Islam, *per se*, but rather with the effectiveness of their leaders in dealing with the modern World, in the context of unholy political truces between fundamentalist Muslim clerics and secular leaders. This is not so different from the unholy alliance between the current Administration, and fundamentalist Christian leaders in the United States, who claim to control the keys to the White House. Margaret Atwood described the consequences of such alliances, in her chilling novel, *The Handmaid's Tale*, in which healthy young women become baby factories for privileged older men while young men are sent off to war.

In many parts of the Muslim World, repressive regimes, with little understanding of economics, in the modern sense, have forced their populations into poverty with their regressive policies. Young men, filled with testosterone, have no access of any kind of release for their energy, except the mosque, and what few video games and boring television programs they are allowed. There are few local sports teams, their education is lacking, which means that they do not have the skills to perform the jobs their governments inadvertently give to foreigners, and there are no women, with whom they are allowed to pass some time, regardless of how benign the activity. As a result, these young men are not adapted to reasonable and productive lives in society. Their lives, and the chance to "make a difference," leaving their contributions on great ledger of mankind, are dead ends.

Given this hopeless scenario for millions of ignorant young men, and given that much of the paltry social life they are permitted is at the mosque, it is little wonder that their psyche's tell them that, if they cannot make a difference in this life, then at least they can die as a hero, and count on *Allah's* ledger book. Furthermore, they have been told with great authority, by their elders (who have never tried it), that heaven is beautiful, and filled with the young virgins they cannot meet in this life. There are stories, too, that some misdirected individuals and governments pay thousands of dollars for a suicide bomber, so it is not surprising that these misguided young people, men and women alike, are attracted to the idea of, at least, being a family hero by leaving a financial legacy behind.

The problem of terrorism and suicide bombings, therefore, boils down to hopelessness. To the extent we stand by and condone the policies of governments, which keep their populations in ignorance and poverty, we too are to blame for the results. In my view, Americans need to understand that it is not alright, as long as poverty and ignorance are far from our shores. Those factors drive terrorism, which is the greatest threat to our way of life. When everyone can live in dignity, and provide for their children in a reasonable manner, the threat of terrorism will subside. Until then, we are destined to live in fear. It does not take much to destroy our prosperity. One hundred dollars worth of box cutters cost our society $1 trillion, according to some estimates. We need to find ways to spread our prosperity around the World, and will include confronting some of our allies about the deficiencies of their domestic policies. In my view, if we are going to "stay the course" until "final victory," that is what it will take.

Chapter 10

RESPECT

My business trip to the west coast, in mid-October 2005, gave me occasion to interview two additional intellectuals on the topics of terror and intercultural relations. These were Dr. Philip R. Harris, who, as co-author of *Managing Cultural Differences*, now in its 6th edition, has provided the gold standard in facing our differences globally, for over 40 years; and Dr. Jeff Greenberg, Professor of Psychology at the University of Arizona, Tucson, who co-authored *In the Wake of 9/11: The Psychology of Terror*, with Sheldon Solomon and Thomas Pyszczynski.

I am fortunate to have known Phil Harris for over 4 decades, even before he began writing *Managing Cultural Differences*. When I first met him in Kamakura, Japan, in 1962, he was already a respected author and academic, but he was like a deer in the headlights when it came to intercultural issues. For almost 25 years, he had been encapsulated in the Franciscan Order as an educator. But it was my mother, Jeanne, who introduced him to the concept of culture, by giving him the book by anthropologist Ruth Benedict, *The Chrysanthemum and the Sword*. It was a turning point in his life and lead to his many writings on the concept of culture and its impact on human behavior. While a Fulbright professor in India, he traveled around the world, suffering in the process both "culture and re-entry shock."

After lecturing at Sophia University in Japan, Phil spent three weeks with my family, and was introduced to our pseudo Japanese lifestyle of sleeping on the floor, with only a single space heater to warm an entire house, entirely devoid of weather stripping, in the middle of December. My mother was teaching English to Japanese businessmen in Tokyo, while my father served with the U.S. Navy, in Yokosuka. Phil was fascinated with the kaleidoscope texture of our lives, which included dealing with Japanese citizens in their own communities, only 17 years after World War II. All of us loved Japan, and my mother, who relished the entire experience, can be credited with insisting that we lived in a totally Japanese community.

When I boil it down now, in the fullness of time, I can say that what we all learned, in 1962, is that different cultures must first learn to *respect* one another. Only then can we ever hope to understand one another, and find peaceful and reasonable ways to live together. The differences among us are truly inconsequential, when compared to the similarities.

Subsequently, this cosmopolitan author and educator would marry my aunt, Dr. Dorothy Lipp, and together they managed dual careers in universities and international consulting. I interviewed him in October 2005 for my *Words Matter*™ television project. By the time of our interview, Phil had come a long way in his thinking. He left the Franciscans, in 1963, and had long since given up the fiction of the infallibility of the Catholic Church. His message was one of tolerance for all religions. He urged that Muslim Americans stand up for their rights as Americans, and help the rest of us understand the differences between their faith and the politics of their former countries, which all of them have left behind to find a better life, just as their predecessors of other faiths and nationalities have always done. Here are some of the key observations he made in that interview:

> "Our problem is that a lot of Americans, who haven't had the advantages of international education and travel, are rather myopic in their views of other people, who are different from them."
>
> .....
>
> "It amazes me how our own political leadership, at times, is so blind to the historical and cultural implications of some of the things we do in the Middle East, and especially in Iraq."
>
> .....
>
> "Once you begin to shift the mindset, then you get the changes in attitude and behavior."

When I boil it down now, in the fullness of time, I can say that what we all learned, in 1962, is that different cultures must first learn to *respect* one another. Only then can we ever hope to understand one another, and find peaceful and reasonable ways to live together. The differences among us are truly inconsequential, when compared to the similarities.

Jeff Greenberg is the gentleman in the "Mad" hat, in *Flight from Death.* He has been instrumental in much of the field research, which has led to Terror Management Theory. Much of this research has been done with a concept called "reminders of death." Normally, the subjects are divided into two groups. One group is subtly "reminded of death," in some manner, while the other group is not. Then the subjects are asked to perform a task. Most often, the subjects with the "reminders of death" respond more aggressively, with a strong tendency to withdraw into the teachings of their cultural groups, however they may be described (religion, nationality, ethnicity, tribe, etc.).

Two examples, described in *Flight from Death:* The *Quest for Immortality,* are as follows:

1. Municipal Court Judges in Tucson were asked to complete a questionnaire. Half of the group received questions with "reminders of death," while half did not. They were then given a "charge sheet" for a defendant accused of solicitation, and asked to set the bail. The average bail set by the judges, who did not receive the "reminders of death," was $50. The average bail of those reminded of their death was $450.

2. Tabasco sauce is sometimes used by parents to punish their children. This is a form of child abuse. Participants were given a shot glass and a bottle of Tabasco sauce, and asked to put sufficient sauce into the glass to provide a sufficient punishment for someone (not a child, in this case, and the punishment was not actually inflicted on anyone). The participants, who did not receive "reminders of death," put one or two drops into the glass, while those with the "reminders of death" put in elephantine doses, with some of them filling the glass, but only to people who did not share their same political attitudes. Seeing this tendency in the experiment, which appears on the DVD, is sobering.

The researchers have pointed out that at the time of 9/11, a monumental "reminder of death" for all of us, American flags flew off the shelves of every merchant. Everyone wanted to own more symbols of our culture. I recall that, a few days after the event, an airline cabin attendant sat down beside me and literally grabbed my arm, as if for comfort, because I was wearing an American flag tie.

Our President's re-election team probably used this research, to their advantage, during the 2004 election. All of us remember that many of the President's campaign advertisements contained images of 9/11, "reminders of death" for this purpose. The objective was to manipulate voter psyches back toward this "defend the culture" point of view. Unfortunately, getting everyone whipped up in that way, does not serve our long term interests, though it got the Administration elected again, which was their objective.

Now we are faced with the task of getting all of our citizens, and everyone else in the World, to recall that the key to the survival of the human species is, very simply, *respect.*

Chapter 11
"Sectarian" Is No Better

I have decried the use of "Islamic terrorist," "Islamic extremist," "ethnic Pakistani," and later "Islamist," as descriptors of the media to describe what is happening in our troubled World. As I pointed out in Chapter 2, these terms do not reasonably describe Islam, which I regard as a religion of peace and moderation, and they are defamatory to more than 99% of Muslims in the World. You can find my 12 minute talk on this point at www.wordsmatter.tv.

My public campaign to end such usage has had its effect, but I feel like I have been squeezing a balloon. My first public complaint was registered during my Kalmbach Lecture at The William E. Simon Graduate School of Business Administration, one of my *alma maters*, on November 10, 2005. You can find some of what I said in Chapter 2, and hear it on www.wordsmatter.tv. Since then, though I do not claim exclusive credit for this, I have not heard the first three terms used on CNN. Instead, they morphed into using the term "Islamist." I heard this first used during President Bush's trip to Pakistan, earlier in 2006, when I complained bitterly about that term. They stopped using that term too, but now have morphed again, with most other media outlets, to "Sectarian."

They just cannot help themselves. These lazy journalists have tied Islam and terrorism together in their own minds, without adequate experience or research, and have therefore offended and defamed most of the 1.3 billion Muslims in the World. "Sectarian," as in "Sectarian violence in Iraq," is no better, because the innuendo is that the Iraqi population is killing one another because they are one sect or the other. I know many Muslims of both groups, and not a single one of them has suggested that there is anything whatsoever, in the religious differences between the two groups, which would justify killing one another. Just as the Christian Protestants and Catholics in Ireland were fighting over political control—read "power"—so it is with intra-Islamic disputes in the Muslim World. They are not religious fights; they are political fights. Or, they are *vendettas* or feuds, but at their base, they have nothing to do, so far as I can tell, with the true tenets of Islam.

Indeed, in my opinion, The Prophet would be appalled at what is going on among his followers. I admit to being ignorant about 99.999% of all of the teachings and dictates of Islam, but my many years of experience in the Muslim World and dealing with Muslims of every variety, tells me that my conclusions are true. If I have a reader, who believes my conclusions are wrong, please write me at skip@wordsmatter.tv.

There is a rub. According to several non-Muslim scholarly authorities I have consulted, Islam has always been combined with politics, very much as an organizing factor, since the time of The Prophet, just as happened in Christianity over centuries. As a result, many political ideas have been smeared into the minds of Muslims by politicians seeking secular power, much as Christian fundamentalist preachers smear hate into the minds of their "flocks" this very day.

This brings me back to the superficiality of the mainstream media, and their insistence upon using terms which mix the religion and the politics. By tying the religion into the violence, they are offending over a billion peace loving Muslims, while giving everyone else the wrong impression about the Muslim World in general, thus causing more distrust and hatred.

Just over a century ago, a "yellow journalist," William Randolph Hearst, was able to influence the American public into insisting our federal government enter the Spanish-American War, by publishing inaccurate "facts" about what was going on, in a very inflammatory way. The battleship U.S.S. Maine had blown up in Havana Harbor, killing 256 members of the crew, and he demanded action. He got it! And as a result, the United States took control of The Philippines and Puerto Rico from Spain. He did this with a very small newspaper readership, in the tens of thousands. One version of the story I have heard is that a naval inquiry, a decade later, concluded that the explosion aboard the U.S.S. Maine was caused by a sailor dropping (probably accidentally) a cigarette or cigar into the powder magazine, causing the explosion. But, Hearst was happy, because he sold lots and lots of newspapers and advertising.

Today we have a more difficult problem, which is much more serious than the failure of William Randolph Hearst to require thorough reporting. We have several mainstream media channels (CNN, BBC, MSNBC, *Al Jazeera*, and *Al Arabiya*, to name a few), which reach a billion listeners in each broadcast. Their reports influence the public at large, politicians and theologians alike. The problem is, they do not present an accurate picture of the World, so they are causing more and more unnecessary hatreds and misunderstandings, and leading us into an inferno.

I want to avoid suggesting that the media be controlled by our politicians. That's a slippery slope in another direction, which can lead to even worse consequences. Indeed, I consider myself to be among the most dedicated believers in the 1st Amendment to the United States Constitution, which guarantees our Freedom of the Press. Without it, the tempering of the United States, which has built its strength by allowing all ideas to be aired, and the bad ideas to be beaten out of the system on the forge of public debate, could not have been possible. This does not mean, however, that the media are immune from criticism. As a member of the public, each of us can criticize their coverage, and any apparent bias, which I am continuing to do publicly here. And, importantly, nothing stops the media, our schools of journalism, pundits and writers of professional juried articles from evaluating their own craft, and improving on their own sense of responsibility and ethics.

No one seems to want to think through the consequences of how they choose to report a story. The crisis over the Danish cartoons, last fall and winter, is a case in point. While I surely do not condone the cartoons, I feel the media coverage was irresponsible, leading to the deaths of hundreds of people around the World. By repeating, over and over again, close ups of angry demonstrators, rather than indicating how small the early demonstrations actually were, they inflamed other repressed Muslims to vent their anger in a violent way. To the extent that Muslim countries chose to boycott Danish products, I thought that was a reasonable response to the cartoons. It clearly gave the message to the media that such cartoons were considered blasphemy in the Muslim World, something many westerners, including me, did not know before the event. But the drumbeat of coverage inflamed the matter into a conflagration of unprecedented proportion for satire, causing many unnecessary deaths.

Much later in my story, I asked Dean Dianne Lynch of the Roy H. Park School of Communications at Ithaca College, whether she would consider that it would be irresponsible to continue to publish the offending cartoons, once the impact of the incident was known. She responded, "Absolutely!" But she also said that the news has a right and obligation to report events, such as the demonstrations, to which I agree. And the fact that people were killed in the demonstrations was newsworthy. But, I am talking about a matter of degree here. I am talking about journalists and media executives asking themselves always, "Does my story report the news or inflame the news?" If it inflames, the ethical answer about the report should be obvious. Inflaming the news crosses the line into propaganda, but for whom and for what? It seems to me that, if you inflame the news, you lose sight of the high minded ideals for which the 1st Amendment was put into the U.S. Constitution.

All of this brings me back to the use of the term "sectarian." It is true, I do agree, that much of the fighting in Iraq is between people, who are either Sunni or Shia. My heartburn is that I have yet to see a western media outlet, which acknowledged that, at its base, this fighting has nothing to do with the differences between how these two groups follow their faith and the teachings of The Prophet. Rather, the fighting is about control of oil revenues, about politics, about revenge for what has gone on before, tribally and otherwise, but it is not about religion. If we can make that distinction, we can lower the decibel level and the concept that we have a conflict going on between the Muslim World and the Christian World. We do not! Indeed, according to my understanding, Islam recognizes Jesus Christ, though it denies that he is the son of God.

But lazy reporters ask, "How can I describe what's going on, if I can't use the word 'Sectarian,' or some other word that relates back to Islam?"

"I don't care," is my response. "Call them the Green Team and the Blue Team; the Hatfields and the McCoys; the northern fighters v. southern fighters; or whatever your imaginations might like; BUT, whatever you do, avoid making it a battle between two parts of a peaceful religion, which serves the spiritual needs of most Muslims very well, and which does not cause them to attack anyone else, or interfere with anyone else's Worldview or way of life. Whatever we do, we must never acknowledge that murderers, criminals, and demagogues are anything but what they are. They are aberrations against civilization, which must be stopped before they cause the cockroaches to inherit the Earth."

Chapter 12

Reality Check

How badly has American prestige eroded since the invasion of Iraq? We don't know, but it occurred to me that I should be speaking with typical citizens from around the World, to put together some sort of matrix of an answer. I began my research by speaking with two students in the United States. Ms. Michaela is a foreign student, from Romania, while Ms. Alma is in the first generation of her Mexican American family to be born in the United States. I spoke to them together.

I first asked each of them for their views on Governor Romney's speech about national security, in which he rhetorically suggested the wiretapping of mosques, and surveillance of foreign students (discussed in Chapter 8).

Both spoke of the unintended consequences of surveillance. Ms. Michaela implied that behaviors like surveillance were among the factors which caused communist regimes to fall, further implying that such behavior could cause a similar result in the United States, while Ms. Alma pointed out the "blow back" effect of repressive behaviors toward certain groups, where resentment is likely to build.

Here is what Ms Michaela's said:

> "I come from a [formerly] communist country, where people were surveiled (*sic*), and where some people chose to report to the government about their neighbors or families or whatever; and that has not made the system to survive. It may have made things happen at a slower rate, but eventually the system did not survive. So surveilling people, and keeping them quiet, and watching what they're doing didn't really help the system."

Here is Ms. Alma's reaction:

> "The U.S. government, by following this course of action, is doing to these students, maybe, what these students are running away from, so that, as opposed to coming into a nation where they are following "the American Dream" of trying to pursue liberty and the pursuit of happiness, they are being persecuted, and therefore that may cause anger, which may cause some type of reaction against the U.S., against the government, against the people."

We spoke about misunderstandings between the American Muslim community and the remainder of the population, which has caused politicians to suggest such draconian measures.

Ms. Alma said that, "There hasn't been enough interest from the American public to learn, not even to understand, but just learn about the culture [of Islam]. Therefore, people [in the United States] are guided by stereotypes. And that's what I believe develops in any type of conflict."

I asked Ms. Michaela what she felt was the main reason for the general success of the United States in the World. After two years of studying in the United States, coming from Romania, this is what she said:

> "I think it is the 'American Dream'." I think that each individual believes that if they want to accomplish something, if they want to achieve something, they can do it. And I think that over time the society has evolved so that each individual can allow each other individual to become whatever they want to become. I come from a culture where we were all supposed to be the same, and therefore if you want to be more, or you want to be better, you are not a good person. People will not hate you for it, but they will not necessarily help you become what you want to become.
>
> "Because the United States has this culture, it has attracted the smartest people in the World. It's not the money; I don't think it's the money. I think it is the fact that you can come here and achieve what you want to achieve; make the most of whatever you want to do; have people accepting you. Since I've been here in the States, I've had numerous upon numerous people helping me when they didn't have to help me."

I asked Ms. Alma how she felt about America's role in the World. We spoke of the perception that the United States is somehow intentionally trying to rule the World. After several months in a leading business school, she responded, "I believe that politics and business go hand in hand. You cannot separate one from the other, and that they rule the World."

We then spoke about perceptions of Muslims in the United States. Ms. Michaela had the most experience, and responded: "I lived three months in Turkey. I think Muslims are very warm people, very family oriented, very good people. A lot of Muslim countries are poor. Poverty does very weird things to people. Makes them do things they would not normally do.

"I think the Muslim community should do more to allow the Americans, the non-Muslims, to understand who they are as a culture. I think that a lot of the conflict is because the two cultures just don't understand each other. I don't think Americans want to hurt Muslims; I don't think Muslims want to hurt Americans. But I think that in the whole process of trying to figure out what's happening, a lot of people fall into the trap of having to prove that they're not bad, and ending up doing something that looks like it's bad."

I am pleased to say that these two articulate young women, neither of whom is the stereotypical American, renewed my faith that the American "system" does work to give people the opportunity to realize their dreams in an environment of hope. One key to peace, though, is recovering the belief that this is true in other parts of the World. It seems to me that these were among the qualities that led to the prestige of the United States in years gone by; but somehow, in the hurry to judge peoples and cultures in moments of passion, we have lost this reputation in the rest of the World. Fortunately, I feel that the qualities, which have always made the United States strong, do survive, and will re-assert themselves as the American public has an opportunity to change the direction of our country at the polls.

Chapter 13
Abu Yousef

Debbi and I are privileged to travel the World, but rarely together. The end of November 2005 brought one of those rare instances, when we could be in the same city, this time in Egypt, together. Debbi was inbound to Alexandria, for her typical task of facilitating an international NGO conference, and was expecting to meet me in Venice, a few days later. I had 3 days free in Dubai, and decided to surprise her in Egypt. I called her hotel, left a message, and jumped on an Emirates flight.

Debbi met me at the door of the hotel, thrilled that I made the trip. We went for a walk along the Corniche of Alexandria, and ran into the driver of a horse drawn carriage. We immediately hit it off, but we were too tired to take a ride that first night, November 29, 2005. Debbi knew what was coming, when I asked the driver to take me alone, while she worked the next day, on condition that he agree to be interviewed on my topics of interest. He was unsure about what I really meant, but we agreed, and set a time.

Abu Yousef ("Father of Yousef") was right on-time the next morning, and we had a fun four hours together, touring the ins and outs of Alexandria. He was an excellent guide, who had been plying his trade on the Corniche for 30 years, during which time he has worn out 20 horses, and 4 carriages. Such people have a wealth of wisdom, if one gives them a chance, so I enjoyed his company.

When we stopped for tea, he had the impression I was from a major network, when I began unbundling my two Panasonic GS400 cameras, tripods, and *Sennheiser* wireless microphones. I very soon disabused him of such a myth, but it being the first time anyone had ever asked for his opinion, he was thrilled to be talking.

He immediately wanted me and my audience to know that Muslims are peace loving people. He said:

> "Muslim people have very, very, very, very wide hearts. ... Very big hearts! Muslim people like everybody in every way. Muslim people not like danger; not like trouble."

Being dependent on the tourist trade, he commented on how the last 15 years have been difficult for him. Speaking of many profitable years gone by, he said:

> "A lot of American people came here on Navy ships. John Kennedy, Nimitz, Coral Sea, Roosevelt, Iowa .... Maybe 11 years [since they came]. I don't know why they don't come."

He pointed out that there was an Italian destroyer in the port that very day, and throughout the day pointed out all of the Italian sailors enjoying their liberty in Alexandria. Like the Chamber of Commerce, he promoted his city, urging:

> "I think [that if] American people come back, Americans very happy. No problem."

I have to agree with him. Alexandria, Egypt, is a remarkable city, once the home of Pharoahs, Cleopatra, Mark Antony, and many others. Cleopatra's city is accessible to divers, just off shore. Alexandria's ancient library, burned 2,500 years ago, has been replaced by, in my view, the most remarkable library in the World. The *Bibliotheca Alexandrina* has a reading room on 5 levels, beneath its sloping glass roof, and 5 museums within the building, containing artifacts like no others in the World. Thanks to the eminence of Debbi's hosts, we were treated to a private tour, which can only be described as astonishing.

Abu Yousef apparently felt that I have more clout than I do, because he urged me to help the city attract more tourists:

> "You tell them. Tell all American people, Egyptian people like Americans."

By the end of our time together, two old men, of an age, had learned to respect one another as men, and not as some grotesque caricature, foisted on the World by those who think we can have any World civilization based on hate. Abu Yousef told me:

> "I'm very happy because you're talking to me."

Isn't that what the whole World needs?

Chapter 14
Where Are Our Leaders?

Snapped back into the present by the inanity of our current leaders, I cannot believe that I live in the same United States of America in which I grew up, and for which I served 23 years in the U.S. Marine Corps.

This morning, June 28, 2006, news media are reporting that yesterday the United States Senate spent some of its valuable time debating whether there should be a Constitutional Amendment banning the burning of the flag of the United States, all of them forgetting that the flag is the only such national symbol, which stands for the right to burn the flag. The 1st Amendment of the United States Constitution, as interpreted by the Supreme Court of the United States for over 230 years, stands for our freedom of expression, and by suggesting that we curtail this means of expression of dissatisfaction with our leaders, 66 Senators are ignoring the principles upon which our Republic is founded.

In fairness, I should point out that most of them are educated enough to know better. Unfortunately, the policies they have been jamming down our throats recently, have destroyed the American educational system so badly that they think our electorate is too ignorant to know better. They think they will help themselves at the polls, by wasting their time on something that is only symbolic, while ignoring the real problems of our country, like poverty, healthcare, and tolerance for all of the residents of our country, which was why they were elected to serve in the first place. Fortunately, there are enough educated patriots left, to know the difference between action and obfuscation.

Another example of this inexcusable behavior is the repeated attempts to pass a Constitutional Amendment against gay marriage. I ask everyone reading this, "Does it really matter to us how people spend their time together, in the privacy of their own home? If two people choose to commit themselves to one another, why should society stand in the way? After all, don't spouses take care of one another in illness, for example, thereby avoiding larger healthcare costs to our government? Why don't we demand that our leaders find means to solve a real problem, like AIDS, which is killing millions of people globally?" It seems to me that solving real problems, rather than fake symbolic issues, is what we elect our leaders to do. Let's make a list of all those politicians, of whatever party, who wasted a single minute of their precious time on fake issues, rather than issues of substance, and let's make certain we throw the bums out in the fall. This is the just reward for failing to solve the real problems, which they were elected to solve.

And then there is our Administration, many members of which missed the civics lesson in which was taught how our Founding Fathers created a separation of powers. The President is incensed because his citizens object to his willy nilly looking into bank records. His toadies say that it's OK, because a different department of the Administration is overseeing the process. I object!

I do agree that examining bank records seems a viable means to detect terrorists. I object to the idea that the Administration can police itself. The President's program is a slip down the slope to totalitarianism. We have other branches of government, the Congress and the Judiciary, to oversee the plans and actions of the Executive Branch, and these have been ignored every bit as much as The Constitution of the United States has been ignored.

The same thing happened in the President's wiretapping strategy. There is nothing wrong with wiretapping for national defense, *per se*, but when it is done by ignoring the Judicial oversight that was mandated by Congress, effectuating the protections of the balance of powers our Founding Fathers had in mind, any properly educated American will naturally object.

They tell us that it is alright, because the Court always approves the wiretapping in the first place. Perhaps they approve it because, knowing that they will have to acquire Judicial approval, the Administration is careful to only wire tap those where a case of risk to our national defense can be made. I worry, though, when there is no such oversight. Is the Administration as careful about whom it wiretaps then? Or have we come so far toward the time of "Big Brother," that the majority of my fellow citizens think this is OK? I don't think so! I want our judges, even if they have been appointed by our President, to review such matters, and make sure our Freedoms and privacy are protected. That's their job!

Chapter 15

Mohammed Abbas

My brief two days in Alexandria ended with two more "man-on-the-street" interviews. I never drive when traveling outside the United States, so as to avoid having a problem with an accident abroad. My limousine driver from the Windsor Hotel, which seemed a strange name for a hotel in Egypt, to the Alexandria Borg Al Arab airport, was a young, neatly dressed, and articulate Arab. During our drive to the airport, I persuaded him to let me interview him. We arrived at the airport early, and I could not check in anyway, so we decided to leave the airport premises.

I asked him where we could go to conduct the interview. He said, "We have two choices. We can go to McDonald's," he heard me gasp in disbelief, we were out in the middle of a desert and refinery area, after all, "or we can go to a hotel for foreigners, I know."

"Please let us go to the hotel for foreigners," I said. "It would be too sacrilegious to do my interview about the views of Arabs from a McDonald's franchise." I suspect that even my readers would be shocked, if I described such a thing. American "culture," and I am using the term loosely, has dogged my steps everywhere. I have a wacky picture of my daughter in front of the golden arches rising over Tiananmen Square in Beijing, but I was in no such mood on this day, December 1, 2005.

We went to the Adham Compound Hotel, which has a lovely garden and swimming pool, and began setting up the equipment. Very shortly we were confronted by a man, who told us that we had to have the owner's permission. I was a bit apprehensive, but said I would go and speak with the manager, who I felt could not object, since I was doing my project for the benefit of Muslims. At least, so I felt.

It turned out that the 60-year-old owner, Mr. Adham, spoke perfect English, and had lived for many years in Canada. He had no problem with my interviewing at his hotel, but he objected to me interviewing my limousine driver. He said, "Why should you interview someone like that? We are descended from the Greeks! You should interview my son. He is very articulate."

"I would like to interview your son," I replied, as he walked in the door.

Teymour Adham was not really ready for an interview that morning. He sells Sahara adventures, and surfing experiences on the Egyptian coast, but he agreed to talk with me, if I gave him a few minutes to clean up. "Of course," I responded, and immediately returned to my limousine driver, to begin that interview.

Like so many average and unprivileged people, Mohammed Abbas did have his own level of personal wisdom to impart, though he was only 24 years old. He assured me that Egyptians like Americans, as follows:

> *"My opinion about American people? We like American people. There's no problem with us with American people. But maybe we don't like American government, because, you know, the news in Iraq and Afghanistan. We feel American government push[es] Muslims, or Arab Muslims. Maybe I don't [understand well] American politics, but that's my opinion."*

He described to me his perception of why Americans are misinformed about the Middle East by the international news media. Here is how he put it:

> *"I met 3 or 4 Americans, and worked with them as a limousine driver. They were saying that before coming to Egypt, they think that the whole Arab World is one country, and that the Arab World is a big desert, and that a few people make their transportation with camels, only. So the media sees only the problem: bomb, fire, and killing people; but, for example, they don't see the River Nile or the Cairo Tower. So the American media needs to be here, with the normal people.*
>
> *"Firstly, Arabian people, not Egyptian only, welcome [very well] their guests; that's the rule in Arabian countries. Secondly, for Egyptians, tourists mean jobs and money to a country for tourism, which is a good business. A lot of people are working in this business.*
>
> *"So we want the American media to come here, and take a view for the American people, that Arab people are not only fighting."*

For his part, he explained how he formed his opinions of the United States:

> *"Most of the people of the World like American from movies."*

Somehow, I didn't find his source of information so comforting, but I had to acknowledge the reality.

Chapter 16

Three Kinds of Muslims

Teymour Adham, the son of the owner of the Adham Compound Hotel (www.adhamcompoundegypt.com), was a remarkable find. Because I have opened my mind to the idea of interviewing anyone who is willing to speak with me about these issues, I benefit from great wisdom held in the repository of every day citizens of the World. All of the three men I spoke with in Alexandria, during my two-day visit, were extremely articulate in their own way, but, because of living in the United States for many years, Adham was a wealth of articulate knowledge. Like his father, who returned to Egypt from Canada in 1994, to begin his hotel enterprise, Adham had returned to Egypt to take a hand in building his country in another generation. I have always admired such people, the small minority of those who come from the Developing World to the West to find opportunity and then return home, because they chose to live more difficult lives in order to build their own countries. They reap the benefits of understanding where the World economy is ultimately going.

I am of the opinion that reasonable people, such as Abu Yousef, Mohammed Abbas, and Teymour Adham, are ubiquitous throughout the Muslim World, meaning that I would find them nearly everywhere I turn. Indeed, that would no doubt be true if I approached average people in the United States, as well. Certainly, that proved to be true in Alexandria.

Operating out of his father's hotel, Teymour Adham has built a tourist business out of his love for surfing, which he learned in Hawaii, and his love for adventure in the desert of Egypt (www.saharaadventurecompany.com). I asked him whether he experienced terrorism every day in Egypt, and this is what he said:

> *"No, no! Just on CNN, BBC, Al Jazeera. It affects people's lives in certain ways. I'm working in the tourist industry, and I would have a huge market with America. A lot of Americans would love to come out here and surf, and sand board, and go out*

in the desert but due to the conflict nobody comes. Mainly we have a lot of Italians, Greeks, Germans, British. They come here like September 11th never happened. To them life goes on. It seems like the only thing that has really changed in the World is America's point of view on the rest of the World. But to be honest, [as compared to] pre-September 11th, everything is pretty much the same here, except that we don't have as many American tourists."

Then, spontaneously, Adham started to talk about the influence of American policies on Islam, and where that is leading the World today. He said:

"Moderate Muslims are becoming more extremist. There are three kinds of Muslims: there are spiritual Muslims; there are moderate Muslims; and then there are extremists. Now, prior to September 11th the extremists were a minority. They stemmed from the little villages in the oasises, out in the desert, that had a rule for the last 500 years of not allowing foreigners or anybody in. It was mainly because of disease. The extremists took that another step. There were not a lot of them.

"But then after September 11th, a lot of moderates felt they were being culturally accused. Like, 'Your culture is wrong!' You know, you tell somebody that and they'll want to say, 'No, my culture's not so bad.' So a lot of the moderates are becoming a bit extremist. You know they're putting on the veil, when before they didn't put on a veil. They've stopped drinking, when they used to drink.

"They're starting to share the opinion of Free Palestine. And they're starting to really push for those things, because ..... What happened is that a small minority of extremists has made the World accuse the majority of Muslims ..... and if you accuse me of being something that I am, culturally, I'm just going to want to show you the good sides of it, and if you refuse to see it, I'm going to insist."

"Now that's horrible, because now the moderates, who are the majority of the Muslim World, are becoming more extremist in a way that they want to identify themselves culturally. That's who they are.

"Spiritual Muslims are different. Spiritual Muslims identify themselves by faith; it's a personal thing. They do not talk about their religion; they do not preach their religion. It's like Zen Buddhism. Someone who practices zen buries himself into his work; that's his religion; that's his thing. A lot of spiritual Muslims are like that. A lot of Muslims that live abroad; a lot of Muslims that live in Egypt; for them it's just a spiritual thing."

Chapter 17
One for the "Good Guys"

When I was growing up, in the 1950s and 1960s, America's self-image was that we were "the good guys." Our industrial might had been brought into the fight between living free and living under rigid totalitarian rule, and had prevailed. All of our movies clearly set up "the good guys," as we called the protagonists, and "the bad guys," those evil doers, who wanted to kill our men and rape our women, while repressing our population to their will. "The good guys" always won, in those celluloid fantasies, of course.

I remember the first time I began to doubt the purity of our "good guy" image. My father was stationed in Japan, with the U.S. Navy. One evening, in the summer of 1962 or 1963, he took me down to the docks at the Yokosuka Naval Base, and showed me a line of ships leaving Tokyo Bay in a convoy, like I had seen in World War II movies.

"See that?" He asked me.

"Yeah, Dad," I replied.

"That's the Marines," he said. "They're going to Vietnam. Every man and woman in the military has been to Vietnam, is there now, or is going there." My father was in charge of Navy audit, in that particular incarnation, and he had just returned from Saigon, where he had the responsibility of auditing the books of the PX of a small military contingent in the Cholon District, the Chinatown of Saigon, in those days. He obviously had some inside scoop, based on rumors being passed around the Officer's Club.

"Why, Dad?" I asked.

"Because the generals need more medals, for their careers," he responded cynically. "It's been 17 years since World War II, 10 years since Korea, and many of the senior officers at the Pentagon have never seen combat. They need to serve in combat, in order to get promoted."

I formed my opinion, that America's involvement in Vietnam was a "bad guy" thing to do, from that moment, nearly three years before most Americas even knew Vietnam was a place on the planet. Later, I served a tour of duty there, spending most of my time as an interrogation officer. Because of my father's service, there was never a thought that I would refuse to serve, as many did. In fact, in my Navy high school class, only one male graduate did not serve in the American military. I knew that American involvement was wrong, but having little choice and still be my father's son, I did feel that it would be useful to know why, from my personal experiences. And so it has been. But that's a different story.

On June 29, 2006, "the good guys" won an important victory. The United States Supreme Court (the head of our judicial branch of government) ruled against the Bush Administration (our executive branch), in the case of *Hamdan v. Rumsfeld.* I am sure "the bad guys" think America lost, in that case, but actually, the process of the *Hamdan* case, handled entirely in public, with lots of debate and comment, including in this chapter, proves the merits of the American system of government.

Justice John Paul Stevens, in his majority opinion, ruled that the United States must abide by the Geneva Convention, particularly "Common Article 3," which provides standards for trying individuals captured during armed conflict. He wrote that, while the provision "tolerates a great degree of flexibility in trying individuals captured during armed conflict," it does contain requirements, by which the United States is bound. He went on to say that, "in undertaking to try Hamdan and subject him to criminal punishment, the executive is bound to comply with the rule of law that prevails in this jurisdiction."

In all of my years associated with the practice of law, I never imagined that the Supreme Court would have to tell the President of the United States that he must obey the law. But it has come to that.

This is not over, by any means, and the Court invited the President to go back to Congress (our legislative branch of government) to seek appropriate permission for his style of military commission. Indeed, the Republicans were in a hurry to act to support the President yesterday morning. But, there will be a lot of embarrassing public debate; the Congress will have to be prepared to stand up for a lame duck (on his way out) President; and, if it does, our system could take that decision back to the Supreme Court, to see if any new law meets the standards of "the rule of law that prevails in this jurisdiction." [At this writing, the new law governing military commissions has been pushed through the Congress, just before Election 2006. Someone or more will be tried using it. They will appeal, based on the idea the law is flawed once again, and The Supreme Court will once again have to decide whether the Congress and the President overstepped their authority. I think they have, but it will take another 2-3 years of litigation, before we know what the Court thinks.]

It is a long and messy process, as I have described earlier in Chapter 6, but ultimately history will record that "the good guys" will prevail. At the time of 9/11, it was predicted that the President would assume extraordinary powers to defend the United States, and that over successive years these powers would be trimmed away through our judicial and legislative systems. Exactly this has occurred many times before in American history. *Hamdan* is one example of this prediction coming true.

In the "system of checks and balances," within the American Constitution, this is how our government serves Americans. Many inputs from many sources finally hammer out the overall best course of action for all Americans. This is why we Americans are committed to "democracy" as we practice it, because we know that ultimately "the good guys" do win through.

There will be more rebukes of our President, and his high handed policies, which offend me and many of my fellow Americans, in addition to what seems a majority of the rest of the World. I am heartened by the fact that the system does work. I believe that within my lifetime, we will see America's prestige in the World restored, and President Bush will seem like an unfortunate aberration on the way to forging an even greater nation.

There is a dark side, however, which must be acknowledged. In the *Hamdan* vote, the three votes against the decision came from the three "conservative" ideologues. Furthermore, the Chief Justice took no part in the vote, because it was his decision, when he was a lower court judge, which was being overruled. If he had voted, we may presume that the tally would have been 5-4. This means that the balance between right and wrong is clearly on the shoulders of each of the 5 Justices who voted with the majority. If any one of them changes their mind, the decision of the Court could be a step backward for mankind.

As a lawyer for over 30 years, I pray daily for the continued health of these 5 Justices, in the hope that God will grant that President Bush will never again have the duty of appointing another Justice to the Court.

Fortunately, every time we vote, the American people get to decide which politicians are "the good guys," based on all of our experiences and history. This is a privilege we cherish, as we know that few other people in the World really get to decide. The results are for all the World to see. While we have our slums, and bad moments in history, our cities are not falling down around our ears, as they are in so many countries.

All of us have our faults, both as politicians and as citizens of countries, but over time, all of us in the World have our way of voting. Everyone living in the Americas is here because we or our ancestors voted with our feet, to leave oppression or hardship, and come to a place where we could be free to live our lives as we wish. It isn't a "free pass" for aberrational behavior; but it is a system that works over time to benefit all mankind. One can easily assess the esteem in which a country is held by the World, by counting the balance of immigrants vs. emigrants in a given year. Speaking only for the United States, most people in the World will accept that our applications for immigration always far exceed the number of people who want to leave. This is an election America will always win, and for very good reason!

I am an optimist! Even after what is going on in our World, I still believe that "the good guys" win.

Chapter 18
Contradictions

Returning to my interview with Teymour Adham, in Alexandria, he offered a perfect example of our World schizophrenia today. Teymour had lived in Canada and the United States for so long that he actually speaks like an American. On the podcast of this book, you cannot tell that he is not as much an American as me. He also talked about how some parts of the Muslim spectrum are dividing Muslims against one another, along political lines:

> *"It's horrible what's happening in the World right now. The Islamic Brotherhood is up in Egypt right now, big time. And now it's like I'm not Muslim, because they're the Muslim Brotherhood. So if I support the other party, then I'm not part of the Muslim Brotherhood; I'm not Muslim."*

Teymour pointed out that American policies are aiding and abetting this process of making such groups stronger.

> *"America's Policies are just wrong. You can't expect democracy to work in countries where the majority of the people are not educated enough to understand what democracy is. First they need a leader, to bring their living standards up. They need to live well. Their children need to be educated. And then maybe their children's children, who have university degrees, and understand what good government is, and what good government is supposed to do; those people can have democracy.*
>
> *"But the moment you throw democracy at people who earn $20-30 dollars per month, and tell them choose your leader. Sometimes I just think they want the Islamic Brotherhood … 'well I pray every day; I fast; maybe if I choose the Brotherhood, God will help me.' I mean,* ***these guys are hoping for anything. They're so poor; and they're so down and out.*** *So religion is their only sanctuary.*

"America turning it into a war of religion; and Italy backing up America, which means the Vatican backs up America .... So if it's not a war for religion; and it's not a war about Islam; and it's not a war for Jerusalem; and it's not a crusade ... ***then it must be about money.*** *If it's not about money, if it is idealistic, then it's about religion. But if it's not, then it's about money. It's about selling guns, and selling weapons and starting conflicts."*

Teymour claimed that **America's proclivity to violence** is one of the big culprits in the whole process.

"I think we're smart enough now, and we have enough communication with the Internet, and everything, to know the evil side of mankind; how savage we can be. I don't think our televisions should be full of that. If you look at Al Arabia TV, for instance, it's all either drama or comedy. We don't have violence in our movies. If I watch an American movie, very violent! American television, very violent! Your culture is based on violence and materialism in many ways."

While I do not agree with every word of what Teymour has to say on these topics, I do have to acknowledge that perception is reality in many ways; and this is the way Teymour perceives American culture, even after living in the United States for many years. He blames America for turning friend against friend in the Middle East, as a matter of policy, since inception of Israel.

"My father's best friend, and my uncle's best friends in Alexandria here were Jewish. In North Africa, here, we all lived—Christians, Muslims, and Jews—we all lived together just fine. We lived together just great, in fact!

"If you hear some of the stories about Egyptian Jews, and Egyptians; and the Israeli conflict you'd be amazed. I'll tell you a little story. A friend of my father's was in the Egyptian military during the war. His whole platoon was wiped out, and he was walking back to Suez, which was 2-300 miles from where he was. When he was walking back an Israeli tank drives right up to him, puts the nozzle down in his face, he puts his hands up in the air; then the Israeli army guy gets out, comes down from the tank, looks him right in the face, and gives him a big hug. Because they were friends, they went to school together at a French school in Alexandria called St. Mark, which was in the Jewish quarter of Alexandria. They were best friends growing up. So he sat the Egyptian soldier on top of his tank, and drove him all the way back to the border. There are hundreds of stories like this. Friends were divided. People were divided. We lived with the Christians and the Jews and everything was just fine.

"What is it then; the old divide and conquer; the old Anglo-Saxon strategy? They want to divide us up. If we were still living together, Muslim and Christian and Jew, maybe we would be the First World, and America, you guys would be the Third World."

He then commented that the way Americans and Europeans live is just an illusion:

> *"I moved to Egypt in 1999, because I didn't want to live in North America anymore, because it was just not the place I wanted my daughter to grow up. At least out here it's a little dirtier, and maybe it's a little more dangerous on the road, and there are not as many rules, but I feel like I have a lot more control over my daughter's life, and her upbringing. We go out into the desert a lot; she sees nature.*
>
> *"I really feel like the Third World is the Real World. I feel that the First World is really just a dream. Everybody that's living in the First World is living in a dream. It's not real. When I go to America on vacation, or I go to France, and I wake up in the morning and see how everything is just in place, I feel like I'm in a dream. And the fact is that 10-15% of the World live in Europe and America. Only 10-15% of the World live in that dream. The real World is the rest of the World. It's us. It's Africa; it's Asia; it's the Middle East. The population of the World is living like this."*

I have to describe Teymour's demeanor as a bit rueful that living near an oil refinery in the desert of Egypt is his reality, rather than on the North Shore of Oahu. It seemed, somehow, that he was trying to justify to me his life choice of coming to Egypt to work side by side with his father. But I felt that many of his observations were poignant, and right on the money, so I feel obliged to include them in detail here, so my fellow Americans can understand his sincerity and intelligence about the World situation. In the next chapter, I will present Teymour's feelings about what needs to be done politically.

Chapter 19
Corruption

Teymour acknowledged that the West is not the only source of problems in the Muslim World. Beyond the Muslim Brotherhood suggesting people are not good Muslims if they do not vote for their party, there is corruption in many governments, which have impoverished many of the people of the Middle East. Teymour summed up the problem quite succinctly:

> "To improve the economy in the Arab World would be to create a paper trail for all of the money. I think Egypt is supposed to do that in 2010. It's just difficult to get it implemented when it hasn't been implemented. Egypt needs to do economically what America did in the 30's. You know, when you guys busted all of those Mafia people; Al Capone and all that. Egypt needs to do that. At lot of North African countries need to do that. You need a paper trail for the money. You walk into any bank in Egypt and there's suitcases of money going in and out of the bank. No real paper trail. So the government really can't collect taxes properly."

There are very many cases of fraud, waste and abuse in many Middle Eastern countries. They are beyond the scope of this chapter, but they are widely reported. Since the United States government has its own examples, it is not for me to point fingers. But, in the West, we do try to correct such problems, as they surface, and there are many prosecutions annually. A government that does not even envision passing banking regulations to provide "paper trails" for money until 2010, does not seem to be a government that is looking out for the best interests of its people.

The standard defense to such an assertion is to say that we Americans should mind our own business. The United States has similar problems. To which I do respond, "Yes, we do, but the order of magnitude is quite different, and we regularly send our scoundrels to prison." Furthermore, we do this publicly, for the World to see. Meanwhile, the corrupt practices of many governments around the World are putting peace at risk. When such matters threaten the national security of our country, they become issues our government can no longer ignore.

I believe that the rules diplomacy in the World are changing, and will change much further. Until recent times, the general rule of diplomacy was to leave "hands off" the domestic issues of other nation states. Today, I am doubtful that is an appropriate strategy. We need to be aware of the demographics and internal politics of other countries, and begin to push their governments to improve the living conditions of their citizens. Several tens of millions of disenchanted and impoverished Muslim youths, throughout a region as volatile as the Middle East, can no longer be ignored as a domestic problem of another country. Such a "head in the sand" strategy can only lead to greater troubles for the whole World.

Still, my two days of interviews in Alexandria made me feel quite optimistic again. Each of my three randomly selected "men in the street" were articulate in their own way. Each responded quite reasonably to what needs to be done. A common theme was the urgency of improving the economy of Egypt, and I extrapolate that response to the rest of the Middle East. Each was derisive of American policy, which is spending tens of billions of dollars on making war, but is afraid to make a matching investment to assure a just peace in the future. Each man did, in his own way, demonstrate that Muslims are peace loving people. They have genuine concerns, which are close at hand, and American policy needs to orient itself to help common people in developing countries solve their very real everyday problems.

Chapter 20
Lubna Hussain

I first became aware of Lubna Hussain, the courageous columnist for *The Arab News* (www.arabnews.com), on July 8, 2005, as the hateful coverage of the London bombings of the previous day were being pumped into my hotel room in Jeddah, Saudi Arabia, by CNN and BBC. As I have said earlier, I had reacted viscerally to the fact that, beginning immediately, and continuing for a couple of weeks thereafter, the mainstream media was bombarding their viewers with the terms "Islamic terrorist" and "Islamic extremist." I was upset that these terms amount to defamation of nearly everyone in the Muslim World (www.wordsmatter.tv), and I immediately recognized that they would engender more undeserved hate toward Muslims generally, and cause Muslims to react defensively, because they would feel that they were under attack, which they clearly were.

I was paging through *The Arab News* when I came upon Lubna's article, "The Opiate of the Masses." She was railing against the mainstream media, and particularly describing an incident in which she was asked to be a network's "reporter on the scene," during the Alkhobar terrorist incident the preceding May. Her outrage was that she was in Riyadh, not Alkhobar, and had no information to impart. She proceeded to inform the anchor of that fact "on the air." She went on to say in her column,

> *"Unfortunately, in a world where there exists a sordid intimacy between the media and realpolitik, it is becoming increasingly arduous to discern what the truth at the heart of the matter is. Sure, all the news channels relay "facts," but it is the manner in which they are presented that has become increasingly important. In some, there is no longer much scope for us to judiciously assess through a process of impartial reporting what is going on in the world around us as it has become the job of the producers of the piece to make up our minds for us."*
>
> .....
>
> *"ETA is not synonymous with the Spanish. The IRA is not symbolic of ordinary Irish people. The Red Brigade is not representative of fashionable Italians. Who on*

earth would dare equate the KKK with Americans? But the actions of Al-Qaeda speak for the entire population of Saudi Arabia."

.....

"...This constant bombardment of television news, that we are subjected to round-the-clock, has slowly but surely eroded our ability to distinguish between fact and opinion. ... We see the same reports repeatedly, over and over again. We lose our ability to reason and, as I have said before, "a lie repeated often enough becomes the truth."

Lubna surely wrote this article before the news of the London bombings, since it was in my morning paper in Jeddah the very next day, which adds further credibility to my assertion that Muslims have consistently felt that they are under attack from the Western media. By the time I read her article, I had already decided to express my dissatisfaction publicly, in my Kalmbach Distinguished Alumnus Lecture at The Simon Graduate School of Business, which was scheduled for the fall of 2005. I wrote to Lubna, noting my admiration for her ability to articulately express the same outrage, which I was feeling that morning. She never responded, but then, I did not expect that she would, imagining that she must receive hundreds of e-mails per day, which later proved to be the case.

Nonetheless, I began to follow Lubna Hussain's writing, and have been consistently amazed by her passionate style and erudition. She frequently takes on instances of injustice in Saudi society, especially those aimed at women, which few other writers would dare to touch, though most of those writers' work appears in *The Arab News*. The fact that these pieces have been published at all is a credit to *The Arab News*, which I regard as one of the best and least biased newspapers in the World. All of Lubna's articles can be found on *The Arab News* web site (www.arabnews.com) by typing her name into the internal search engine, and they are fully accessible to anyone outside of the Kingdom of Saudi Arabia. Regretfully, and this was a topic of another Lubna Hussain article, they are only available by subscription within the Kingdom. My favorite Lubna Hussain column was published on November 25, 2005, "Anything He Can Do... She Can Do Better," but that is a topic for a later chapter of this book.

All of this chapter is prologue for my fortunate experience of meeting Lubna, in late November 2005, and the privilege of interviewing her on December 12, 2005. For those who cannot wait to hear that interview, it can be found on the *Words Matter* web site at www.wordsmatter.tv.

Chapter 21

"America" is Self Correcting

July 4, 2006 (Beginning the 231st Year of Independence)

To all of my "Big Brothers," and the wannabees out there, I send you greetings! I am able to see the IP address of people who access this book online. This is a service provided by my host computer. The last few days, when I search certain IP addresses, I get "access denied," which is a spooky experience, if ever I saw one.

Some may think that I am critical of the President. *Au contraire!* Like many of my fellow Americans, I have thought for many years that his father bobbled the task of ridding the World of Saddam Hussain, in 1991. Given the demographics of the Middle East, having his regime in play was definitely a wild card. Allowing terrorist training camps to exist in Afghanistan for over a decade, in hindsight, was definitely an error in judgment, for both parties. These situations had to change, to defend our country. To his credit, President Bush was up to the task.

The regretful truth, though, is that our politicians of both parties, though they knew this truth, were afraid of the political fallout from taking the necessary action before September 11, 2001, just as Franklin D. Roosevelt could not take action against Japan until after December 7, 1941. Only after such shocks did they have the moral fortitude to stand up and be counted, and then they were practically unanimous. For what, we may ask, were they waiting?

Very shortly after 9/11, newspaper articles were written, which predicted what the President would do, and, in effect, predicted *Tsunami of Blood.* We knew that the President would take strong action, very likely contrary to some of our guiding principles, to protect the nation. We also knew that, soon enough, there would be a backlash, if he went too far.

I do believe that wiretapping American citizens is a good idea, to protect our national defense. Indeed, I assume my wires are tapped. I do believe that examining bank records is a good idea too. I feel certain that, except for the briefest time, these actions should have taken place through our system of laws, checks and balances. This would have been quite possible. This was not done.

Instead of insisting that our laws be obeyed, and indeed, enforced by our Executive branch, as called for the The Constitution of the United States, Members of Congress and Senators put their collective heads in the sand, and said to the President, "Let us know when everything is alright." Instead of taking appropriate steps to protect our national values and solve real problems, they chose to waste too much of their time on symbolic gestures, which have no meaning in our lives as we live them. I have never physically seen anyone burn an American flag. I have never seen a homosexual act in my community. I have seen poverty in America, within three blocks of the United States Capitol Building. I have seen Marines and Soldiers die for the wrong reasons, because the Congress would not do the necessary to save their lives. Politicians, who think they can keep their jobs by wasting time on symbolism, should be shown the door as quickly as possible. We need men and women of action and courage, who will insist on doing their jobs of solving the problems of our nation and the World. Many of our politicians have let us down!

There is good news, though! "America" is self correcting. On this 4th of July, the 230th Anniversary of our Independence from tyranny, what do I mean by "America?" On September 25, 2001, Professor Peter Ferrara of the George Mason University School of Law, published a short op-ed called, "To Kill an American." What he meant by "American," in this case, was anyone, in any nation, who carries the human spirit of Freedom. Every human being in the Americas has come, or their ancestors came, with that spirit in their hearts. Professor Ferrara's point was that every human being carries that spirit deep inside, regardless of their birthplace, and "America" is simply a metaphor (a symbol) for that spirit.

If we look at the broad span of history, we can see that the direction of values has always been toward honoring the human spirit of Freedom. Sometimes, this direction is misguided and misdirected by venal leaders, but always, over time, human beings have trended toward a society of Freedom and mutual respect.

Many Americans believe that the President has gone too far in wiretapping and violating privacy without oversight. He could have gotten the necessary permissions, and followed the necessary processes, but he chose a different path. Now he will suffer the approbation of history, but we all have to acknowledge that he has kept the nation safe during the past 5 years of the War on Terror.

Eventually, enough of us do see the right path, and take it. Eventually, enough Americans saw the truth about Vietnam, so we swallowed our pride and left.

I think we need to look at what needs to be done, to honor the human spirit of Freedom:

1. We must demand that our politicians solve real problems. If you had a choice of allowing the burning of a flag, a symbol, or saving the life of a poor child, by providing good healthcare for the impoverished, which would you do? Is there anyone reading this, who thinks that the integrity of a piece of cloth or paper is more important than even one human life? Speaking for myself, I will be as much an American regardless of how many flags are burned. But that child's life can never be recovered. Nonetheless, this is what we let our politicians get away with, if we allow them to misdirect our attention with symbolic gestures.

2. We must make certain that the media understand the danger of their behaviors to the peace of the World. Does their reporting add to information, which can be used to solve problems, or add to the problems on which they report?

3. We must make our fundamentalist clerics, of all religions, remember that God made everything and everyone within view. We must stop the fiction of fighting one another over how we pray, as God taught us all to pray, or not, each in our own way. Is there any cleric out there, of whatever religion, who thinks their religion can convert everyone else before causing a mass conflagration? Write to me! I'll publish your reasoning, and make it part of the record of mankind. There is an account, in Daniel Boorstin's *The Discoverers,* of how Galileo knelt before the Inquisition, and swore on a Bible that the Sun does orbit around the Earth, which is the center of the universe. Good records were kept of his speech, even then. He made monkeys for eternity of those Inquisitors, who accused him of blasphemy, because of his science. Reading his words now, no one could believe that he was sincere in his oath, even when sworn to on a Bible, before high clerics of the church.

4. We must insist that our executive branch of government enforce our laws. Last week it was reported that the Bush Administration is not enforcing 750 statutes of the United States, a task they were elected to perform. They are not the legislators of our laws; they are the enforcers of our laws. This is their role in our checks and balances. And yet, they have established a reputation for thinking they are above the law, both nationally and internationally. This is not acceptable!

5. We must be aware of the demographics and motivational dynamics of other parts of the World. Some of our allies have ignored the needs of their people. We must hold them to account, or reap the unfortunate consequences. The French riots of last fall and winter are only a prologue for the type of conflagration that will come, if we do not insist upon change. In America, we suffered through this type of conflagration in the Civil Rights movement. Must we repeat history, and risk the species, because we cannot see the inevitable and move to correct the injustices? 9/11 proved that we are not safe just because we are oceans away from the injustices.

I have every confidence that, in America, we will make the necessary changes in our behavior, to save the human spirit of Freedom. I have the Freedom to write this into the collective unconscious, so that we may hear this message again and again, from every quarter.

Will you be "an American," in the Peter Ferrara sense, and do the necessary to make the World a safer place? The World has gotten more dangerous since 9/11, not safer, and the momentum is in the wrong direction. We have a President who doesn't enforce the laws passed by Congress; we have a Congress that thinks talking about symbols is more important than solving real problems; and we have idealogues on the Supreme Court, who think it's OK to violate our laws and our treaties. Only if like minded individuals stand up and say that we must reverse the direction, will we be safe in our homes. America is self correcting! We must correct it! We are God's manifestation of that human spirit of Freedom!

Chapter 22
We Can Close Gitmo

The good news for President Bush is that we can close the prison at the Guantanimo Naval Base, and send all of the prisoners back to the custody of their home countries.

If we presume that the premise of this book is true, that it would not be in the best interests of Muslim countries to allow hardened fighters back among their general population of frustrated young men, then we can rely on these countries to do the necessary to keep them incarcerated on their own soil. This would be more humane, as it would allow for family visitation.

It appears that the reason for intended long term imprisonment was to keep hardened fighters out of the battle. I am in agreement with that! Indeed, I believe it is the job of the Administration to make judicious decisions on who should be retained, although perhaps not at Gitmo, and who should be allowed to serve their incarceration in their own country.

I feel it is clear that releasing prisoners to the custody of their home countries will not be a free pass to release. Indeed, their home countries are more likely to retain them indefinitely.

If the home country governments will agree that this is the correct idea, then we should do all in our power to empty Gitmo, so that we remove that unfortunate stain from our honor.

Chapter 23
Ahmadinejad Makes Monkeys of Western Press

Shortly after my brief visit to Alexandria, I returned to Saudi Arabia for business. I was thrilled on the morning of Saturday, December 10, 2005, to open my *Arab News* and find several stories about the summit of the Organization of the Islamic Conference ("OIC"), which had just concluded in Makkah. King Abdullah had hosted leaders of the 57 Muslim nations in an extraordinary conference, the culmination of which was the "Makkah Declaration," which espoused principles of moderate Islam for all of the World's Muslims.

Since 9/11, commentators in the West have been calling upon Muslims to come forth and take a stand on where Islam should be in terms of its principles as they relate to the rest of the World. Here were many heads of state doing just that, and in writing. "This is a wonderful breakthrough," I thought.

Since I was in my hotel's coffee shop when I first read this, I hurried back to my room to see how CNN was covering the conference. Nothing! BBC? Nothing! I was crestfallen. I went on about my business, contemplating how the news from a meeting of 57 Muslim countries, with such an important result, could have been missed entirely.

12 hours later, I checked again. This was the moment when I first began to appreciate the artistry of President Mahmoud Ahmadinejad of Iran in his manipulation of the Western press. CNN was carrying a story, which said that Mr. Ahmadinejad had suggested that, since the Jews in Israel had come from Western Europe, and Germany had been their oppressor, Germany and Austria should make room for a new state of Israel within their borders. (*Arab News* had carried an *Agence France* report about the statement on December 10th.) There was still no sign of news about the OIC Summit at Makkah.

24 hours after finding news of The Makkah Declaration, CNN was still carrying the Ahmadinejad story, but was mentioning that he made the statement at a meeting of the

OIC, thereby implying that somehow the other members of the OIC were concurring. By then the rumors among my Saudi friends were that King Abdullah was furious that the conference had been upstaged by Mr. Ahmadinejad, but this is not what the Western press was reporting.

36 hours after, CNN was finally carrying a 10-15 second video clip of the OIC Summit, which showed Mr. Ahmadinejad walking next to King Abdullah. I guessed that it was the only 15 seconds in the entire two days, when Ahmadinejad was anywhere near the King, but that was conjecture on my part. They were still commenting on Mr. Ahmadinejad's remarks, and not mentioning the Makkah Declaration at all, thereby implying by the juxtaposition of the King and the President, that the King was supporting the Iranian's position. According to my Saudi friends, nothing could have been farther from the truth, but this is what everyone watching CNN International was led to believe. While I was not able to watch the US domestic version of CNN, I have to believe that my friends in America were seeing the same type of shameful reporting.

I have since asked many friends whether they have ever heard of the Makkah Declaration, and not one of them has. This is a classic example of why Americans and other Westerners have an entirely skewed perception of what is really going on in the Muslim World.

I give Mr. Ahmadinejad my "Press Manipulator of the Year" award for 2005. I give CNN my "Dupes of Venal Politicians" award for 2005.

Chapter 24
Lubna Hussain's Comment

When I spoke with Lubna Hussain about the Organization of the Islamic Conference Summit, and the incident with Mr. Ahmadinejad, two days later, this is the exchange we had, when I was questioning press responsibility:

Skip: *"Something like the OIC Summit, which was the culmination of requests from Western governments, and so on, for a period of time: for the Muslim World to speak up and say 'we are a tolerant religion, we are a moderate religion, we're not a religion of extremism and terrorism,' and I've heard all kinds of calls for that, but when the King pulled together a huge conference with all these heads of state, it wasn't reported."*

Lubna: *"Nobody wants to know."*

Skip: *"Right. I observed the development of that story in the last few days. I read about the conference in the morning in Arab News, and I was impressed, I was thrilled by the good news that was coming out of that summit, and so I immediately went up and turned on CNN. It wasn't even mentioned. I don't know if CNN had a reporter there, but up until then, I don't think it was even going to be reported on at all, I mean the conference itself."*

Lubna: *"Of course, in fact most of the major networks chose not to carry it. They said it wasn't important."*

Skip: *"That's shocking to me!"*

Lubna: *"That's what I'm saying. Do you see that therefore, they talk about how Arabs are resentful of American policy, all Arabs are resentful. This is the point I think that the American people have to understand. Arabs actually are not resentful towards American people. They love American people. We think that American people are, in fact, 'salt of the Earth,' and are actually some of the nicest, friendliest, kindest, most generous people in the World. But, it is not the American people that we have an issue with; it is their government and it is their media; and we see their media as being a vehicle of their government."*

Chapter 25

My First Meeting with Lubna Hussain

I am blessed with friends in Saudi Arabia, who know important individuals. Over the months since July 7, 2005, I had discussed with one such friend my admiration for the writing of Lubna Hussain. He said he knew her (slightly), and would be happy to see if he could persuade her to interview me, about my mainstream work in Saudi Arabia. He delivered on this promise, so there came a time in the last half of November 2005, when Lubna and I had arranged to meet in a public place, to interview me.

There was a somewhat funny incident, because no one had mentioned to Lubna that I am in the habit of wearing Saudi attire when working in the Kingdom. When Lubna arrived, looking for me, she did not recognize me as an American, so looked right past me. I approached her and said, "Miss Hussain?"

"Oh, my God!" She responded, grabbing for her throat. She looked desperately around the room, saying, "I must be on Candid Camera!" We both had a laugh about her reaction, and then went to begin her interview of me.

At that time, my mind was filled with what I had learned from Sheldon Solomon (*In the Wake of 9/11: The Psychology of Terror)*, just a few days before. I had the interview on video tape on my camera, and a headset with me, so I said, "I know you came to interview me, but I think we can do nothing more important than having you listen to the first part of this interview with Sheldon." She agreed to listen, so I gave her the headset, and started the camera running, with it's mini 2.5 inch screen. This is what Sheldon was saying:

> *"One of the things Becker points out in a very powerful book called Escape from Evil is that if these ideas are correct, if we really do subscribe to our views about the nature of reality that culture gives us in order to minimize concerns about death, then we're naturally going to have problems when we run into people who are different than ourselves, because if we accept the validity of an alternative conception of reality, that*

undermines the confidence with which we subscribe to our own, and that in turn opens us up to the overwhelming terror that our beliefs were designed to reduce.

"So according to Becker and other theorists, what we do when we run into people that are different than ourselves, is we tend to belittle them as an inferior form of not quite human life. We try to convince them to drop their beliefs and adopt ours instead, and if that doesn't work we just literally kill them, as harsh as it sounds. According to Becker and terror management theory, a good deal of the ongoing strife that we see in the world, not only today but throughout history, is the result of a psychological inability to tolerate those who do not subscribe to our own death-denying ideology. I think underlying all of the problems that we see in the world today, I think central to understanding is just recognizing that it's very tough when we run into folks who happen to be different than ourselves.

"What is it that causes terrorism in the first place? Our understanding of that is that in every culture, and in every religion, most people are quite decent and even very noble. They subscribe to their beliefs about the nature of reality, and by having them and living in accordance with them, I think it brings out the very best, generally, of what people are capable of becoming. Unfortunately however, in every time and place, in every culture that we've seen so far in history, in every religion that we know of, there is always a very extreme, I'll call them at the risk of offending some, 'lunatic fringe,' that subscribe to a malignant, fundamentalist brand of their secular or religious ideology.

"Always in these cases what you find is some other individual or group of individuals that is designated as the all-encompassing repository of evil that must be eradicated, and if we're able to do that, life on earth would be just like it would be in heaven. During the Crusades, of course, the Christians thought if they could recapture the Holy Land, life would be great. Of course, in some Islamic countries today, all of the problems in the world are ascribed to the evil-doers in the West. I don't think this is confined to one group or another, nor is terrorism. You have the Hindus duking it out with the Muslims in India; you've got the Protestants and the Catholics in Ireland, as you know; and so history is riddled with people that say if we can only get rid of these other people, life would be fine."

"My understanding of terrorism is that it usually comes into play when a group of individuals does not have either the numerical or military power to fight in conventional terms. What they then try to do is to literally disrupt the symbolic fabric of cultural life by heinous deeds that just shatter cultural Worldviews in seconds. So, when you can fly an airplane into the World Trade Center, or attack the Pentagon, it's not only the loss of life that's so egregiously psychologically discombobulating, it's really that you're poking holes in the cultural symbols that sustain folks. So I would say that what makes terrorism so profoundly and disarmingly effective is not only the carnage, but on top of that you've got the random and arbitrary nature of it, and on top of that, it appears to make a mockery of the kind of psychological security that our cultural Worldviews

provide for us."

It was interesting that, during our taped interview, two weeks later, Lubna and I were talking about the power of the media, particularly television media, to "disrupt the symbolic fabric of cultural life" in one shot, very much as Sheldon described what terrorists do. This is what we said:

Lubna: *"Media is the most potent Midas for corrupting the minds and hearts of millions of people in an instant. In a five minute piece you can actually change somebody's perceptions, pretty much. And so, there has to be some kind of rebalancing."*

Skip: *"CNN has done a very good job over many years, twenty-five years now, presenting a story from around the world with very courageous reporters, no doubt about that. But I think that they've lost the fact that they are so influential today, that they really have to put another layer of consideration on what it is they do."*

At that point I had to ask Lubna to stop listening, so that we could proceed with her interview of me. In the course of that, it occurred to me that I should have the courage to ask Lubna to let me interview her on tape. She was kind enough to agree.

Chapter 26
CNN Compared to Hitler's Propaganda Machine

1,000,000,000! One Billion! That's a one with NINE zeros after it. That's a lot of people to be able to reach in one go with your "Midas" (magical) ability to change minds with one brief story. But that's how many people CNN, BBC, *Al Jazeera*, *Al Arabiya*, MSNBC, and Star TV, to mention just six networks, can reach in EVERY broadcast.

Before I write this chapter, I want to be very clear that there is absolutely NO time, and I mean ZERO, when I believe it is appropriate for ANY government to attempt in ANY way to control the content of ANY media outlet. America's Founding Fathers were a lot smarter than I am, and they wrote into The 1st Amendment to The United States Constitution, and it was ratified by the people of the United States, that there would be Freedom of the Press and Freedom of Speech in my country. This provision has been interpreted, by The Supreme Court of the United States and hundreds of lower courts, for 230 years, to mean that this provision also applies to the States, and to all forms of expression, including *Tsunami of Blood*, published on the Internet. It was their belief, and it is mine, that where published words or images are unacceptable to the public at large, the public can express its Freedom by turning away from them, or criticizing them, until they are discontinued.

The five Freedoms contained in The 1st Amendment of The Constitution of the United States, are the bedrock of The United States of America. Without these, the tempering process from Diversity, which I spoke of earlier, which allows America to accept the best ideas and eliminate the worst ideas of our society, would not be functional. It is painfully obvious that this process is not functional in most countries of the World. The living standards of most people on Planet Earth speak for themselves. Because people are intimidated by their governments from mentioning controversial ideas, they also are reticent about airing good ideas, so their societies do not advance as quickly toward higher living standards, as the American society does constantly.

So, as I criticize CNN, in the next few lines, I want to be clear as crystal that there is absolutely NOTHING, which would make me suggest that any government should intervene to interfere with absolutely ANYTHING they, or anyone else, including *Al Jazeera* and *Al Arabiya*, might choose to put on any "air," cable, transmission or in printed form.

BUT, those same rights give me the privilege, indeed the responsibility, to make my case to the World, that CNN, and many other outlets of the mainstream media, have gone too far, and need to reconsider their approach to the news. They need to reconsider their responsibility to report the news, without inflaming the news. As *Words Matter* began, CNN and BBC were defaming practically all of the World's Muslims, over and over again, for weeks on end. This is VERY dangerous! People who are defamed, on any pretext, become understandably angry.

On December 12, 2005, this is how *Arab News* columnist Lubna Hussain expressed the same idea:

> *"I think, as you know, the impetus and the importance of the press has increased with satellite television. ... I think it's interesting because the level of responsibility and the level of accountability has actually gone down as the importance of the press has actually gone up. There's been this exponential rise in the prevalence of the press, and a corresponding decline in the responsibility that the press takes towards disseminating information as is. So there's become this really, I think, skewed view of the World, and unfortunately reporters, I feel, should be impartial in an ideal World. Of course they should actually have the ability to criticize; they should also have some procedures within their own countries that protect that level of criticism."*

Lubna is never one to "pull her punches." As my readers know by now, Lubna is quite articulate in expressing the frustrations of more than a billion people in the Muslim World. This is what she said:

> *"When you're reporting a story, it should not have a slant. I think that the Western media, as I said, go in with an angle, and they corroborate that angle through stories that actually match that angle. That, therefore, is not impartial reporting, that is not a reporting job, in my estimation. I don't see any difference now between what was going on in World War II, in terms of Hitler's propaganda machine, and what is going on in, for example, a network like CNN, which 24/7 bombards you with, as I said, massaged stories and massaged facts and figures that correspond to the very thing they're trying to prove in the first place. So it's a question again of deduction and induction. It's no longer this sort of impartial, wanting to bring the truth to the World. It's wanting to bring your truth, and making everyone else believe it."*

Several Americans in journalism have told me that the Bush Administration has used intimidation to control reporting of the press. Ron Suskind, in his recent book *The One*

Percent Doctrine, implies that the American government intentionally attacked *Al Jazeera Satellite Channel*, as a means to "send a message" about its coverage. I am doubtful that such behavior will stand the test of time, in the face of fully enforced international law. But the strength of our 1st Amendment Freedoms is that Mr. Suskind can suggest such a thing openly, and I can add my comment here. Here is how Lubna Hussain and I expressed the same concern, during our interview:

Lubna: "The point is, is that in the Western media, you are also seen, I think, as almost a traitor if you report something that is contrary to what the general belief is, more so in the United States than in Europe.

Skip: "I'm afraid that's true. One of the things that I've observed recently, as I've been becoming more interested in what it is to be a television journalist, is that all of the CNN shots, or most of their shots, are very tight shots. They're shots like we have in this interview, where they're head and shoulders. So, if someone's angry at the US for example, they'll be shouting like crazy, but they won't be showing the wider shot that has McDonalds over here, and Kentucky Fried Chicken over here, and people driving past in Chevrolets. Unfortunately, if Americans could see that, and see that there is American influence, that has been accepted in Saudi Arabia completely, for example, they might see Saudi Arabia in a different way. But they don't see it that way. They only see it as talking heads, and very often they're angry talking heads, and so that creates the news in a certain way."

Lubna: "This is the power of rhetoric."

Chapter 27
Bad Dream, Good Dream

It is often sobering, as an American, to hear the raw reactions of people in the Middle East to behaviors of the United States government during the Iraq War. Speaking to someone as articulate as Lubna Hussain makes this somewhat easier, but when one considers the perceptions of the average Saudi, Egyptian, or Syrian man-on-the-street, who has no access to or actual experience with Westerners, one has to wonder how anyone can believe that this will all end well. I'll just give a small sample of Lubna's stream of consciousness, during our interview, to give you a sense of the perceptions that exist:

> *"When you're talking about diminishing people's existence; when you're talking about removing basic human rights from people; basic civil rights from people; you're talking about children, who have starved to death in Iraq; you're talking about hospital facilities that have been bombed; you're talking about various assassinations; you're talking about people who cannot live and function on a daily basis; you're talking about people being shadowed by death at every single point; and you're talking about all of this in the name of Democracy. To me it's absolutely repugnant and incredible that this level of hypocrisy; this level of real hypocrisy that can claim 100,000 lives, in the name of Democracy, is exercised, when pure democratic rights are being rescinded [by] people who are supposed to be bringing them in the first place. This to me is so outrageously unbelievable that I feel I have to slap myself awake to actually believe that I'm reading this.....*
>
> *"Sometimes fact is stranger than fiction. The designs and machinations that went on behind the Iraq War, that are all emerging, and everyone is just saying, "So what, we're there now. So what do we do next? The actual accountability is zero! The atrocities that have gone on in torture camps and these stories that have leaked out about the torture camps in Eastern Europe; it's OK if we don't do it on our soil."* ....

As I have pointed out earlier, there are literally tens of millions of young people in the Muslim World, who hear no counterpoint from Americans outside of the official line from the Bush Administration, and are totally disenchanted by the palpable realities in their own lives. Our government has made it too easy for *Al Qaeda* to recruit and radicalize these young minds.

As I take a step back from the situation, I ask myself, "What can be done to change the direction of this very dangerous trend?" Intellectual Noam Chomsky (*Manufacturing Consent*) says that the government, in effect, creates an environment of fearfulness about our security, so that the Americans will support a large portion of the national budget going to our Defense Department, which in turn promotes research and development, which is then useful in our peaceful economy. He claims we would not support research, if we had to pay for it directly, as a free standing budget item. All of this helps the American economy, which in turn drives the World economy. I infer that he means that a certain level of death and destruction is acceptable, because it keeps military industry humming, thereby providing plenty of jobs to keep politicians in office.

What I fail to understand is, "Why is not the opposite idea, one of peace, also equally effective? Now that we understand the premise of *Tsunami of Blood*, that we should be very fearful about the aftermath of our military adventures and aggressiveness in the Middle East, why can't we use that fear to drive new efforts to enhance living situations peacefully?" We know that governments everywhere will envision an outside enemy, to distract their population from focusing on domestic issues (besides the US, Iran would be another excellent example today). BUT, we also know that massive economic efforts, such as the Marshall Plan, in the period following World War II, have served as the basis of long periods of stability and peace. Indeed, the primary beneficiaries of that effort, Germany and Japan, are today among the best friends of the United States.

Those efforts of rebuilding Europe stimulated two decades of successful industrialization and modernization of the American economy, while absorbing millions of weary soldiers returning from the war. We need to envision this kind of effort for the impoverished and volatile areas of the Middle East. We will need the collaboration and cooperation of our allies, in order to make this happen. Without promoting this "good dream," I fear the "bad dream" is likely to continue and get worse.

Chapter 28

Lori's 9/11

On July 9, 2006, a long time friend of Debbi's and mine visited our home. We were talking about the *Tsunami of Blood* project, and its "irresponsible media" theme. She responded that perhaps she should tell her 9/11 story. It became obvious that her story needed to become a part of the project.

Many Americans will remember that, on 9/11/01, there were images, on several news channels, of Palestinians celebrating and shouting in happiness after hearing news of the events in New York, Washington, and Pennsylvania. I'm sure few of us ever challenged the validity of those images.

Lori's story demonstrates both the tendency of the media to go for the most inflammatory images, and the tendency to be irresponsible in their reporting. One could forgive media people for being upset, and feel the need to get anything on the air on 9/11, but this is a cautionary tale. It is a story, which tells us that we must always be somewhat skeptical of stories we hear on the news media, especially in the heat of the moment, at least until we can have enough sources of information to make our own judgments. Hearing Lori's story made me change my mind about what was happening in Israel and Palestine, nearly 5 years after 9/11.

This is what she said:

> *"On 9/11 I was in Jerusalem on business. We were in the middle of a meeting when The Towers were hit in New York. Obviously, our meeting ended once we heard the second Tower had been hit. We went throughout the hotel, to find a TV we could watch. As soon as we saw what was happening, obviously, the meetings were over.*
>
> *"I asked my colleagues whether we could go into the Holy City. I'm not Jewish, but I wanted to go to pray. They agreed to make those arrangements. They took me to*

the edge of the Holy City, but you have to walk part of the way through. As we were walking there were a lot of shops, and the shopkeepers are primarily Palestinian. One of them came up to me and said, 'Are you an American?'

"'Yes,' Lori responded.

"'Are you here to take revenge?'

"I was kind of taken aback, and I said, 'No, I'm here for prayer!'

"Then they said, 'Can we join you?'

"My little entourage was like a parade, as we went down into the Church of the Holy Sepulchre. I went in to say some prayers, and the shopkeepers stayed outside in the courtyard and did their prayers. When we finished there was a lot of shaking hands and hugging, and just concern for one another. It was just a solemn, solemn moment.

"When we got back to the hotel, looking at some of the television coverage, CNN was showing people celebrating in the streets. That may have happened on some street in Jerusalem, but where I was, that was not the situation at all. It was a very quiet time; it was a very solemn time.

"We were to have a reception that evening, and we decided to go ahead and do it anyway, because I think most people felt that we needed to be around other people; a sense of humanity; a sense of what had happened, not only to America, but to the World. It was definitely a life changing moment for us; a very historical moment for everyone.

"A little bit later, I was in Lebanon. We turned on the TV, and we were watching either Lebanese or Syrian television. The story they were reporting, as many people were trying to speculate what 9/11 was all about, and one of the local staff was translating the coverage, on this particular newscast they were speculating that 9/11 was not about the Middle East or some sort of home grown terrorist. But, it was about a Vietnam War protest. The conclusions were based on the fact that all of the pilots of the planes were Vietnam War veterans. And of course, hitting the Pentagon was all about a statement against the Vietnam War.

"That's just one more view on the different perspectives that were being reported around the World at that time. We were given to wildly divergent opinions, and also wildly inaccurate opinions about what was going on. The suggestion that this was about the Vietnam War was, of course, very incredulous to all of the Americans who were watching this broadcast, because, of course, the Vietnam War had been over 20 some years ago. And any pilot, who would be flying any of these major routes, most likely is a veteran of the Vietnam War [which meant that they would have had an opposite position to protest], so we found this a bit strange. But, I guess that some of

the other coverage that people saw around the World can be considered strange as well.

"My take away from being in the Middle East at that time, was that it was a very solemn time. *It was a time of great uncertainty; of concern about what was happening. Not just what was happening in New York, and to people in Washington and Pennsylvania, at this time, but also what was happening to the World."*

Chapter 29
Planting Organs

My friend, Mohammed, lives in Doha, Qatar. He is an Egyptian systems engineer, who I have met so many times in my work, that we have become bonded as personal friends. Though I am old enough to be his father, and nearly his grandfather, I always feel a special kinship to him. Even when I think of him, as I am doing now, tears come to my eyes. He is a man of great compassion and intelligence, who, like me, has been set adrift in his thinking about how to guide our political leaders to solve the World's problems. I am certain that there are many hundreds of millions of Muslims, Christians, Jews, Buddhists, Hindus, Jains and others, who feel the same quandary.

Every time I meet Mohammed, I am moved by the clarity of his thought about the World situation. On December 15, 2005, he was gracious enough to come to my hotel, just as I was leaving for home, and give me a 45 minute interview. The impetus for the interview began in the morning, when Mohammed told me two incredible stories, when we could take a few moments from out work. This was one, which I feel must be told and retold to the World:

Skip: *"You were telling a story this morning, that you had seen in the media, about a Palestinian man who lost his son, I believe and, I wonder if you would relate that story."*

Mohammed: "Of course. It was a very touching story. This man, this Palestinian man, last November his thirteen year old kid got shot in the head by one of the IDF troops. The kid, of course, died instantly. One day they were in the hospital and they said 'He's declared dead, what do you want to do now?' He did an amazing thing. He said that 'I will donate all that can be donated from my son's organs to anybody, including the Israelis.' And in fact, six Israeli patients got all of the possibly donated parts from this Palestinian child.

"This man said, 'I know my loss cannot be compensated by any means,' he lost his small kid, but he meant to give a message to them, that, instead of planting an olive plant as a model of peace, he planted his son's organs into Israeli children, and now his heart is beating in an Israeli child.

"It was so touching, so touching when the mother of one of the Israeli children, who got the organ, hugged the mother of the Palestinian kid. It was a very touching incident, and what was even more touching was an Israeli man, who had lost one of his children in one of the Palestinian bombings, had hugged the Palestinian man and told him 'I exactly understand your grief and your loss.' This really touched me, and it showed that at the end of the day, we're just human beings, and it is so sad, it is so sad, it is so disappointing, in fact, killing each other, instead of killing other things: disease, poverty, starving nations."

Chapter 30
In Memoriam: July 11, 2006

I wish to express my sincere regret for the deaths of more than 140 people in Mumbai today. I am relieved to know, at this writing, that none of my many business associates and colleagues, were among those hurt in these horrific bombings. I wish to express my condolences to all Indians, for these unfortunate losses today.

As my readers would expect, I checked CNN and Fox News's coverage of the events this afternoon. I am pleased to report the both kept their reporting to a reasonable length, as dictated by the press of other World events, and that both networks showed due care for how they were reporting, particularly in mentioning any religious connections to these events. This is a vast improvement over the reporting we experienced one year ago, which was the impetus for the *Words Matter* project.

We can all hope that this reasonable level of restraint, on the part of our networks, will continue.

Chapter 31
Pyrrhic Victory

Humanity won a small pyrrhic victory on Tuesday, July 11, 2006, when the Bush Administration ordered that all detainees would be afforded the minimum rights required by common "Article 3" of the Geneva Conventions. While it would be a travesty to suggest that this decision now puts the Administration into the "good guy" column of World opinion, at least this decision does prove that the President will change a firmly held position, when he finally believes that it is time for the change to be made.

Hooray for the five majority Justices of The United States Supreme Court, who exercised the checks and balances contained in The Constitution of the United States, and gave the President the rationale for implementing this standard of humanity in *Hamdan v. Rumsfeld.*

My readers must understand that I make no statement about the final disposition of Mr. Hamdan's case. That is for a properly constituted authority to decide. My point is only that America must be seen as standing for The Rule of Law, even when that is sometimes not easy, in individual cases. I thank the President for proving the point I made in Chapter 21, that "America" is self correcting. There are still many neo-conservative members of his party, who think that we should be above this minimum standard, in the face of terrorism, but the good news is that their views will not stand the test of time, and their standard bearer is already leading them in a different direction.

Let me offer a brief comment on how lawyers are trained to follow The Rule of Law, and what that means to society. Before I became an attorney, I often wondered how a criminal, who was obviously not innocent, could be found "not guilty." The reason is that there is a difference between innocent and "not guilty."

In order to be found "guilty," in a criminal trial, one must not only be not innocent, but our system of justice must have operated in the proper manner, to establish "guilt." It is the role of the defense attorney, in a criminal case, to use any means possible for his client to be found "not guilty," even if he knows that his client committed the heinous act, so that the integrity of our Rule of Law can be maintained. He defends The Rule of Law as much as he defends the defendant!

Attorney Johnny Cochran, who led O.J. Simpson's defense in his criminal case, defended our system of The Rule of Law, because he pointed out many shortcomings in how our system of justice applies. His arguments caused police departments everywhere in the United States, and perhaps everywhere in the World, to re-evaluate the training they give their officers, and the rules of procedure their police officers follow. This was a significant contribution to the civility of "America." Without tens of thousands of Public Defenders and paid defense attorneys, who are willing to take the defense side in criminal cases, our society would very quickly devolve into a police state, as Nazi Germany did in the 1930s. We must be ever vigilant to prevent that from happening in "America." So, the next time you wonder how a defense counsel can take the case of a heinous criminal, remember that s/he is not only defending the criminal. S/he is also defending you and your rights as they exist in the very foundation of "America," our Rule of Law.

I know many who are outraged that O.J. Simpson was found "not guilty." They think The Rule of Law "lost" in his criminal case. I think it won, because we further secured the place of "America" as a unique place for humanity in our World.

O.J. Simpson was assuredly not innocent. A later civil case found him responsible for the murders, and awarded damages against him of approximately $8.5 million. Furthermore, he can never go anywhere in our World, without most people he meets thinking he is a murderer. Whether this is sufficient punishment for such a crime, only God can finally say. But, his case did prove, for all to see, that "America" is self correcting.

When President Bush said, immediately after 9/11, that "You are either with us, or against us," he did not mean that one would be disloyal to our country, if we disagreed with his Administration's opinions and policies. Dissent is the very bedrock of our Democracy! What he meant was that all humanity is either for The Rule of Law, as embodied in the idea of "America" (discussed in Chapter 21), or you are against The Rule of Law. The heinous murderers, who killed more than 190 of the World's poorest people yesterday in Mumbai, will surely find their place in Hell. They were not expressing dissent, they were expressing **inhumanity** of the worst type! A dissenter can surely find a place in Heaven; a murderer never can.

Praise be to God that "America" is self correcting, and that President Bush and his Administration accept that idea, and are willing to make the necessary adjustment, while he is in power to do so. If you are reading this chapter outside of The United States of America, when was the last time your national leaders took a stand like that, to protect the rights of the common man by The Rule of Law?

Chapter 32
Wrong Move

As I found my pillow on July 12, 2006, I knew that I would not even want to turn on my television this morning. The media was in the process of telling us that the World is in trouble, with frightening crises everywhere. Yes, this is true, but it has always been so; men just didn't know it, for lack of the technology we "enjoy" today.

Today's topic is the response of Israel to the capture of 3 of its soldiers. According to my friends who have developed "Terror Management Theory" (Chapter 5), by overreacting, Israel has given its enemies in Hamas and Hezbollah exactly what they needed.

Historically, what does a government do, when it is failing at its domestic duties? It creates a foreign enemy, which causes everyone to rally around "the flag," thereby distracting their citizens from their day to day squalor. By its lack of proportionality, in its response to the capture of three soldiers, Israel gives its enemies exactly what they need to gather strength.

Israel and the West should trust in the democratic process they espouse! It is easy enough for murderers to get guns, and whip up passions in the masses. The psychology of mass movements are well established in the literature. What is harder is actually making a better World, by installing sewers, fresh water supplies, and providing education. Indeed, the psychological evidence that every revolution in history has been betrayed by the corruption of its leaders. The initial objective of "equality" is impossible to achieve. The United States Constitution did the best job of creating a viable "equality," by making it an "equality of opportunity." Perhaps this is the best humanity can achieve in the long run.

The people of Palestine have been misdirected, by the rhetoric of passion, into voting for a group, which western governments accuse of being murderers. One hundred Israeli air strikes in southern Lebanon, reported last night before I went to bed, beg the question. Who are the murderers? Who are the attention grabbers? Who represents Evil?

Israel should create an atmosphere, which is as peaceful as possible, and then just let Hamas try to govern. If this is done, soon enough the people will understand that their needs are not being met, and in the next election cycle, throw the bums out. But, by giving Hamas passions against an non-peaceful solution, they give Hamas exactly what it needs to gain strength—a foreign enemy, on whom they can blame their inability to deliver real benefits to the Palestinian population, and a recruiting poster to bring more young men to the cause.

I know little about the men who govern both Israel and Palestine. What I do know is that these methods of tit for tat murders and gangster behavior, have not brought their people peace in 100 years. The results speak for themselves! It is time for a different approach, by both sides. Everyone knows what does not work!

President Bush was quite right, yesterday, in expressing concern for the stability of the democracy in Lebanon. As long as Israel insists on behaving like the regime from which the Jews were delivered at the end of World War II, the results will be the same. Such behaviors are not solutions for Jews any more than they were solutions for Germans.

Ernest Becker, in his land breaking works, *Escape from Evil* and *The Denial of Death* (for which he won a Pulitzer Prize in 1974), exactly predicted, in the year of his own death, the consequences of all of the behaviors in the Middle East today. If we cannot learn from his intelligent insights, and from the work of his disciples, we are destined to continue to live in a troubled World. The magic about what Becker said is that his work in social psychology is devoid of religious doctrine, as a means to prove his case, allowing people of all faiths to internalize his lessons. And his lessons, though as difficult to face as death is for most of mankind, are undeniable by any thinking person. We must have enough intellectuals, on all sides of the calculus of the Middle, who can aspire to rise above the hurly burly of the moment, and start talking about how these ideas and others can be used to solve the problems.

At one stage of the *Words Matter* project, I commented to Sheldon Solomon (*In the Wake of 9/11: The Psychology of Terror*) that, because "Terror Management Theory" offers its solutions without relying on any religion, it would not be well received by those who use religions as instruments of control. Sheldon responded that Becker's view was that psychology drops one off at the doorstep of religion. If we understand psychology, we can see how evil doers use religion for inappropriate ends. At the same time, we can accept and appreciate the proper role of religion in our lives.

One of the reasons I respect Islam is that one of its dicta is that each Muslim has a direct relation with God. To me, this is the right answer! It is only when intermediaries get involved, to tell us what religions mean, that mankind has gotten in trouble over the centuries. We should all ask God directly, "What is the solution to the troubles of our World?" When we receive the answer directly and privately from God, we should act on that Wisdom. We should be very suspicious of those who want to tell us what God told them. Are they relating God's Wisdom accurately? I don't know.

I've played the "Telephone Game," at parties, in which everyone sits in a circle. The leader tells a secret to the person sitting next to her. Each person, in his or her turn, tells the secret to the next person in line. By the time the secret gets back to the leader, it is completely distorted. This happens in a game with no agenda, other than to demonstrate the phenomenon. It seems to me that if we are expecting someone to tell us what God told them, we should be very worried.

Chapter 33

Mohammed's Honeymoon

My Egyptian friend, Mohammed, celebrated his wedding on August 2, 2005, and I knew he planned his honeymoon for Sharm al-Sheik resort, at the northern end of the Red Sea. I was very worried about his plans, because on July 23, 2005, murderers killed 88 people in and around 3 hotels there. When I met Mohammed again, in December 2005, it was the first time we had seen one another since the London bombings, which occurred on the day I was leaving Doha, Qatar, on my previous visit. Naturally, as a friend, I was asking him what he had done about his honeymoon.

I include the story here for two reasons. Firstly, because it demonstrates the **courage of ordinary people** in facing the horrors of gangs of murderers roaming our Planet; and secondly, because of **Mohammed's remarkable story about St. Catherine's Monastery**, which is located in central Sinai. (http://interoz.com/egypt/Catherines.htm) Here is our conversation:

Skip: *"Earlier today you and I were talking about the incident which surrounded your wedding, which was in August of 2005. I wonder if you would just describe what was happening in Egypt at that time."*

Mohammed: "Well, my wedding was on the 2nd of August, and a week earlier, three devastating bombings occurred in Sharm al-Sheik resorts in South Sinai. We were all shocked. Eighty-eight people died there. I won't really say how many Egyptians died and how many foreign people died, they were all human beings; they were all there to work, to have fun, to seek what's good in life, and somebody just ended that, and this is unacceptable in all manners. My wife and I decided, when we heard the shocking news, it was one week before our honeymoon, and my wife and I decided that we would not change our plans."

Skip: *"You were planning to go to Sharm al-Sheik."*

Mohammed: "Yes, we already had the reservations made because it's a peak season at that time, and we had our reservations made two or three months earlier. We decided we would not change even a bit of the plan, including going to secluded areas like St. Catherine's, driving the roads where you are the only car there for one or two hours, before you encounter another vehicle.

"We decided to not change our plans, and this went against all of the family recommendations, and we said no, we stand for principal here, we're going to set an example. If we are, Egyptian people, nationals, afraid to go to Sharm al-Sheik, because of bombings or because we are afraid of the terrorists, what would be the opinion of the tourists? We decided to set an example for them. We did everything in the book, we just went for it. What was really amazing is that instead of really seeing that lots of people ran away from Sharm al-Sheik, lots of people didn't change their plans, and they stayed there, from all over the world. Later on, when we went to St. Catherine, it's a very special place in my heart, because it has one of the oldest monasteries in the world."

Skip: Could you describe where it is?"

Mohammed: "OK, it is in the middle southern part of the Sinai Basin. It is surrounded by mountain terrain, and somewhere in these mountains is where God spoke to Moses. St. Catherine was a Christian martyr who was killed in this place, I think it was by the Romans, but I don't remember the history now. This is where they built the monastery. The monastery is built on the roots actually from people coming from Saudi Arabia and Jordan and Israel all the way to Egypt. During the Islamic Era, Islamic troops came through this part. They secured people over there, the monks and the priests, and until today, a Sinai tribe, which is a Muslim tribe, is taking care of all the Greek monks and priests over there, and this has been going for the last maybe 1,000 years.

What's so amazing about this place is that all religions live in this place, and it is so peaceful. As we were talking earlier today, when I told you, just look at why God chose this place over any other place in the World to speak to a human being, you won't find out that answer except if you go there yourself. What is really amazing about this monastery is that you can find inside a chapel, a church, mosque, and a place for Jewish ceremony. You find people from all over the World, all nationalities, all religions, all beliefs, and they all the have same common feeling; it's the feeling of peace. This is why I said this one point on earth where you'd speak to the other person that you meet as a fellow human being, regardless of his religion, regardless of his beliefs, even within the same religion. Everybody is treating this place with sacredness and respect, and out of that comes the human to human respect as well.

Chapter 34
Distressing News

What is the solution for the Palestinians and Israel? All of my thinking friends struggle with this question. I have friends who are Christians, Muslims, Arabs and Jews. I have met one or two Israelis. I have never been to Israel. I have many friends who are Saudi, Sudanese, Qatari, Egyptian, Palestinian, Syrian, and Pakistani. The company I founded employs 5,200 Indians, directly or indirectly, many of whom are Muslims. So far as I am aware, none of us has an answer! All of us share our lives together in a peaceful manner; each of us contributing to the lives of one another in various ways, each according to his or her skills and abilities.

I feel that intelligent decisions arise from facing facts as they are; not as we might wish them to be. In order to find an answer, let us consider some realities:

1. Israel is a reality as a nation state. It is not going away, regardless of what populist politicians like President Ahmadinejad might say or do. Regardless of what we might think of "The Jewish Lobby" in the United States, there are no circumstances under which the United States can allow behaviors by Israel's neighbors, which would truly threaten its existence.

2. A variety of misguided political, religious, secular and criminal leaders in the Middle East have held out the hope among their followers that, if they keep the pressure up, eventually Israel can be extinguished by its more populous neighbors. In so doing, they have actively or passively encouraged murderous and gangster behaviors, aimed toward Israel, while keeping their people in squalor and ignorance. Some of these leaders, including Israeli leaders, have used this strategy to distract their populations from their very serious domestic short comings—see point 11 in Chapter 35.

3. Overreactions, such as that pursued by the Israelis in Lebanon and the Gaza Strip

in the summer of 2006, put the whole World at risk, because they radicalize even more disenchanted Muslim youth, throughout the World. News reports coming to me from CNN said that Lebanese youth were being radicalized by the Israeli attack, and more and more of them are favoring joining Hezbollah. This behavior is exactly predicted by "Terror Management Theory," as illuminated by the intellectuals who have followed in the footsteps of Ernest Becker (*The Denial of Death* and *Escape from Evil*). The implications are much farther reaching, however. The youth of Lebanon are just the "tip of the iceberg." These behaviors are radicalizing young people throughout the Muslim World. From this, there will be much more serious consequences than any of us can predict. Radicalized youth can be dangerous to their own governments, which in turn can affect oil prices, which will hit Americans in the pocketbooks.

4. All of us have condoned the rise of gangster behavior somewhere. The United States is still condoning war lords in Afghanistan, if not actively supporting them, and by so doing has given up on the "war on drugs." The United States government, by its behavior, condones the growing of poppies, even though it knows the consequences to our poor and undereducated populations. Is that the point? BUT, if we spin the needle on a parlor game, wherever it points, we will find governments and intellectuals doing the same thing (by analogy), with slightly different patinas. So, there is no reader of this that can say that their leaders take the moral high ground. I call on all Citizens of the World to "Think Globally, Act Locally," as the Buddhist bumper sticker goes, and squeeze murderous and gangster behavior out of our systems, wherever we find it. I understand Israel's point, of wanting to stop gangster behavior along its border, but they put us all at risk by radicalizing the World at large. Those governments, which condone Hamas and Hezbollah, put themselves at risk, because their radicalized youth live closer to them than they do to the United States.

5. Feuds are stopped, when the participants decide they will live in Peace. There is no such thing as "even" in a feud, especially one that has been going for a century. No one possibly knows what "even" is, so feuds cannot end by a balance of carnage. Feuds end when communities decide they will make some compromises, and live in peace.

6. The solution is in the future! It is NOT in trying to find restitution for the carnage of the past. All sides have lost. Who has won? Was it venal leaders? The winners have surely not been mothers, who have sacrificed their children. And for what? The solution will only be found when our leaders decide to start their negotiations on those matters on which we can agree; and then find ways to compromise differences to achieve agreeable solutions. In the same sense that I am willing to give up revenge upon Hezbollah, for the 241 Marines and Sailors killed in Beirut in 1983, with regret, but acknowledging today's reality, so must we all draw a line in the sand, and say that the first priority is peace. That is the

course of humanity!

7. Lt. Col. Rich Higgins, USMC, was a classmate and friend of mine. He was captured by Hezbollah, in southern Lebanon, on February 17, 1988. At some later point he was murdered by Hezbollah, and photographs of his body, hung by the neck, were broadcast throughout the World. Rich was commanding UN Observer Group Lebanon—he was a peacekeeper. Indeed, the United States government would not allow him to participate, except as a peacekeeper, under the circumstances that existed at that time. With regret for the loss of my friend, I favor the members of Hezbollah being allowed to live as peaceful citizens of Lebanon, helping to build their country into a nation state that can fully attend to the needs of its people in the World. I do not favor tolerating Hezbollah's criminal behaviors, by the Israelis or the Lebanese.

8. All nations, and aspirants to be nation states, must stop gangster behavior, wherever it exists. It cannot be justified. It cannot be tolerated. It must be stopped wherever it is found. Only then will be all live in peace.

Chapter 35

An Open Letter to Nick Robertson

Subj: Stop Helping Murderers and Gangsters with Their Recruiting

Dear Nick,

You are, in my opinion, the best reporter in the World. You are courageous, you are tenacious, and you obviously care very deeply about the difficult stories you are called upon to report. The World would be a better place, if there were 100 reporters as courageous as you are.

I want to enlist your help in changing the way the mainstream news media reports World War III. First of all, it is important to understand that the battle is really between civilization and Evil. It is not a battle between religious World Views. BUT, our enemies very much want it reported in those terms, because they are using a misrepresentation of Islam to recruit their followers. Therefore, every time you or one of your colleagues uses a term in your reporting, which seems to equate criminal behavior with Islam, our enemies take a step forward, and civilization takes one step further back into the Dark Ages.

Two days ago, I heard you refer to the criminal gang, Hezbollah, as "Shiite Hezbollah." Last week, *The Washington Post* referred to Hezbollah as a "Shiite Muslim" group. If you were reporting on the mythical Corleone Family, you would not refer to them as the Catholic Corleone gang. Would you? It seems to me that if you did, you would have 700 million Catholics down your throat in a heartbeat. The Pope would never stand for it, because that method of reference would smear the entire Catholic Church.

Immediately following the London bombings, on July 7, 2005, I began a campaign to stop you and your colleagues from using terms like "Islamic terrorist" or "Islamic extremist." To your credit, you morphed your reference to "Islamist," but this was no better, and I pointed that out. You morphed that into "sectarian," but this is no better either. Why? Because all of these words make reference back to the religion at large. Unless you have a legitimate representative of Islam, who says a behavior is "Islamic," then it is not appropriate to use religiously charged words in your reporting. You play right into the hands of these gangs, who want to be able to recruit disenchanted youth at the Mosque. Just because a group calls itself "Islamic" this or that, does not make it so.

Finally, it seems to me that all of you should discontinue the use of the terms "terror" and "terrorist," which elevate murderous gangster behavior to the level of some sort of extreme, but valid, political movement. They are nothing better than murderers and gangsters, and we should begin to refer to them as such. Why should you promote their cause, by helping them hijack a religion, which supports the spiritual needs of about a quarter of the World's population quite peacefully?

You and your colleagues have an instrument of great power in your hands. You reach a billion people every week. While I acknowledge and honor the right of the press to deliver the news in any manner it deems appropriate, I urge you to consider these thoughts. I think you will find them sensible. If you are persuaded, then I am sure you can help me persuade others. Let's stop the media from giving aid and comfort to the enemies of civilization.

Best regards,
Skip Conover
Producer, Words Matter, LLC

Chapter 36
Recognizing Reality

On July 17, 2006, *The New York Times* carried two of the most heartening reports I have seen in many years. The first reported that Saudi Arabia, Jordan, Egypt, and several members of the GCC, had chastised Hezbollah for its criminal behavior at a meeting of the Arab League. The second reported that Sunnis in Iraq are suddenly acknowledging that it might be a good idea for the United States military to remain in Iraq for the foreseeable future, and perhaps even increase its presence.

These facts represent a sea change in perceptions about how the World of the 21st Century will operate. The stress fissures between strict solidarity with any Arab entity, regardless of behavior, and the maintenance of the status quo operating in a global economy, have finally become apparent.

Average Americans have long been mystified by the idea that after we came to the rescue of Kuwait, Saudi Arabia, and the GCC in Gulf War I, we were treated as pariahs in Saudi Arabia. This was not completely true in commercial business, of course, as my experiences demonstrate, but the American military was invited to depart forthwith.

It is my understanding that Osama bin Laden, and certain other interests, were using the presence of the American military as a wedge to challenge the Saudi government. It was their position that it was "impure" to allow "infidels" to remain in Saudi Arabia. Of course, this was only a problem after about 140 Americans gave their lives to defend the Kingdom from an invasion by Saddam Hussain.

My reading of the situation is that the Saudi government chose to appease these groups within its own ranks, in the great tradition of Neville Chamberlain, whose appeasement of Adolph Hitler, in 1938, gave the dictator another year to plan for war. Of course, American diplomacy, not wanting to "rock the boat," went along with this appeasement. The fig leaf of moving the main body of America's forward deployed military to Qatar was devised. Americans could continue to defend Saudi Arabia from Saddam, while not actually offending these powerful interests in the Kingdom.

But, the developing situation in the Middle East will not support such an appeasement forever. No one wants what is happening in Iraq to spill over into other countries. So finally, there is recognition that there is merit in having the United States attempt to restore order in Iraq.

The news today is that more than 50 ordinary Iraqis, waiting in line to get jobs, so that they could care for their families, were murdered by thugs in Kufa. Obviously, no society can function under such conditions. If any Arab state were to attempt to intervene, to defend those with the closest affinity to them, it would be seen as a major provocation by countries, which have other political ambitions. It is, therefore, in their best interest to have the Americans stay, and clean up the mess.

Is America to blame for the mess? I don't think so! Yes, the United States provided the catalyst for the current state of affairs, by invading Iraq. But, any thinking person in the Arab World must acknowledge that Saddam Hussain was a "loose cannon," who could have brought on another major conflict, of far greater proportions than what we are seeing today. He had already carried on an 8 year war against Iran, which killed a million of people or more on both sides; and he had invaded Kuwait, an American ally—big mistake.

The existence of weapons of mass destruction in Saddam's hands begs the question. We may not know, for a very long time, whether they actually exist. Obviously, the United States government was played by a group of Iraqi exiles, who wanted to take over Iraq, but average citizens do not know what the truth really is. I speculate that in the run up to war, certain items were moved into Syria, and perhaps even Iran. [We never understood why, in Gulf War I, the entire Iraqi air force escaped to Iran, just a few years after the Iran-Iraq War. There is more there than meets the eye, but it seems evident that Saddam had made certain arrangements with the government of Iran. Why else would he send billions of dollars worth of fighter aircraft to the Iranians? Did they give them back? I think so, but I don't remember ever hearing.]

Do we think that America does not know what happened to the weapons of mass destruction? Of course, we do! [Since Saddam murdered a large number of his own citizens using them, it cannot be argued that they did not exist at all.] Until now, it has not been in our interest to disturb the balance of power by pointing a very accusing finger at Syria. But the fact that Syria now appears inclined to slow down the behavior of Hezbollah, suggests that certain pressures are being used behind the scenes. Whisper who dares!

All of these governments have been using Israel as a convenient scapegoat, to keep the attention of their people off of their domestic problems. This is "the oldest trick in the book," as Ernest Becker pointed out 32 years ago, in *The Denial of Death* and *Escape from Evil.* The World has finally reached a tipping point, however, beyond which it can no longer accept these fictions. As I pointed out in Chapter 34, the domestic results cannot be hidden forever. Ultimately, the people will understand that they are being held back by silly policies. It is not about religion! The United Arab Emirates is ahead of the United States in per capita gross domestic product, and has successfully changed its economy from a 45% reliance on pumping oil to a 9% reliance on oil, in just a decade.

Humanity will either find a way to live in peace, with everyone ruefully accepting the plain fact that we must let others, who do not believe as we do, live in peace; or we will fall toward conflagration, which will consume all of us. The potential for a global conflict is horrific. We have seen the edges of it throughout the World in the past year. As some commentators have pointed out, World War III already began some years ago.

Now is the time to continue the reevaluation of what is important! We either stop murderous and gangster behavior, wherever we find it in the World, and attend to the real needs of our peoples; or we face the prospect of many countries falling into purgatories as bad as Iraq or worse. In my opinion, the risk is just as big in the United States and Western Europe, as it is in the Middle East. The events of the past 5 years prove my point!

Chapter 37
"Under God"

Shame on the Congress of the United States! I learned, during my travels in L.A. today, that the Congress spent some of its precious and insufficient working hours yesterday creating a bogus debate on a statute that would make it illegal for the Supreme Court to rule that the words "Under God" are inappropriate to be included in our Pledge of Allegiance, recited by every public school child, and the 8:00 a.m. guests of Chick & Ruth's Deli in Annapolis, every day.

Whoever came up with such a time waster should be run out of Congress on a rail, regardless of party. It is, on its face, unconstitutional, since it proposes to limit the power of another branch of government, leaving the issue of "under God" moot. Meanwhile, work on solutions to REAL problems languish. Simply outrageous!

Our modern patriots have forgotten that we, in the Western World, have learned by painful experience that combining Church and State is a recipe for tyranny. Such combinations give rise to Inquisitions of the worst order. It is our enemies, on the other side of World War III, who want to impose ideology on the peoples of the World. We must stand for Freedom of Religion, which means, no combination of Church and State.

I do not favor changing the Pledge of Allegiance, because I feel it is a bogus issue, which is not a REAL problem, as practiced in the United States. But if ideologues continue to try to make it mandatory that "under God" stays, I will stand against them any day of the week. They need to do the work they were elected to complete; not waste their time on phony window dressing!

Chapter 38

Sunni v. Shia

One question that mystifies Westerners is, if Sunni and Shia are both sects of Islam, why are they killing one another in Iraq? In my view, the insurgency in Iraq has nothing to do with religion at all. It is, rather, a vendetta; or a feud; or a struggle for power among criminal gangs, but it is not about differences in their religious practices, and therefore it is not "sectarian." We must change the trend of making World War III a war of religion. It is a war between human civilization and gangsters! We will only start to find the solution, when we work through all of the major religions of the World, not one against another.

For many months, I have been asking interviewees whether there is anything in the difference between Sunni and Shia, which would justify killing one another. The answer is always no, regardless of who I ask.

It is time for our capable media reporters on the scene to start unraveling what is really going on in Iraq. It seems to me that non-Muslims must begin to help Muslims distinguish their religion from the criminal behaviors, which are running rampant throughout the World. At 13:02 Eastern Daylight Time, on July 21, 2006, CNN Headline News was reporting that three people have been arrested in Mumbai, in the investigation of the Mumbai train bombings. At the end of the report, Chuck Roberts said, "All three are Muslims." That is gratuitous content, with no place in the report, unless there are facts known which connects the criminal bombing murders to the religion of Islam. Just because someone calls there organization "Islamic," and wraps their leaders in symbols of "Islam," does not make it so. Unless we clear up some of these misconceptions, we can never reduce the level of hatred, which is zinging around the World with every news cycle.

On March 17, 2006, I was privileged to interview a Saudi woman, Ms. Kawther, who expressed to me that the solution to World peace must come through Islam, not in spite of it. I agree with her analysis. When we were talking about the difference between Sunni and Shia, this is what we said:

Skip: *"Of course there's something going on in Iraq, whether we call it an insurgency or civil war or what it is, but it's spoken of by the mainstream media as "sectarian" mainly between the Sunni group and the Shia group. I wanted to ask you whether, in your perception, there is anything in the two sects of the religion, leaving politics aside, is there anything between the Sunni and Shia which would justify killing someone else?"*

Kawther: "No. From my point of view, a Sunni is as much a Muslim as a Shia, and a Shia is as much a Muslim as a Sunni. Like in Christianity, you have Catholic or – "

Skip: *"Protestant. We have many flavors of Protestants."*

Kawther: "You have all kinds of different sects. So it is exactly the same way, Sunni and Shia are sects of Islam. Maybe they have a different view of Islam, Shia from Sunnis. That doesn't make them non-Muslim. They are Muslims just as [among] Christians: Protestant is a Christian and Catholic is a Christian, Methodist is a Christian. In the same way, we are all Muslims. Basically, we believe in our God; we believe in our Prophet (Peace Be Upon Him); we pray the same way; we fast the same time. The five main pillars of Islam are done the same way. If they have a different view or a different way in some things, there will be differences. Basically, the religion is the same. So there is no difference between a Shia or a Sunni."

Skip: *"So, to the extent that there's fighting in Iraq, in your view it really has nothing to do with religion at all."*

Kawther: "I don't think so. I don't think it has anything to do with religion."

So, a valid investigative report for CNN, or any other reporter, is on how and why we all came to the point of equating Islam with criminal behavior, and the insurgency in Iraq about religion, rather than what it is really about. This distinction is VERY important! If we do not correct this injustice, things will continue to get worse, because impressionable young people are being recruited by civilization's enemies; by criminals, who are improperly twisting a religion to their own ends. Our media is making this just too easy for them!

13:32 EDT, July 21, 2006. This problem is pervasive. Sylvia Choi, on CNN Headline News, just referred to Hezbollah as "the Muslim militant group." Sorry, my opinion is that Hezbollah is a gang of thugs, which ignores Islam. If they were truly faithful Muslims, they would find peaceful ways to achieve their goals, to the extent that they are legitimate. If CNN feels the description is apt, why do they not refer to the IDF as "the Jewish military organization," thereby applying to all Jews the same brutal behavior as the overly aggressive Israeli government?

Chapter 39
Very Little Time

On July 20, 2006, I interviewed a leading journalism educator in the United States. In discussing the irresponsibility of the mainstream press, he said that he was of the view that the best answer is to accept the press as it is, and let responses such as *Words Matter* cause them to change their behaviors over time. I pointed out to him that there was a quantitative difference between CNN and *Words Matter*. CNN reaches one billion people every week, while I have reached one thousand people in 6 weeks. It is going to take a very long time to see reforms in the media, if we must rely on such mechanism. He acknowledged that the process will take decades.

I cannot accept that! In my opinion, schools of journalism must immediately work to reform the attitudes of the working press. There must be a concerted effort, immediately, to instill a value that the press will not intentionally, or by unacceptable policies, add to the problems they report. It seems to me that this is the minimum standard that we should expect from our working journalists. The cartoon controversy of last winter was blown out of all proportion by the major news outlets, and I am convinced that hundreds of people died because the press was inciting people around the World to demonstrate, which, regrettably, led to unfortunate deaths, where those demonstrations devolved to riot.

Yesterday, CNN reported that the Saudi government has agreed to remove bigoted and intolerant references from all textbooks within the Kingdom, and to advance religious freedom, as long as other faiths are practiced privately. I look forward to the day when CNN admits its own bigoted and intolerant reporting, and moves to correct the misperceptions it has itself fostered about the Muslim World. As I have pointed out, CNN's anchors and reporters are regularly defaming Islam, by combining references to the religion with sacrilegious and gangster behavior.

As a World of humanity, we must all step back from the edge of the abyss, and begin to respect one another. Because the mainstream media control the thought of most people around the World, it is they that must lead the way into a new era. Only when they themselves understand how dangerous it is, to continue to foster intolerance, will we begin to see a change in the way our populations view one another. I have seen perceptible changes in the past year. I have not seen CNN use the term "Islamic terrorist" since 2005. BUT, they still apply religious connotations to gangster behavior, both in Iraq and Lebanon. Hezbollah is not an Islamic organization. While its members may consider themselves Muslims, and follow certain practices, I do not believe that Hezbollah follows the teachings of The Prophet, Peace Be Upon Him. In my view, there is no stretch of the imagination which can justify calling the gangsters and thugs, who are murdering 100 Iraqi civilians daily, Muslims. They are murdering Muslims! The violence in Iraq is largely caused by gangster claims to power. When CNN starts reporting it that way, and stops referring to it as "sectarian," we will have begun to see the truth as it really is.

Chapter 40

Tinkering with Population

I pointed out, in the Introduction of *Tsunami of Blood*, that the burgeoning demographic of young males with little to do in Saudi Arabia seems to me a crisis waiting to happen. In my reading, I have come across a sobering confirmation of my analysis.

University of Chicago Economist Steven D. Levitt, in his *Freakonomics, A Rogue Economist Explores the Hidden Side of Everything*, tells the sobering story of Nicolae Ceausescu of Romania. In 1966, he banned abortions, thereby causing Romania's birth rate to double. In 1989, his people began to protest their conditions (pp. 117-119). Most of the demonstrators were thirteen to twenty. Older Romanians reported that they had courage to participate because of their children. Ceausescu lost control of his country. This was certainly an unintended consequence of tinkering with population.

Meanwhile, in the United States of the 1990s, most theorists were expecting a huge upsurge in crime. Instead, the crime rate dropped precipitously. Levitt attributes this unexpected consequence to the January 22, 1973 result in *Roe v. Wade*, which allowed abortions in the United States. As a result of that ruling, many of the criminals, who would have driven that crime wave, were never born.

From personal experience, I know that crime is becoming a problem in Saudi Arabia. In February 2006, much to my surprise, because of the severity of criminal penalties for theft, my laptop computer was stolen in Riyadh. It seems to me that this is a symptom of the much bigger problem, which I perceive in countries with large populations of young people, and not enough activities to keep them busy.

Noam Chomsky, the World's most quoted living intellectual, argues that sensible governments make it possible for their people to be distracted by a wide array of activities. In the case of men, much of their aggressiveness is absorbed into supporting and participating in sports teams at every level, from elementary school to professional teams. Even the Romans knew this, as they conducted major events in the Coliseum, to keep their populations busy.

Chapter 41

Where Are the Muslim Clerics in Iraq?

I am blessed to have many Muslim friends. Every one of them assures me that Islam is a **Religion of Peace**. Every one I have asked says there is **nothing** in the difference between Sunni and Shia, which justifies murdering one another. I have always accepted these assertions as absolutely **true**.

I have asserted that if the fight in Iraq is not based on religious matters, then it must be a feud, a vendetta, or tribal warfare. I have asked myself, "How do you end a feud?" I have responded that you cannot end it by "getting even." What would that be? Would it be an equal balance of the carnage on each side? No one could possibly tell us what "even" is anymore!

In the Western world, we have had many feuds, and some of them were religious. Some of my ancestors left Holland in 1625. They were simple farmers. They were tired of the carnage caused by the Spanish Catholics coming up to Holland every summer, to try to convert the Protestants to Catholicism at the point of a gun and a sword. The Dutch, in response, every summer flooded their country, to chase the Spanish out. After 80 years of this, the Spanish finally wised up and stopped coming. My ancestors didn't wait that long, though. Like many humans since (and a few before), they chose to come to the New World, and became among the first 200 settlers of Manhattan Island. 381 years later, Holland remains Dutch and Protestant; Spain remains Catholic. What was the point?

On July 23, 2006, I visited the Vancouver Museum, and learned again about human resilience. The Haida nation, a "first nation" of North America, lived just north of Vancouver. When Europeans came, they brought disease, which killed all but 600 of these people, who had been there since the end of the last ice age, when they apparently came across the frozen Bering Strait from Mongolia. Christian missionaries took their children away from them, and tried to brain wash them to Christianity. They were not allowed to practice their religious rites from 1900 to 1950. But, today their art and culture is celebrated everywhere in western Canada. Indeed, their revived cultural area is a major tourist attraction of British Columbia. They had kept their traditions alive, in secret, doing their celebrations disguised as birthday and wedding parties.

My point is that the spirit of the Haida, even though they were severely repressed, could not be crushed, even with concerted effort by so-called "well meaning Christians." I see no way, therefore, that any side in Iraq, regardless of what we call the sides, can crush any other. All that will happen, by the continuing effort to suppress the other, is that many people will die, and those that live will live in misery. For what? I really wonder what these people are thinking! It is evident to me that they are not thinking rationally, and they are certainly not spiritually guided.

How do you end a feud? You end it when the society decides it will live in peace. It is evident that the society has not so decided in Iraq. Six months ago, everyone was blaming everything on the Americans. Today, no one can say that the Americans are responsible for the current carnage. What I want to know is, "Where did all of these gangsters come from? Since Islam is a religion of peace, and there is nothing between the two sects of Islam, which justifies murder, they clearly are not Muslim.

I just do not understand where all of the Muslim clerics have gone? I see Iraqi "Mafiosi" wannabees, who wear the symbols of Islam, and who falsely allege that they are pious men of Islam; but I see no Muslim cleric in the peaceful tradition, which my real Muslim friends describe. If there were such men, they would be able to calm their communities and find common ground, by a call back to their faith, which has obviously been abandoned in the heat of battle. I see no sign of *Allah* in that place! I see only Evil (or hapless) men, and marginalized women and children, who can do nothing to save themselves from the temptations of Evil. *Allah* has surely abandoned them!

If anyone can show me some evidence that *Allah* has not abandoned Iraq, please respond to this post, and I will give your response equal prominence.

Chapter 42
What Is a Mosque?

The title of this chapter, begs the question. Obviously, a mosque is a religious site serving the spiritual needs of Muslims. Any legitimate military would avoid such a site, if at all possible. But, when it houses missile launchers, it becomes a missile site. You can't have it both ways. When it houses an ammunition dump, it is an ammunition dump, and all of the gangsters waving their hands on international television, cannot change that.

What do we call parents, who intentionally put their families into harm's way? Criminals! When Hezbollah embeds their families within their military power structure, hiding behind the skirts of their wives and daughters, they are sacrificing their families. What civilized person does such a thing? Certainly, no Muslim I know would ever consider sacrificing their family, especially for a criminal enterprise. I cannot imagine anyone suggesting that such behavior is "Islamic."

CNN reported on July 24, 2006, that Saudi Arabia, Jordon, and Egypt, in their criticism of Hezbollah, are out of tune with "the Arab street." The Introduction of *Tsunami of Blood* predicted exactly this. I find sobering the prospect of what will happen in these countries, when the intensity of the battle, which allows energies to be focused on Israel and The United States, diminishes, and allows people to focus on their actual domestic living conditions.

We notice *Al Qaeda* has been rather quiet during this period of "crisis" between Israel and Hezbollah. Why should they rock the boat? Taking a page out of Ernest Becker's book, *Escape from Evil,* they know that Israel has given them an ideal recruiting poster across the Muslim World. Muslim youth are becoming more and more radicalized. The risk of this is not to Israel. As I have previously argued, Israel is here to stay, and The United States will always defend it, if necessary. The risk is that other Muslim governments, which are important to The United States, might well be changed in favor of radicals.

It seems to me that there can be zero tolerance for gangster behavior in any country, regardless of where the behavior is aimed; and it is essential that these countries provide activities to occupy their citizens after the Israel/Hezbollah distraction quiets down. Unless the "Arab street" sees hope about improvement of their living conditions, they will become a very volatile force, radicalized by extensive media coverage, which will make the current troubles in Israel and Lebanon just a side show.

Improving local employment, for example, would be quite easy, if only these governments will realize that their economic and trade policies have been impediments to progress in their countries.

Ibrahim Mousawi, Chief Foreign News Editor for Al Manar TV, is currently responding to the question, "Is Hezbollah's aim to wipe out Isreal?" His obfuscatory answer, by not answering the question, answers it. No one in the World should accept such an answer.

Chapter 43

Saudi Arabia Takes the High Ground

My congratulations to The Custodian of the Two Holy Mosques King Abdullah, and the Saudi Arabian government, for taking the high ground in seeking reasonable and expeditious solutions in the current battle between Israel and Hezbollah. *Arab News* reported gifts in excess of $1 billion from Saudi Arabia to Lebanon, to stabilize Lebanon's currency, and provide relief for beleaguered Lebanese.

It is clear that Saudi Arabia does understand that the continuation of armed gangster groups, which are laws unto themselves, like Hezbollah, cannot be allowed to continue anywhere in the World. The big issue, for all of us in the civilized World, to include Iran, Syria, and others, who like to play with fire, is how to make the adjustment to a World where the Rule of Law is the primary means through which disputes are resolved.

Israel must balance the gain to be achieved by crushing Hezbollah, against the harm done by radicalizing so many of the youth of the entire region. Israelis live in a region where most major players have shown reasonable restraint toward it for decades. Radicalizing the youth of the entire Arab World, however, runs the risk of causing much less reasonable leaders to emerge, which in turn has the potential to cause a *tsunami of blood* beyond the imagination of most civilized people.

I have mixed emotions about the timing of a cease fire. It cannot be seen as a victory for Hezbollah, or we will only see greater adventurism and bloodshed in the future. Other groups might seek to emulate them. Despite my personal grudges against Hezbollah, I certainly would be happy to see a genuine cease fire, in which Hezbollah becomes an effective, but peaceful, political party in Lebanon.

One can only hope that the Hezbollah leadership will soon see the resolve of the entire civilized World in putting an end to the tolerance of gangster groups in the Middle East. Only legitimate political movements need apply for acceptance!

Chapter 44

He's Just a Feckless Old Man in a Turban

On July 27, 2006, Ayman al Zawahri showed us a weakness of *Al Qaeda*. He urged Hezbollah not to allow its battle with Israel to become a secular fight. He repeatedly urged Hezbollah to focus on the differences between Jews and Muslims generally. This proves my oft stated point that he is trying to use Islam for his murderous purposes. What right does he have to do that?

He urged his followers to make themselves martyrs, while not offering to become one himself. Is there no hypocrisy in that? He is a very confused man! In the past, he and his partner in crime have referred to Shiites as "infidels," but now that they are in a fight with Israel, he wants to bathe in Hezbollah's reflected "glory?"

Some news sources say these videos are secret messages to supporters. His demand for worldwide attacks may backfire, if they in fact do not occur. The original idea of *Al Qaeda* was to train terrorists in their camps, and then let them go off to be independent operators. Their problem, though, is that many of the men who were full of aggression in their 20s, back in the 1980s, are now approaching their 40s, with families and children, and real responsibilities. It remains to be seen whether these will rise up in support of any exhortation like this. I think not!

No one can seriously think that the two groups arrested recently for proposed attacks on the Sears Tower and Holland Tunnel were anything but amateurs. What professional gangster would hang out on an Internet chat room, hoping to meet an *Al Qaeda* recruiter? These people were clearly wannabees. I presume that Vice President Cheney's team is probably tracking 15-20 such wannabee groups, and is just throwing one to the press every so often, just to make the rest of us think something is really protecting us.

I'm afraid the reality is much more sobering, or not. I presume that any real *Al Qaeda* professionals are practically untraceable, and have in mind something really dastardly, or they really do not exist. The more time passes without seeing something major, obviously coordinated by the *Al Qaeda* leadership, the less powerful they seem.

I love the fiction that Osama bin Laden is living in the caves between Pakistan and Afghanistan. Who is that kidding, besides the gullible press? Why do they keep printing such stories? They must realize that activities in remote mountains can be easily monitored! Or don't they? Why does everyone forget that years ago Osama was known to have a renal problem, which is reputed to require regular dialysis? If so, those procedures are not being performed in caves! Is he dead? Where are the investigative reports on renal conditions, which would elucidate the probabilities of surviving this long, with the conditions from which Osama was known to be suffering? Unless Osama can appear on video, giving some clear and unambiguous statement that he knows what day it is (perhaps holding up the front page of a current newspaper), it seems to me that there is every likelihood that whatever is left of *Al Qaeda* is hiding its reality from its supposed "followers." It's a clever ruse with smoke, mirrors, and doctored videotape, but eventually someone will say that "the king wears no clothes." Indeed, I just did!

It appears to me that the tired old man, in the dirty cotton turban, is just a has been gangster, who is hoping he can use the reflected glory of a real leader, hoping against hope that his cadre of "fighters" has not evaporated into the realities of living and aging. They cannot stay on message any longer—"infidel" Shiites have turned into allies, in his vision, thereby proving that there is nothing, which legitimately separates the two sects. You can't have it both ways! Either you are whipping up the two sects against one another, to keep things hot for Mr. Bush in Iraq; or you are suggesting joint action to defeat civilization. But, you can't be both. Which is it?

He also emphasized that Hezbollah must be careful not to allow the battle to be referred to as a secular contest for power. If this happens, the entire claim to a religious battle of world views evaporates. I have not heard Hezbollah claiming any divine intervention on its behalf. Indeed, as they steadily lose more and more infrastructure in the current slugfest, it would be hard to argue that *Allah* is on their side.

To the extent that Hezbollah has received good reviews from the ever accommodating media, they have been over the fact that they have successfully provided secular services, like garbage pickup, to their followers. If they stuck to these successes, it seems to me, they would be much more effective in providing a platform from which their followers could live and build strong families. Hezbollah would be much better served to get out of this situation quickly, with their two cabinet ministers still in place, and focus on rebuilding their part of Lebanon. If they fail to do this, eventually their own people will chew them up and spit them out.

As for the tired old man in the dirty turban, his exhortations become more and more lame, the more he exhorts but nothing happens. It seems to me that those of my readers, who hate what I am saying here, should take a moment to reflect. Just what is *Allah* telling you, by giving civilization the opportunity to dismantle Hezbollah's military strength? It seems to me that *Allah's* message is loud and clear, and it does not favor gangster behavior.

Dr. Zawahri: leaders lead! You are not a leader when you try to follow along behind a true leader, in a religious sect you previously vilified. The World is on to your fraud of leadership! Muslim leaders have long ago recognized your fraud on Islam.

Mr. Nasrallah: Now it is time for the true leader to sue for peace, so that he can live to lead another day. Civilization will give you no rest until you pledge your commitment to a civilized World for all peoples, including your own, and then lead them toward that civilization by your example. What ever gave you the idea that a few thousand rockets could somehow subdue Israel? Since everyone is now condemning the United States for not stopping the carnage, everyone must also already have known that the United States will never let Israel be defeated. Why do you waste any part of the rest of your precious life on such a project, when you know it is already doomed to failure, wasting the lives of hundreds of your followers in the process? You have, according to reports, already done many good things for your people. In Islam, there is a saying that we should be known for our good works. I know this because I bought an Arabic print of the saying at the Islamic Museum in Kuala Lumpur, last May. Survivors remember good works much more frequently than they remember "martyrs." It is time to find a way to save face, and lead toward peace.

No matter what happens in the next few weeks, if you fail to do this, you will be destroyed. When the United States could not send Al Capone to prison because of his many murders, he was successfully prosecuted for income tax evasion instead. Civilization (and I don't necessarily mean Western Civilization) will find a way to stop you, and the rest of the gangsters who continue to tarnish the good name of Islam, if you fail to see this truth. Your only hope is to have your signature on a peace treaty, which leaves you with a semblance of dignity, and the right to lead your people toward prosperous lives.

Failing this, you will never sleep a peaceful night again, because you will never be sure that one of your own body guards will not slit your throat. All of the governments of the Middle East have too much to lose from irresponsible behavior. They can never let you continue to create such provocations, for fear that you may bring down their regimes. None of them are advantaged by radicalized youth within their borders. You may well survive Israeli bombs. But, will you survive an Arab or Persian assassin in the dark of night? They will trip over one another trying to get to you; and you will never know when. Your only true solution is crafting a peace, in which you can be seen as a messianic leader of a peaceful and prosperous Lebanon. You need to do this soon. If you fail to do so, you may find yourself trying to persuade *Allah* of your just cause, at a time when *Allah* has already spoken.

Chapter 45

Losing Progressive Arabs

Progressive Arabs and Muslims are the key to establishing peace, and defeating terrorism. The Western World cannot lose their intermediation with the radicals in their countries, since the Western World, and especially the United States, is obviously so inept at maintaining a nuanced policy, which recognizes that there are many more important forces at play in the Muslim World than a few incursions across the Israeli border.

On July 28, 2006, the West received a sobering call for help from this important constituency. *Arab News* Editor-in-Chief Khaled Almaeena, in a scathing article directed at the Bush Administration, clearly stated the stakes, which have heretofore seemed well beyond the comprehension of America's diplomats. By publishing his op-ed, "Mr. Bush Just Doesn't Get It," in *Gulf News*, he intentionally made certain that his Arab audience goes well beyond his own Saudi readers.

Mr. Almaeena's most critical point is that the Arab World has changed. It's highly educated 40-something management class will not stand for the continuation of a *status quo,* where Israel is always right, and Arabs are always wrong, regardless of how loyal they have been as allies and supporters of the United States.

Tsunami of Blood has heretofore been focusing on the radicalization of the undereducated and disillusioned young men, who make up the 15-23 age group across the Middle East. But, Mr. Almaeena is quite right that the educated class can also be radicalized, with sufficient provocation. It is sobering that this warning is coming from a man known for his progressive views, which are often at odds with the very conservative policies of the Saudi government.

Chapter 46
It's the Stupidity Stupid

Politicians seem to think their constituents are stupid. I, on the other hand, favor a campaign bumper sticker for the Fall election campaign, which reads, "**It's the Stupidity Stupid!**"

The days of an ignorant electorate have long passed. The Internet means that even this book can reach practically anyone anywhere (115 countries to date). The issue for writers is only how to get the attention of the many readers around the World, in the face of tens of millions of other offerings. The other day, I did a simple search on the number of blogs existing in the World, and a superficial study said the number was over 200 million.

President Bush says that we are going to "stay the course" in Iraq "final victory," but he cannot articulate what he means. Not only he cannot, that would surprise no one, but his entire policy and speech writing team cannot; OR, they just think that sloganeering is going to keep Republicans in office. Not! As I have long argued, people need to understand their peril, if they are going to support political leaders with vision. In his recent book *The Long Emergency: Surviving the Converging Catastrophes of the Twenty-First Century*, James Howard Kunstler highlights two sides of one idea. He first draws attention to the fact that Carl Jung had once stated that "people cannot stand too much reality." The President's team obviously subscribes to this point of view. On the other hand, Kunstler rails against the fact that Americans are totally clueless about how problems in the Middle East relate to their lives.

Recently, in a non-scientific study, I attempted to determine whether Americans are aware of the potential consequences to their lifestyles of events in the Middle East. When I first asked about the Middle East, I got mostly stammering. Then I asked, "What would be the reaction of Americans to $10-15 per gallon gasoline?" The reactions were quite succinct. While most agreed that, despite perceptions in the Middle East, the United States is not seeking to control Iraqi oil, since we are able to buy it anyway, in the World market, most also said that they would favor the United States taking control in several countries, if prices would go that high. Some thought the higher prices would be the solution to getting alternate energy sources going viably. Kunstler argues, though, that all alternative energy strategies will be too little too late to prevent major catastrophes to the American way of life.

My point is that there is a boundary, somewhere between $4 and $15 per gallon of gas, where many Americans do become imperialists. To those who think that the United States cannot tolerate casualties, I refer them to the experience of Vietnam, where the average death toll over 8 years was approximately 140 per week, and the death toll in the two worst years rose toward 500 per week. It is hard to know what the tolerance level would be, especially if the price is other people's children, if everyone is feeling that their personal economic life style is seriously under attack. Americans are not yet feeling that today.

We need a generation of scholar politicians, who accept Theodore Roosevelt's dictum that we should "Speak Softly, But Carry a Big Stick." That would suggest a generation of politicians, who believe in diplomacy, over brute force, using the latter only when absolutely essential. During the Twentieth Century, we saw the Soviet Union collapse under the weight of its own policies. We prevailed in 40 years of intense, diplomatic chess, where the adversary, too, was a super power. It is hard to imagine what the outcome would be, if the United States had attempted regime change instead. Belligerence merely gives rise to belligerence!

All evidence today suggests that the Iranian theocracy will collapse under the weight of its own repression, if only the United States resists attacking, and allows the process to run. Shirin Ebadi, the 2003 Nobel Peace Prize winner, said so explicitly in *Iran Awakening*. I saw one telling comment, in Nasrin Alavi's *We Are Iran: The Persian Blogs*, where an Iranian blogger said that the one thing the Iranian theocracy had done was prove to all Iranians that there is no God. That's quite an accomplishment, in a country that prides itself on being religiously based. The *Mutawa* of Saudi Arabia have similarly undermined the very purpose for their existence, just as the Inquisition caused its own demise and sweeping reforms in Christianity, in the 16th Century.

Chapter 47

Seven Habits of Highly Ineffective Governments

During a long trip home, yesterday, I listened to an audio version of Stephen R. Covey's *The 7 Habits of Highly Effective People*, and it occurred to me that his prescription for success, if viewed from the opposite end of the spectrum, exactly describes why the Bush Administration is the antithesis of effectiveness in World affairs. Using Dr. Covey's ideas as a model, let's consider what I mean:

1. Not proactive. The United States of America under George W. Bush refuses to have diplomatic dialogue with the very people, with whom we must be talking: Iran; Syria; Hezbollah; Hamas; and North Korea. The Administration seems to have the half-witted idea that all that history of diplomacy in the civilized World means nothing; that we can just bully other peoples into our point of view, without recognizing the fact that we came to our point of view only after seriously bloody conflicts in our own part of the World over millennia. Why should we believe that others, who were insulated from those developments, can change any faster? The Bush Administration seems to believe that diplomacy means having tea parties with our cousins and friends. While, fortunately, there are still capable career diplomats in the ranks of our State Department, they have been totally marginalized. The agencies, which did engage other peoples in positive ways in past decades, like the Agency for International Development, have been eviscerated by the cleptocrats, who are trying to hide the hideous excesses of failed development programs in Iraq.

2. No vision. Dr. Covey urges that, in order to be a leader, one must have vision. It is quite clear that nothing of the sort resides in today's White House. The Bush Administration lacks the vision to see what is possible in the Middle East, in general. Instead of developing a bit of strategic vision, it insists on heinous little chess moves, which have done nothing, in the 5 years since 9/11, except make the World a more dangerous place for all Americans.

3. No management. Without vision, no one can manage! To the extent there are still bureaucrats, who know what a decent plan is, and how to execute it, their authority has been completely usurped by non-leaders, who do not understand that they cannot do everything, and who think things can happen without vision. Why does the World have to wait whilst Condi flies from Malaysia to the Middle East, only to learn that she is *persona non grata*, because she has nothing to offer? A lowly visa stamping bureaucrat (we won't call them diplomats any more, since they obviously have nothing to say) could have done that. But the visa stampers did not get that information, which shows just how badly they have been marginalized by a White House, which thinks it can do everything.

4. No win-win. Anyone knows that in any agreement, both sides must win. Condi hasn't been to the grocery store lately. Even there, where the pricing is "take it or leave it," if the customers choose to "leave it," the grocery store marks the overpriced bananas down until they solve their inventory problem. Our Texan and Wyoming cowboys have watched too many John Wayne westerns, where "my way or the highway" works wonderfully—in fantasy!

5. No communication. Condi flits in like a little bird, defecates and leaves. It is obvious that no one in the Administration has been listening. I have every reason to hate Hezbollah, considering the fact that they murdered hundreds of my friends and fellow Marines, but even I can see that they have been effective in delivering government style services to the civilians in their areas of control. A discussion might help us learn how we could accentuate the positive, and eliminate the negative aspects of their behavior. Discussion does not mean that everything is hunky dory. Leaders, who insist on remaining gangsters, will be ended by the civilized World. But, it would help all of us if a majority of the civilized World agreed that this is necessary, and then it should be done with lethal injection, not a bludgeon, which kills hundreds of innocents in the process.

6. No synergy. As a businessman, I can easily see how the Lebanon/Palestine/Israel part of the World could become a powerhouse economic region very quickly, if only everyone would wake up out of their bad dream. A compromise, which only restores the status quo, could not achieve that. But, if the adults in the region could see what is in their best interests, and the best interests of their people, it could easily compete with Dubai in less than a decade. Indeed, many of the people, who have made the Dubai miracle happen, have been displaced Palestinians. So, if they felt confident that they could make the same thing happen in their homeland, I am sure many would return. I am sure that many moderate Arab governments would be very happy to encourage such a development with their investments. This would, indeed, be considerably better than the subsistence wages, which most Palestinians are relegated to today.

7. We have squandered our power. Few people outside of the United States look to

our country with admiration today, because of our cowboy politics. Meanwhile, the Bush Administration has seriously degraded the very aspects of American society, which have been our strength—our Freedoms are in jeopardy, on the current course. Only when we insist that our leaders go back to the fundamentals of what made America the power it is today, will we change these negative trends. Time is short!

There is good news, however. America is self correcting, as I said in Chapter 21. This morning I was awakened to C-Span radio, which was airing one vituperative call after another from angry citizens. The mood in the United States is vicious, and it is not directed at Hezbollah! It is directed at the White House! It appears clear that the Republicans, who have squandered America's prestige in the World, making things steadily worse, may have reached the end of their "free hand" time in Washington. They may have misled many Americans about their inadequacies in 2004, in the post 9/11 frenzy of fear mongering, but the carcasses of their failures will now be hung around their necks for everyone to see and smell. Even the Christian fundamentalists, who have been running around cheering about the coming of Armageddon, will come to know that life goes on, and even they will have to accept the idea that nothing is infallible.

More good news is that all of the impact of the new media, from "sms" and cell phones to the Internet and video cameras everywhere, means that no one will get away with improper behavior anymore, anywhere in the World; at least not for decades or centuries, which has been the experience in the past. With reporters and commentators everywhere, who can easily ignore the mainstream media propagandists, change is coming in the way people are governed throughout the World.

Chapter 48

Media Shame of the Week

At about 9:15 p.m. EDT, 31 July 2006, I was watching Fox News, just to see what they were saying, and I happened to hear the "Media Shame of the Week." Bill O'Reilly made a reference to "Islamic Fascism" and Oliver North used the term "Global Islamic Terror" at about 9:24 p.m. Can anyone get through to these people that these comments are Defamatory to the vast majority of Muslims, and not helpful to finding peace? Here is what I have to say to Ollie:

Ollie: When you, Rich Higgins, Jim Webb and I were at The Basic School, we all believed in right and justice. Your terminology suggests that you think it is OK to foist a gross injustice on the Muslim community in the United States and around the World. You should know that there are 4 million Muslim voters in the United States (according to the Muslim Public Affairs Council). Since the electorate has been consistently so evenly balanced in recent years, any minority group with that many voters can swing an election. Indeed, it was the Muslim vote that put Our Fearless Leader over the top, in both 2000 and 2004. It was the Muslim vote in Northern Virginia, in November 2006, which put Jim Webb over the top and gave control of the Senate to the Democratic Party.

I want you to know what I was doing during the 2006 election season. I was trying to reach every Muslim voter in America, to point out to them how the President used fear mongering to scare everyone into voting for him in 2004. We all remember all of those campaign ads, in which the President appeared with the burning World Trade Towers in the background. Sheldon Solomon's "Terror Management Theory" predicts that people will vote for charismatic leaders, when such fear mongering is used. But, there is an antidote. That is for me to place an anchor in the subconscious of every Muslim voter, which accomplishes the following, in counterpoint to the President's subliminal tricks: every time a Muslim voter sees one of those fear mongering ads in every election season, it will remind him or her of how voters were psychologically manipulated in favor of the President in 2004. We empowered a grass roots effort across the country, to convince all Muslim voters that they must vote for candidates, who can demonstrate a reasonable amount of international sophistication and nuance in their diplomacy. By electing two Democratic controlled Houses of Congress, we put a speed bump into the President's cavalier cowboy attitude.

It is time for you and Mr. O'Reilly to know that there are many different types of Muslims, and 99% of all of them are peace loving, and most are favoring a just peace with Israel. If I started calling you some of the names that come to mind, you would immediately take umbrage. Knowing your pugilistic history, you would probably challenge me to a boxing match—no need, I'll concede you that one. But, my point is that when you intentionally offend 1.3 billion people, time and again, with no thought of the consequences, their natural reaction is much the same. You are not making the United States safer for Democracy. Knowing your nature, you will probably jut out your chin, and say, "I won't take it back." But that just proves that you and Mr. O'Reilly have become irrelevant, because you are not really interested in finding a solution, you are just interested in pushing belligerence, so that you can have more fodder for your "War Stories" program. Some of us actually advanced our education and perspective quite a lot after Vietnam, but you're still trying to relive your "glory" days (and I use the term loosely). I am simply asking you to wake up and understand the ground realities in today's World. I urge you to read the "Introduction" of this book, which puts the big picture in a little better perspective. If you understand that, you will understand better what really must be done in order to ensure a peaceful World for our grandchildren. What you are doing now, through these careless defamatory comments, is making things worse.

The solutions to our myriad troubles in the Middle East are not going to be found by making every Muslim our enemy, and calcifying views, which went out of style in earlier centuries. The solution will only be found by working creatively with moderate and progressive Muslims and Arabs around the World, who have a much clearer Vision of what World peace looks like than you do.

Ollie, you actually have some influence. I'm really not trying to offend you, here. I am writing to ask you to look at the bigger picture, evaluate our real peril, and then come to some sensible thoughts about how peace can be achieved. I would be happy to work with you toward that end. Until May of this year, I was in favor of an immediate withdrawal from Iraq, because Americans were simply being blamed for everything, and that was contributing to a worse global situation. I was thoughtful enough to not only reverse my position, but advocate for an even larger commitment to Iraq, for the reasons I have expressed in my "Introduction." It seems to me that if you read that one contribution, and think about it for a week, you will begin to see the sense in my views. If you would like, I will be happy to work with you to see where we can find common ground.

You were criticized Mr. Al Maliki, the Prime Minister of Iraq, for criticizing the Israeli attack on Lebanon. But you must understand that the Israeli attack is causing more and more intransigence in the Arab World, thereby making his job, and ours in Iraq, exponentially more difficult. He was quite right in saying to Congress this week that if we cannot defeat terrorism in Iraq, we cannot defeat it anywhere. But the Israeli attacks are making that process far more difficult, because the reactions to the Israeli attack on Lebanon extend FAR beyond the borders of Lebanon, and well beyond Syria and Iran. Let us stop making more enemies, and start recognizing our friends in the Middle East. At the very least, let us respect our friends and their religion. That is the American way!

Chapter 49

Advertisers – That's the Ticket

Many of my Arab friends have complained to me about the coverage of Fox News. It is plain that people like Bill O'Reilly like to taunt their adversaries. But as I pointed out in Chapter 48, some of what Mr. O'Reilly says is, in my opinion, actually defamatory toward most Muslims. Mr. O'Reilly seems difficult to convince by an e-mail campaign directed to him. BUT, there is one thing that would get his attention. If he were to start to hear from his advertisers, that he needs to tone it down and wake up to the ground realities of the World, including the importance of moderate Arabs and Muslims, we might see genuine behavior modification. This would be contributory toward World Peace!

On August 1, 2006, Mr. O'Reilly interviewed Condoleeza Rice at 11:00 p.m. I turned on Fox News about 10 minutes before the program, and watched until 12:00 midnight. While I may not have noted down all of the advertisers, who are supporting Fox News and his program, I did make a list of a few of them. They are:

Boeing—This is one company that can't afford to be making enemies in the Arab world, since many of its projected sales are to Arab airlines.

Chief Executive Officer
The Boeing Company
100 N. Riverside Plaza
Chicago, IL 60606-1596
+1-312-544-2000

Hummer—I'm told the biggest market for Hummer in the World is Saudi Arabia.

Go to www.hummer.com, click on "Contact Us," and fill in the e-mail form.

Acura—Seems to me that I have seen a lot of Acuras in the Middle East.

Chief Executive Officer

Honda Motor Co., Ltd.
2-1-1 Minami-Aoyama
Minato-ku
Tokyo 107-8556
Japan
+81-3-3423-1111

Mitsubishi

Chief Executive Officer
Mitsubishi Motors Corporation
2-16-4 Konan, Minato-ku
Tokyo 108-8410
Japan
+81-3-6719=0059

Southwest Airlines/Chase Bank (Credit Card)

JPMorgan Chase & Co.
270 Park Avenue
New York, NY 10017
+1-212-270-6000

Florida Orange Juice—As with the following advertisers, they need to be aware that there are about 7 million Muslims in the USA, and that's quite a buying block.

Netzero

Chief Executive Officer
21301 Burbank Boulevard
Woodland Hills, CA 91367
+1-818-287-3000

Brinks Home Security

Chief Executive Officer
1801 Bayberry Court
Richmond, VA 23226

Nextel

Chief Executive Officer
2001 Edmund Halley Drive
Reston, VA 20191
+1-703-433-4000

Chapter 50
America's Peril

It is very sad to see that the American media has still not understood America's peril. To listen to CNN and Fox News on August 2, 2006, you could be forgiven for getting the impression that the United States was at war in Lebanon. I commend both channels for attempting to bring in all sides of the Lebanon/Israel story, but I condemn them for failing to see what is really important to the United States. Fox News, in particular, seems to be holding a pep rally for American support to Israel, when that has never been in question. Meanwhile, they ignore the contributions and good will of many Arab countries and Muslims, who are friends of The United States.

Speaking generally (while not addressing the issue of the current hostilities), let me be very clear that I support Israel as a nation-state. Indeed, most Americans do support Israel. I can imagine no realistic set of circumstances, which would make it possible for The United States to withdraw its support of Israel. Indeed, if its existence as a nation-state was truly threatened, there is no doubt that The United States would defend Israel, with all necessary force.

My reason for insisting a cease fire is immediately appropriate is that Israel, by its the continued hostilities, is achieving what Iran and *Al Qaeda* could not do as easily. They are radicalizing an entire generation of young people, across the Muslim World. This is the real danger! President Susilo Bambang Yudhoyono of Indonesia said so in so many words today at the Organization of the Islamic Conference ("OIC") emergency meeting in Putrajaya, Malaysia. This is the premise of this entire book, *Tsunami of Blood*. The August 3, 2006 edition of *Arab News* carries a story entitled, "A Young Man's Struggle with Extremism," which reviews a book entitled *The Twentieth Terrorist*, describing the experiences of a young man, who was in a position to possibly be the infamous "twentieth terrorist" on 9/11, but for the fact that he had turned away from the indoctrination. His story resonates, because it must be the same set of issues facing tens of millions of young people across much of the Muslim World, at this point in time. If the World loses these struggles, which are occurring in the minds of impressionable young people, we can look forward to much worse times in the future. As I said in the opening of this book. In that case, Iraq is only prologue. We must remember that not every battle can be won with guns, and the best victory in battle is achieved by never having to go into the battle, because you have already won—like the fall of the Soviet Union.

Demographics are on our side. Robin Wright, a reporter for *The Washington Post*, reported on one of the news shows within the last 48 hours that 57% of Iran's population of 70 million people is under 16 years old (40 million young minds). This is good news, because all evidence is that the generation just ahead of them is fed up with the Ayatollahs, and thirsting for the voice of common sense, which says that Iran is ready to come into the modern World. Indeed, my statistics suggest that one of the largest followings for *Tsunami of Blood* is in Iran. BUT, the voice of reason can be overcome by the voice of radicalism, if the World does not show sensitivity for the concerns of these large populations of young people. (I pointed out earlier that there are approximately 1.5 million young men in Saudi Arabia, between 15 and 23; and I estimate that there may be as many as 10 million in Egypt. There may be as many as 300 million young people, in this age group, across the Muslim World of 1.3 billion people.)

New technologies have changed the importance of how individuals throughout the World react to events. Hezbollah clearly understands this, because they have been winning the international communications war, so far. One of the leaders of *Al Manar*, the Hezbollah television channel, was allowed to provide his revisionist view of the World on America's National Public Radio, this morning. I think this is a good thing, because everyone gets to hear his views directly, and respond accordingly. BUT, it also means that responses to his assertions must be answered promptly, with equal prominence, or be accepted as fact.

Instead of recognizing, talking about, and reporting on this monumental problem, Fox News, in particular, seems intent on offending as many moderate Muslims, and their children, as is possible. This is VERY dangerous, and not contributing to peace whatsoever. Listening to them talk, it seems that their main concern is the national defense of The United States (and Israel); but the actual effect of their behaviors is exactly the opposite. At 9:16 p.m. EDT on August 2, 2006, Sean Hannity, of the Hannity & Colmes program, once again referred to "Islamic Fascism." This is a defamatory statement to all moderate Muslims, who can be the key to solving these myriad problems. It is a "stick in the eye," which is inexcusable. It was no surprise that Oliver North, who I criticized in Chapter 48, was sitting next to Mr. Hannity, when he used this term.

I have the following message for Fox News, Sean Hannity, Bill O'Reilly, and Oliver North: Guys, you are clueless about what the real peril is to our national defense, and who we need to help us protect our country. You do not need to be making a constant harangue on behalf of Israel on your programs. Israel has proven that it is quite capable of defending itself, and there is no doubt that The United States will come to Israel's aid, if it should ever ask for our help in its defense. The truth, which you are failing to report, is MUCH more sobering. If we don't find a way to influence the young people in the Muslim World in the right manner, Iraq will be prologue. I presume that you have noticed that the American military is stretched pretty thin, because of our involvement in Iraq. How do you think we will be defended, if the kind of violence we are seeing in Iraq spreads across two or three other very important countries? How will your viewers feel about $10-15 per gallon gasoline? Do you think that might influence the American way of life? Perhaps you didn't notice that some commentators have set the cost of 9/11, to the American economy, at $1 trillion. Just how many incidents of that magnitude do you think the United States can withstand? That was done by 19 men, with $100 worth of box cutters. Did you think the President's vaunted Department of Homeland Security has made us all safe? Look again! Does Katrina ring a bell? Have you noticed that even though The United States considers Lebanon and its people our friends, even your reports are talking about how we are radicalizing Lebanese youth to the wrong point of view?

There is just no question that The United States needs a nuanced foreign policy, which recognizes that there is good and bad within every country, and that we need to be engaged with those good elements, to keep the rest of the tinderbox in the Middle East under control. It would be very helpful if our mainstream media showed signs of understanding this point, and focused on reporting which, at the least, does not make matters worse.

I know you will tell me that we have to be very strong with Iran and Syria. I do agree! But, at the rate he's going, I doubt that Mr. Ahmadinejad is going to be very relevant much longer. He successfully upstaged another meeting of the Organization for the Islamic Conference ("OIC"), by making his outrageous comments about Israel. And, rather than give that its own due, in the context of the entire OIC, and its meeting, the media is again giving him headlines around the World. The good news, I think, is that he is probably marginalizing himself, in the process. The OIC members cannot stand for their youth to be radicalized; and they certainly cannot accept the idea that their youth would "look up" to Mr. Ahmadinejad, as a messianic leader. My guess is that he will find his way to the footnotes of history, regardless of what The United States and Israel do about him.

My point to you is that we have many and complex problems throughout the Middle East. The Israel/Hezbollah/Lebanon battle will find an end soon, but the seething problems of disenchanted young people throughout the Middle East will not have been solved. We need to understand what those problems are, and how they can be guided toward the path of civilization. This is the true challenge of the next decade! Civilization hangs in the balance!

Chapter 51
Letter to Advertisers

Many of my Muslim friends around the World have asked me, "What is the solution to the defamatory behavior toward Muslims of the mainstream media?" I agree that writing to Bill O'Reilly, Oliver North or Sean Hannity will, in my opinion, likely do nothing. Even if they see your letter, in my opinion, they would simply disregard it. BUT, there is a way to get their attention! Their programs rely on advertising. What needs to be done is that we must educate advertisers to the harm these people are doing to the peace of the World by their defamatory way of referring to the Muslim World. If there were enough letters from around the World (enough to fill the post office), it seems to me that advertisers would cause the necessary behavior changes, since they control the purse strings for these programs. Here is a letter, you could use as a model:

QUOTE

<Advertiser Name>
<Advertiser Address>
<Advertiser Address>

Dear <Advertiser>:

I see that you advertise on Fox News. I want to bring to your attention the term "Islamic Fascists," which was used by Sean Hannity, on Hannity and Colmes at about 9:16 p.m. EDT on August 2, 2006. A tape of Bill O'Reilly was rebroadcast at 11:02 p.m. EDT on August 3, 2006, in which he used the term "Islamic Killers." These terms defame nearly all of the World's 1.3 billion Muslims, who are not fascist nor killers. This behavior is NOT acceptable to the World's Muslims. Please ask Fox News and Mr. Hannity to find appropriate ways of differentiating between gangsters, and law abiding Muslims, who are a part of the civilized World, and who are seeking the same solutions to "terrorism" that you are. I would appreciate your confirmation that you have taken the appropriate steps. Amazingly, at 11:10 p.m. EDT on August 3, 2006, Bill O'Reilly's substitute host said that the question is, "How do we line up with moderate Arabs?" Stopping the defamation on the same program would be a very good start.

Please note that gangster behavior, which is known as "terrorism," is as much a threat to the Muslim World as it is to the West. All civilized peoples are affected. Working through moderate Muslims around the World is the best way to eliminate the scourge of "terrorism." It is evident that the Bush Administration is far out of its depth in achieving this result. When you allow programs you sponsor to abuse Muslims in general, you are responsible for causing more and more Muslims to become radicals. News programs should, at the very least, not add to the problems they are reporting.

Indeed, your sponsorship would be appreciated by the Muslim World, if you caused the people who are behaving this way to begin reporting on the real problems facing people in the Middle East. Leaving the areas of conflict aside, for a moment, there are very nasty problems, which can cause radicals to be effective in recruiting these gangsters you call "terrorists." Why are you making their job easier, by allowing the network and/or programs you sponsor to continuously and gratuitously cause more, and more, bad feeling? This is only exacerbating already existing problems. Why don't you insist that those you sponsor provide programming, which seeks to solve the problems?

Very truly yours,

Name
Designation (if any)

UNQUOTE

I provided a list of companies, which were advertising on Fox News and the O'Reilly Factor, the night Bill O'Reilly and Oliver North committed the "Media Shame of the Week." That list is in Chapter 49. The following is a list (perhaps incomplete) of the companies that were either sponsoring Hannity and Colmes on August 2, 2006, or were sponsoring Fox News:

Mercedes—Lots of business in the Muslim World.
Office of the CEO
Daimler Chrysler AG
70546 Stuttgart
Germany
Tel: +49-711-170
Fax: +49-711-17 22244

Office of the CEO
Daimler Chrysler Corporation
Auburn Hills, MI 48326-2766
USA
+1-248 576 5741

Lexus—Lots of business in the Muslim World.
Chief Executive Officer
Toyota Motor Corporation
1 Toyota-Cho
Toyota City
Aichi Prefecture 471-8571
Japan
+81 (0565) 28-2121

Jaguar
Chief Executive Officer
Jaguar Cars Limited
Browns Lane
Allesley
Coventry
CV5 9DR
UK

Scott Trade
Call Kelly Doria at 314-965-1555 x 1231
mediarelations@scottrade.com

Double Tree Hotels
Mr. Stephen F. Bollenbach
Co-Chairman and Chief Executive Officer
Hilton Hotels Corporation
9336 Civic Center Drive
Beverly Hills, CA 90210

Red Lobster
Chief Executive Officer
5900 Lake Ellenor Drive
Orlando, FL 32809
+1-407-245-4000

Lowe's
Chief Executive Officer
Lowe's Companies, Inc.

P.O. Box 1111
North Wilkesboro, NC 28656
+1-800-445-6937

UBS—A bank with much business in the Muslim World.
Chief Executive Officer
Bahnhofstrasse
Zurich, Switzerland

Hefty
Chief Executive Officer
Pactiv Corporation Headquarters
1900 W. Field Court
Lake Forest, IL 60045

Comcast
Chief Executive Officer
Comcast Cable
4100 E. Dry Creek Road
Littleton, CO 80122
+1-303-486-3800

Home Depot
Media Relations Department
+1-800-553-3199

Lens Crafters
Chief Executive Officer
4000 Luxottica Place
Mason, OH 45040

Raymond James Financial, Inc.
Chief Executive Officer
880 Carillon Parkway
St. Petersburg, FL 33716
+1-727-567-1000

I do not consider it my role to keep such lists. I'm sure there are many Muslims, who can monitor programs and list advertisers. I am just trying to highlight the kind of peaceful action, which is likely to get results, if it is effective enough. If you feel these ideas have merit, please pass them on to everyone who has an e-mail mailing list, and mail a few letters to actual advertisers.

Chapter 52
Laws of Physics

Events in the Middle East, regretfully reflect the physical law that for every action, there is an equal and opposite reaction. We have Israel attacking Hezbollah (and the peaceful citizens of Lebanon). This is causing more, and more, bad feeling throughout the Muslim World. That caused *Tsunami of Blood,* and thousands of others, to call for an immediate cease fire, in order to slow down the radicalization of the Muslim World. This scared the American Neocons, because they love the idea of a war, which drags us into an actual military action against Syria and Iran. The beat goes on .....

At 10:50 a.m. on August 5, 2006, I heard former New York Mayor Ed Koch refer to "Islamic Fundamentalist Fascists (if you will)," on Fox News' "Head to Head" program. Great, Ed! You are really proving that you lack any real understanding of what is going on in the World.

The Neocon's idea of getting all of the fighting over quickly, including with Iran and Syria, is a non-starter, for the same reason and Mohandas Ghandi said, "An eye for an eye makes the whole World blind." New communications technologies are making it impossible for governments to act just as they like. A major battle with Syria and Iran will surely bring the World's approbation, and exacerbate generations of hatred throughout the Muslim World.

I have this message for them: Guys! Have you noticed that, after failing to grab Mullah Omar in Afghanistan, when we knew where he was, Afghanistan has become a disaster? [Probably not, because the mainstream media doesn't consider that shame important enough. But, for the rest of my readers, we haven't missed the fact that the Bush Administration has just let the poppy crop continue to grow, conceding a loss in the "war on drugs," thereby causing problems throughout the World, not just The United States.] Have you noticed that the American Army would have a serious problem supporting another major battle? Not by insurgents, but rather, because of inept handling of the occupation of Iraq. Because most troops have had multiple redeployments to the Middle East, the only way to keep force levels high enough even to continue the efforts where we are already fighting will be to reinstitute the draft, which will not be popular in the American electorate.

I do agree that it would be bad for Hezbollah to come out of this fight with an apparent win against Israel. We must PROACTIVELY solve these problems! The steps are:

1. Cause a cease fire. Fox News reported at 11:01 a.m., August 5, 2006, that the United States and France have agreed to a UN Security Council resolution. Whoop de doo! The problem is, Hezbollah and the other criminal actors are not members of the UN. So, if it takes us two weeks to get agreement with France, which owes us for saving their bacon in World War II, how long is it going to take to make Hezbollah to agree? I pray there is back channel negotiation going on, which will allow a cease fire quickly, but that is not my sense. A cease fire is needed in order to slow down the radicalization of the Middle East.

2. Stop disengaging! We must proactively resolve our disputes with countries like Syria, Iran and North Korea. This does not mean only by negotiation. What we must do is "Speak softly, and carry a big stick," as Teddy Roosevelt had it. The point is that you must be willing to use the big stick, but only at the appropriate time, and at an appropriate level of intensity. Our diplomacy has been toothless lately, which does make it look like we have been appeasing Iran. The World needs to grow up! Gangster regimes and gangster organizations need to be ended. Iran needs to be given an offer they can't refuse. Everyone must clearly understand that "Crime Doesn't Pay!" Hezbollah has not yet gotten that message, and it is unclear whether they will, especially if they can argue that they won the current hostilities. BUT, that does not mean that you can kill innumerable civilians week after week on international television. Even the military strategies need to be nuanced, but quite firm!

3. The problems of Palestine need to be resolved, and soon! As long as the Palestinian people do not have a just society in which they can live in peace, no one will have a peaceful society. If we have all of the influence with the Israelis, which everyone believes, we should insist that they get this done.

4. We must engage with moderate Muslims and Arabs, and help them to evolve their societies to the point that young people see a hope for the future. As long as the best course for their young people is to kill themselves with a bomb wrapped around their body, we will have no end to terrorism. Therefore, all of these societies need to open themselves to all sorts of international economic interaction. Failure to address these issues expeditiously may cause several of these regimes to be overthrown from within, and this, in turn, is likely to have crushing impact on the United States. What will be the consequences in the United States,

if gas prices go to $10-15 per gallon? We need to forget the fantasy, repeated on Fox News this morning, that America will simply move to alternative forms of energy. The reality is that, if we start right now, developments might start making a noticeable impact in about 30 years. So the issues must be resolved in the context of our oil reliant economy today!

Chapter 53
Media War

Media coverage has become one real battleground in warfare, and henceforward will become ever more meaningful. The killings of bombs, rockets and bullets affect only those in the immediate vicinity and family members, but lies spread around the World can first draw us into global warfare, and gradually eat our freedoms, as we let them do it. Lies and revisionist history can mislead entire generations, guiding them into untold horrors. After everyone is either dead or entirely exhausted by the process, the survivors will gladly give up their freedoms, to be able to live in peace.

I will speak here primarily of American media, with special emphasis on Fox News, but I am sure the same is true throughout the World. Those of us, who can read this and still have our free will intact, must fight back or George Orwell (*1984*) will have proven the prophet of our loss of humanity. No earlier prophet will then seem significant to the survivors.

In August 2006, I heard a give and take between Republican (Neocon) and Democratic commentators on Fox News. The Republican was shameless in the lies he was spewing. He was talking about Jimmy Carter being the worst President in American history, while completely ignoring the present incumbent's claim to that title. He claimed that Jimmy Carter never made any worthwhile contribution, and that he presided over the worst inflation in the history of the nation. The hapless Democratic respondent was only about 35 years old, so she could not remember what was really happening, and she did not remember her history on this occasion. She could not respond that the inflation of those days was given to us by Richard Nixon, who famously and ineffectively tried to slow it down with price controls. It was only when Mr. Carter finally had the privilege of appointing Paul Volcker as Chairman of the Federal Reserve in 1979, that America's inflation was brought under control. In our system, the Federal Reserve Bank controls monetary policy, and the Chairman's term is not concurrent with the President's, so Mr. Carter was stuck with the ineffective policies of Mr. Volcker's ineffective predecessor,

Arthur F. Burns, who was appointed by Nixon! Secondly, it was Mr. Carter's initiative, which organized the Camp David Accords, which caused the warring between Egypt and Israel to be finally settled, with the Israelis withdrawing from the Sinai region of Egypt. In the context of all of the events, which occurred before or since that time, I rate Mr. Carter's accomplishment as the most significant and long lasting.

But, my point is that the Republican commentator was able to spew bald faced lies across the airwaves, shouting down the hapless Democratic representative, who did not have enough information, nor the necessary experience, to shout back. It is evident that in today's context, he who shouts loudest revises history effectively. If his lies are unanswered with the same vigor, at least over time, they can become "truths," in the Joseph Goebbels sense of a lie spoken often enough becomes a truth. His principle technique of *argumentum ad nauseum* now seems the principle means by which Fox News permits its lies to be promulgated.

There are ways we can fight back. The World is now interconnected economically. Many advertisers of news media around the World rely on sales everywhere. The people who spew these lies, and try to foment hatred, rely on their advertisers to be able to have the forum they have. It is time for the advertisers to recognize the dangers of our perilous World, and provide guidance to the programs, which they support. Within the past week, to provide just a few poignant examples, I have seen Boeing, Mercedes, Hummer, Lexus, and Acura all advertising on Fox News. All of these companies have major markets among moderates in the Muslim and Arab Worlds. It seems to me that if the Chairman of Boeing were to learn that certain sales of Boeing were being put on hold, pending receipt by the buyers of certain assurances that Boeing would only support programming that is balanced, and not aimed at fomenting further hatred in the Muslim World, Boeing would either discontinue its support of Fox News, or it would see to it that the programming is amended appropriately.

The biggest reason for my immediate concern is that there is information circulating on the Internet, which says that the Neocons in the Republican Party are now attempting to use the media to draw The United States into a war involving Syria and Iran. They are preparing the psyches of Americans for an expanded war, through their manipulation of the media. Their rationale is that we should defeat these regimes now, before they have access to nuclear weapons. The flaw in their logic is being pushed off the airwaves—Iraq. Have you noticed lately that the terrible news out of Iraq has been practically omitted from the news? Notwithstanding the fact that the carnage in Iraq is far worse than what is going on in Lebanon. The Neocons want us to let Iraq fall out of our immediate consciousness, because, if we are thinking about it we know that Iraq is a failed policy of Our Fearless Leader, and that might slow down their intention of getting us into something even worse.

My readers should avoid assuming that I favor appeasement of the current regime in Iran. I do not! I favor a very aggressive negotiating strategy, with effective consequences for behavior, which is beyond what should be accepted in a civilized World. If we do not have such a firm policy, we have learned nothing from the history of the Twentieth Century. Those who whine that Hamas and Hezbollah, and some others, have now succeeded at the ballot box, may have forgotten that, in 1933, Adolph Hitler was elected Chancellor of Germany by the biggest majority in German history. Just because gangsters are elected, doesn't mean they can continue their gangster behavior. Because of the quaint "Marquis of Queensbury Rules," which were followed in international diplomacy in the Twentieth Century, more than 20 million people were killed in World War II. I pointed out earlier that The United States was foolish in its hands off policy to the development of terrorist training bases from the 1960s to 2001. By the same token, it was intolerable to allow Hezbollah to locate thousands of missiles along the northern border of Israel. If they were such a politically oriented group, which is interested only in civic works, why did they need to do that? The Israelis had withdrawn from southern Lebanon six years earlier, thanks to DIPLOMACY! Civilization can no longer afford to tolerate such gangster behaviors. But, that does not mean that The United States can be the World's policeman, nor behave arrogantly, ignoring the sensibilities of the rest of the World. All of civilization must be brought along, through the media, or we will truly devolve into a New Dark Age of Horrors!

We must remember that sanity and insanity are two sides of the same piece of paper. I give Oliver Stone high points for focusing on heroism rather than conspiracy in his new movie "**World Trade Center**." He could have used it as a vehicle to foment more hatred and misunderstanding, which I am sure others, who do not understand the peril the World faces, will do. Mr. Stone's approach is what is needed, and more so. As I am writing this, I am listening to an interview with the two men, whose real life story is depicted in Stone's movie. One of them underwent 8 surgeries, as a result of his injuries. He said that it is his hope that people will leave the theatre with a message of "faith, hope and love ... and see the positive things of that day." Now we need a courageous movie maker who can envision weaving the needs of Muslims of all backgrounds and nationalities, and Americans of all backgrounds and national origins, into one peaceful whole.

Chapter 54

The Conover Doctrine

Civilization does not tolerate gangsters.

Corollary 1: God created all beings on Earth, and all methods of worshipping God.

Corollary 2: The Glory of God is the Diversity of God's creation.

Corollary 3: Religions support the spiritual needs of their followers.

Corollary 4: The role of theologians is to care for the spiritual needs of their people.

Corollary 5: Theologians, who see themselves as politicians, are politicians, governed by Corollary 7.

Corollary 6: Places of worship are for the spiritual support of the followers of a religion. To the extent that they are used for other purposes, they revert to the status of the other purpose.

Corollary 7: All political leaders, who rule by fear, intimidation and intolerance, must be retired.

Corollary 8: Gangsters, who wrap themselves in the clothes of theologians, and claim to get their authority from religion, are gangsters.

Corollary 9: Media organizations must be held to a reasonable standard of responsibility by God's people.

Corollary 10: God's people are civilized by God's guidance over millions of years. Those who are not civilized are gangsters, regardless of their claims.

Corollary 11: Hospitals are for the healthcare support of their patients. To the extent that they are used for other purposes, they revert to the status of the other purpose.

Corollary 12: All negotiations begin from our common humanity.

Corollary 13: The definition of "Civilization," is the definition given it by a reasonable man or woman, who is free from coercion.

Corollary 14: The definition of "Gangster," is the definition given it by a reasonable man or woman, who is free from coercion.

Corollary 15: Gangster organizations, which do good works, are gangster organizations.

Corollary 16: Communication creates common ground for all mankind.

Corollary 17: Compassion must be tempered by wisdom.

Corollary 18: One, who blames another, is not blameless.

Corollary 19: The "Righteous" must examine themselves.

Corollary 20: First seek wisdom from God. Hear what God says from within.

Corollary 21: Civilization is a work in progress.

Corollary 22: All humanity has freedom of choice. If you think you don't have it, get it!

N.B. "The Conover Doctrine with Corollaries" is a work in progress. If you would like to submit suggested amendments or other corollaries, please do so. I will give you credit for your contribution to strengthen this idea.

Chapter 55
Leadership Shame of the Week and Corollary 23

On August 10, 2006, authorities in London arrested 24 British subjects in an alleged gangster plot to blow up 9-10 American aircraft as they fly across the Atlantic Ocean toward the United States. President George W. Bush, in the process of making a statement about the investigation, referred to the defendants as "Islamic Fascists," thereby defaming 1.3 billion inhabitants of the Planet Earth. In my wildest dreams, I never imagined trying to make enemies of 1.3 billion people gratuitously, but this man obviously believes he is above the law. I therefore give him my "Leadership Shame of the Week" Award.

In considering The Conover Doctrine, I am sure it is difficult to look at ourselves, and see our own shortcomings, but that is what is called for if civilization is to survive. Those of us who aspire to see civilization progressing at the time of our deaths, must first examine ourselves, and then work toward changing the situation. For my part, I spent yesterday afternoon preparing for and interviewing Nihad Awad, Executive Director of the Council on American-Islamic Relations, because a *Washington Post* article on August 9, 2006, had reported the difficulty Muslim charities are having raising humanitarian aid funds for Lebanon, during the current conflict between Israel and Lebanon. At the same time, the Jewish community in The United States has been able to raise over $300 million in humanitarian aid for Israel, according to the article.

Fear was the principle reason given for why American Muslims have not made gifts in like quantity. Let me here urge that Muslims have every right to make donations to the legal charity of their choice. What is the risk of having your name on a list (the primary fear) compared to the damage to lives and property, which has been suffered by the Lebanese? By the end of this chapter, you will see that I clearly am putting my name on lots of lists, but I firmly believe in civilization, so I think that risk is most worthwhile.

The fear is caused because The United States government has discontinued the activities of certain Muslim charities, whose funds somehow made their way into the hands of gangster organizations. I cannot comment on those actions, as I know none of the facts. But, I think it is fair to say that if a Muslim charity is still in operation, it has at least passed the bludgeon of the Bush Administration, and should be a reasonable risk for getting funds to the Lebanese most in need.

Corollary 23: Gangsters, who use high political office as a subterfuge to commit their crimes, are gangsters. People who lie, cheat, steal, conspire to commit murder, and commit murder, fit within the definition of "gangster" in Civilization.

I nominate President Bush and Vice President Cheney for the label of Gangster, within the definition, which I believe all civilized people would acknowledge as reasonable. They:

Lied:
About weapons of mass destruction, leading The United States into war;

Cheated:
In diplomacy, because they slither about behind the scenes, allowing murder and mayhem to come down on hundreds of innocent Lebanese civilians, while they cheat the American people of future peace by instigating hatred among moderate Muslims, who are the key to peace;

Stole:
They stole the 2000 election from the winner of the popular vote (whisper who dares); and they manipulated the result in the 2004 election, by using fear to intimidate the American people;

Conspiracy to Commit Murder:
Regardless of what may be said about military action, Ron Suskind, in his book *The One Percent Doctrine* alleges that they conspired (Pp. 137-38) to "send a message" to *Al Jazeera* Satellite Channel, by attacking its offices in Kabul and Baghdad, an action which would likely cause loss of life. One of the strongest allies of The United States in the "War on Terror" is Qatar, where the forward headquarters of Central Command is maintained. *Al Jazeera* is a business operated in Qatar. Therefore, in my opinion, there was no legal "nation state" justification for an attack on *Al Jazeera*.

Murder:
The attacks on *Al Jazeera*'s office in Baghdad resulted in the death of Tariq Ayoub, on April 8, 2003. To the extent that Suskind's allegations, and the logical inferences which follow it, can be proven, this is murder, in my opinion. President Bush and Vice President Cheney are currently immune from prosecution (although I do not know the true legalities here), but it will not always be true. They will leave office

in 2009. They might some day have to face criminal prosecution for Mr. Ayoub's murder, once they leave office. That would be a media circus of the first order!

All of us, who see ourselves as part of the Civilized World, must examine our own societies, and make the necessary changes to prevent gangsters from taking us into an Age of Horrors. No one is above the law!

Chapter 56

Fifty Questions for the Women of Iraq, Lebanon, Israel, Palestine, Iran, and Syria

Non-Muslim non-Jewish westerners have a few questions for the women of Iraq, Lebanon, Israel, Palestine, Iran and Syria:

1. Why did God create a World with so many religions?
2. Why did God create so many viewpoints about religions?
3. Why did God create a World with so many races?
4. What does God say to you today?
5. How do you feel about the West?
6. What do you see as the future of the Middle East?
7. What are your hopes?
8. What are your fears?
9. If you could change one thing about your life, what would it be?
10. What are your hopes for your child on the day of your child's birth?
11. What are your husbands hopes for your child on the day of your child's birth?
12. What contribution will you make to Civilization?
13. At the time of your death, what will people say was your contribution to Society?
14. What contribution will your child make to Civilization?
15. What have you and your husband done to help and guide your child toward making that contribution?
16. What contribution will your husband make to Civilization?
17. At the time of your husband's death, what will people say was his contribution to Society?
18. What have you and your husband done to realize your vision for the future?

19. If you have sacrificed a child to the goals of Society, how do you feel about your sacrifice?
20. How would you feel if the dead child was the child of your best friend?
21. How would you convince your best friend to allow her child to die instead of yours?
22. Who first suggested that your child's death can benefit Society?
23. Who did they approach about the idea?
24. When did they first approach your child?
25. How did they first approach your child?
26. How do you feel about that person?
27. How do you feel about the Faith of that person?
28. What were the teachings that person gave your child?
29. How do those teachings compare to your Faith?
30. How do those teachings compare to your belief about Society and the future?
31. If you have healthy children today, which one will you sacrifice?
32. Which child will your husband sacrifice?
33. Why would you sacrifice that child?
34. Why would your husband sacrifice that child?
35. When you meet that child in heaven, how will you justify your choice?
36. When your husband meets that child in heaven, how will he justify his choice?
37. When you meet that child in heaven, what will your child say about you?
38. What will your child say about your choice?
39. What do you know about how followers of the various faiths live in the United States?
40. What do you know about your rights as a woman?
41. How do these rights differ from the rights you would enjoy if you were in the United States, while still being a faithful and righteous woman within the context of your religion?
42. Who taught you what you know about your rights?
43. What were the motivations of the person who taught you?
44. What are your rights according to God?
45. What are your children's rights according to God?
46. When will there be Peace among the followers of all Faiths?
47. What have you done for the future of Society?
48. How do you feel about your contribution to Society?
49. From today, what will you do to contribute to Society?
50. From today, what will your husband do to contribute to Society?

Chapter 57

Costs and Benefits of Confrontation with Hezbollah

Let's consider the costs and benefits of the attack on Hezbollah:

FOR CIVILIZATION:

Cost:

- Civilization took a giant stride backward! Israel's viscious attack on Hezbollah caused the further radicalization of many millions of Muslim young men. Unless cooler minds prevail with them, these can easily become the gangsters of the future, throughout the World.
- News reporting caused the further polarization of the West. Neocons gained strength too!

Benefit:

- None.

FOR ISRAEL:

Cost:

- Shamed itself by demonstrating callous disregard for civilian casualties.
- Soldiers, civilians, equipment and stores lost or expended.
- Lost moral high ground with other countries of the World, gained after unilateral withdrawal from Gaza in 2005.
- Gave an inept demonstration of military prowess, or lack thereof, against Hezbollah.
- Inexcusable excess damage to Lebanese infrastructure, causing untold bad feeling across the Muslim World.
- Lost the propaganda war.
- Proves Israel does not understand the secret to its survival, because it enraged moderate Muslims across the World, while infuriating many non-Muslims. All of the money in the World will not buy Jews peace in the Holy

Land, until they start behaving like they understand that they are surrounded and outnumbered.
- Created more new enemies than it killed by a factor of 100,000:1. This is a very bad result.

Benefit:
- Demonstrated to Hezbollah that crime doesn't pay.
- Degraded Hezbollah's offensive capability.
- Proved strength and depth of "Israel Lobby" in the USA, where at least one vote in the U.S. House of Representatives was unanimous in favor of supporting Israel.
- Proved strength of alliance with USA.
- Proved it can restrain itself from all out attack by only having about 10,000 men in Lebanon, equivalent to a reinforced regiment [very small organization by the standards of warfare].

FOR HEZBOLLAH:

Cost:
- Demonstrated that it can miscalculate in its adventurism against Israel.
- Fighters, civilians, equipment and stores lost or expended.
- Reputation for "good works" destroyed by fundamental gangster behavior.
- Proved that nation states should control national defense, not private armies.
- Brought death and destruction down upon followers.
- Brought death and destruction down upon people of Lebanon.
- Proved the weakness of the Lebanese government.
- Proved Israel is not paranoid; the threat of 10s of thousands of rockets pointed at Israel's civilian centers is real.

Benefit:
- Proved it can withstand the attack of a reinforced regiment for 30 days—a pyrrhic victory.
- Proved its depth and preparation for Israel's attack.
- Proved the weakness of the Lebanese government.
- Won the propaganda war.
- Radicalized millions of young Muslims, to help its recruiting, probably ensuring more generations of Muslims living in poverty, thanks to the knuckle headed ideas of the leaders of these organizations.

FOR HAMAS:

Cost:
- Lost the propaganda war; they disappeared from the reporting.
- Proved they too can miscalculate in its adventurism against Israel.
- Brought into question their ability to govern and solve the problems of Palestinians. What does kidnapping Israeli soldiers ever get them, except the approbation of the World, on which they are dependent for survival.

- Brought death and destruction down on people of Palestine.
- Proved Israel is a tough adversary, which will not be intimidated by small injustices.

Benefit:

- None

FOR THE UNITED STATES:

Cost:

- Highlighted ineffectiveness of Bush Administration diplomacy.
- Proved Condoleeza Rice as a diplomatic light weight and embarrassment.
- Proved ineffectiveness of Bush Administration Middle East policy.
- Highlighted strength of the "Israel Lobby."
- Gave President Bush the opportunity to defame the entire Muslim World, thereby enraging moderate Arabs, who are our friends, and the key to the solution of the myriad problems in the Middle East.
- Demonstrated callous disregard for human life.
- Proved we have forgotten the lessons of the "Cold War."
- Permitted inexcusable excess damage to Lebanese infrastructure, causing untold bad feeling across the Muslim World.
- Lost the propaganda war.
- Proved the "Israel Lobby" does not understand the secret to Israel's survival, because the conflict enraged moderate Muslims across the World, while infuriating many non-Muslims.
- Created 100,000 new enemies for every 1 Hezbollah adherent killed. This is not the proper formula for maintaining and enhancing a free World, with human rights for all.

Benefit:

- Clearly demonstrated that the United States will stand by Israel, regardless of cost. 435 Congressmen voting in lockstep can't be wrong! Why is that? Whisper who dares?

FOR IRAN:

Cost:

- Saw strength of America/Israel alliance.
- Gave President Ahmadinejad populist fodder for the rest of his career, thereby allowing him and his theocratic buddies the ability to keep Iran's per capita GDP rating (how it's government is doing for its people) at $7,000 per person (in 2003), and 99th on the list of all countries. It's a shameful performance, but nobody notices if he just shouts about nuclear weapons. Is God trying to say something to the people of Iran, through the economic performance of the Islamic Republic? Where is it that religious authorities rule, where the people are better off economically?
- Proved ineffectiveness of weaponry. When your friends shoot hundreds of

rockets you manufactured and kill only 3 people, you have an ineffective weapons system.
- Proved to the people of Iran that their government is wasting money on ineffective weapons systems, rather than improving the standard of living of the Iranian people. What will happen when those 40 million young people born since 1990 get a little older? How bad can it get?

Benefit to President Ahmadinejad:
- Assured President Ahmadinejad of a win in his next election.
- Won the propaganda war through reflected glory from Hezbollah.
- Made monkeys of the World's press yet again!

FOR SYRIA:

Costs:
- Proved Syria is a non-entity in global power politics.
- Proved Syria is Iran's door mat.
- Allowed me to highlight the fact that Syria's governmental policies are even worse for its people than Iran's. In 2003, Syria ranked #149 on the World list of GDP performance, at $3,300 per person. Why is that? Whisper who dares!
- Showed just how ineffective President Assad can seem to global television viewers.

Benefits:
- None.

FOR *AL QAEDA*:

Costs:
- Lost leadership of World's gangsters.
- Looked like a "me too" non-entity again.

Benefits:
- USA and Israel behaviors enhanced pool of potential recruits. They'll get second pick, after Hezbollah!

Chapter 58

The Hypocrite and The Charlatan

It comes as a surprise to no one old enough to read this that the Bush Administration is riddled with hypocrisy. The demand for Hezbollah to disarm is contrary to the very tenets of Freedom, which the Bush Administration holds dear. I quote:

> *"Second Amendment to the Constitution of the United States*
>
> *"A well regulated Militia, being necessary to the security of a free State, the right of the people to keep and bear Arms, shall not be infringed."*

In the United States, we have debated for 215 years whether citizens should be allowed to maintain Arms. It's a big issue! The Bush Administration opposes restrictions on gun ownership.he

And yet, they expect Hezbollah, in a much more dangerous part of the World, to freely give up all of its arms, which it surely will not do, though why they would want to hang on to those ineffective rocket weapons systems is beyond comprehension. Perhaps someone should suggest to Condi that she read the 2nd Amendment.

This should not be taken as my endorsement of the idea that Hezbollah should be allowed to operate a separate army, beyond the reach of law. Please note that the 2nd Amendment says, "A well regulated Militia ....." This suggests, to me, a Militia, which does recognize and accept the authority of the government of their country to regulate their actions.

Meanwhile, the Charlatan is Mr. Ahmadinejad. I asked my wife tonight, "What do you call a magician, who has no magic?" Her answer was, "A Charlatan." Indeed! Like a magician, Mr. Ahmadinejad uses the distraction of his populist rhetoric to lead the international press around by the nose, while hiding the fact that his "Islamic Republic" has been unable, despite its natural resource riches, to improve the lot of its population.

Is God trying to tell Iranians something? In 2003, Iran was #149 in the per capita gross domestic product, in the World, at approximately $7,700. It seems to me that God is trying to tell you something when your people are, by and large, living in abject poverty, by World standards, while you mouth off about things, which will not change, despite your fondest desires. It's a magic trick to get yourself elected, in spite of the fact that your government is incompetent to help its people. It's no wonder you have given Hezbollah all of those missiles. They're so ineffective, no one in their right mind would buy them as a weapons system. Is this the best Persian civilization can achieve after thousands of years of development? Mr. Ahmadinejad, you are a successful magician/politician, but you are not helping your people! Why not take a lesson from the Japanese, and turn your attention to letting your economy develop according to its substantial potential. When it takes hundreds of rockets to kill 3 people, you are clearly wasting your time trying to build weapons! You are an impediment to Progress, not a leader of it!

Chapter 59
Worse than a 9.5 Earthquake!

Tsunami of Blood is about the consequences of allowing the Muslim World to become further radicalized against the West. As I have traveled in the Middle East, I have seen the moral standing of the United States fall steadily. And this is because of the people, who claim we are oh so moral. Everything our President touches seems to turn to lead, or too often, to blood!

The *Washington Post* carried a story in August 2006 about how Condi Rice's "birth pains of a new Middle East" are turning into something far worse than she ever imagined, and the child is not to her liking. Meanwhile, humanitarian aid is having difficulty being dispersed in southern Lebanon, because the Bush Administration won't allow aid agencies to deal Hezbollah. Who are we kidding here? I trust that this restriction only applies to aid, which is provided by our government, and not humanitarian aid, which is provided by private citizens.

On August 30, 2006, my interview with Nihad Awad, Executive Director of the Council on American-Islamic Relations ("CAIR") was broadcast on BridgesTV (www.bridges.tv), appealing for humanitarian aid to Lebanon.

When I started this book, I was worried about young men becoming radicalized in dark allies, by junkyard dog "foreign fighters" returning from the "insurgency" in Iraq. That would have been and will be bad enough; but Mr. Bush has done it on prime time television, for the past six weeks, with no care for the consequences. God help us!

The worse this gets, the more likely becomes my prediction of a *Tsunami of Blood.*

Chapter 60
Counterpoint Needed

CNN Never Learns! On August 23, 2006, CNN broadcast an informative report, "In the Footsteps of bin Laden," anchored by Christiane Amanpour, their Chief International Correspondent. It seemed well balanced coverage, right up until the end, when it was asserted that bin Laden has received religious approval to kill up to 10 million people in the West. They did say that this approval came from a "young" Islamic cleric, but they provided no counterpoint from the Muslim World! They later amended this segment to show a written document with the name of the cleric.

This type of insidious comment is exceedingly dangerous! It implies that the so-called religious person was acting according to the tenets of Islam. If he was not, then his action does not constitute religious approval, but this issue was not explored at all. The report suggested that as a pious Muslim, bin Laden felt he needed religious cover for such a heinous crime, and that he feels that he now has it, because of the position this so-called theologian took. I did not hear the identity of the individual in question on the original broadcast. One could reasonably infer from the report that Islam does provide for such mass murder!

I really want to know what's going on here! Is CNN the dupe of the Neocons, and preparing us for a major war between the West and some other Muslim country? Or, are the editors and producers of CNN, not to mention Ms. Amanpour, just stupid!? Or, as I argued in my Kalmbach Lecture last fall, is CNN just the "Mother of all War Mongering Networks," and they're simply trying to whip things up into another war? Their ratings must have been very good during the conflict between Israel and Hezbollah. Boy oh boy, they just ate that stuff up, with most of their key reporters coming to us, in the middle of the night, from some dusty road side in Israel or Lebanon. Poor them!

If we weight the damage done by such an irresponsible report, how do the real Muslims, as opposed to the charlatans, who have hijacked the symbols and accouterments of the

Religion for their nefarious aims, fight back? How do we correct the record?

In the law, we have an observation that if some attorney says something objectionable in a trial, and the judge sustains (agrees the objection is correct) and directs the jury to disregard what was said, that doesn't really correct the damage done. We say, "You can't un-ring the bell!" Sometimes, such incidents are the cause of a mistrial, which causes the whole trial to start over again, with an entirely different jury, and the attorney in question is held in "contempt of court."

But what the media does, day in and day out, doesn't provide us with such remedies as a new trial. Instead, the poison they plant in people's minds remains there, gradually becoming toxic. We see how that happened to us in the current Iraq War, when we were lied to across the board, by politicians and credulous media outlets.

This is why I call for a broad based Arab or Muslim "Voice." Because, unless information of equal "weight" is disseminated, contradicting the assertion of CNN's program, nearly everyone watching that program will accept it as true, and completely within and acceptable to the tenets of Islam. If good Muslims are not heard to contradict such assertions, the rest of us take it as "silence is consent," meaning we believe you agree that such behavior is acceptable within Islam.

How do you respond with as much weight as CNN in prime time? That's a conundrum! You can't respond on *Al Jazeera* or *Al Arabiya* in Arabic, because then you're only talking to yourselves. You can't do it in newspapers only published in the Middle East, whether Arabic or English, for the same reason. In order for your response to have weight in the balance of truth, in the dark corners of people's minds, it must be heard by the same audience as CNN, and that is global, because I presume CNN will broadcast that program numerous times on CNN International, as well as probably repeating it in the USA, and selling it as a DVD.

One way, I suppose, is for CNN to produce an equally prominent program, which explores the truth of the statement in detail, and gives Arab and Muslim voices the opportunity to respond in detail. I hope they will do that, but I'm not holding my breath!

We all need to find the answer, and very soon, or our problems are going to steadily increase. There's a reason this book is called *Tsunami of Blood.*

Chapter 61
SOWING SEEDS OF DISTRUST

I had an opportunity to hear a wide variety of responses to CNN's "In the Footsteps of bin Laden," which was aired for the first time on August 23, 2006. They raised numerous other issues. While most people in my group of friends feel Israel's behavior, in its recent conflict with Hezbollah, was outrageous, and that American unquestioning backing of Israel is unsupportable, questions remain about the Arab perspective. Some of them are:

1. What does the average person in the Arab World think about *Al Qaeda*, which is regarded as the greatest threat to our grandchildren?

2. Why do Arabs seem to unquestionably support any Arab group, even when they behave like gangsters? "Silence," [which in this context means failure to provide counterpoint of equal weight to assertions like CNN's statement that a Muslim cleric has approved and given religious cover to *Al Qaeda* to kill 10 million people in the West] appears to amount to support of *Al Qaeda*.

3. When I assure that my moderate Arab and Muslim friends all denounce the positions of *Al Qaeda* categorically, the response I get is, "How would we know?" My assurance does not seem to be convincing among this skeptical group. While I heard acknowledgement that Arabs must broadly feel besieged, the point was made that most Arabs are not communicating their positions well, with the exception of Osama bin Laden. Are Arabs really quietly supportive of *Al Qaeda*? What about Mr. Ahmadinejad and his outrageous rhetoric? Aren't the Arabs really at risk in their neighborhood?

4. Could it be possible that such a "Fatwa," legitimizing mass murder in the West, is in any way legitimate under the tenets of Islam? If not, why have the various examples of "hijack" of Islam not been denounced noisily and continuously by noteworthy clerics? What percentage of Arabs supports such a finding? What

percentage feels that it is proper within Islam in the 21st Century?

5. Who is seeking either global or regional hegemony in the following spheres: political, religious, military and economic? USA? Israel? *Al Qaeda*? Iran? Saudi Arabia? GCC? What does the average person in each of these countries or organizations believe?

6. Most believe that there is a "point" beyond which Israel will not go, stating that there is no evidence that Israel is trying to capture the entire Middle East, while multiple full scale invasions against Israel in our lifetimes suggests that the opposite is not true. Where is the evidence that Arab groups are not going to persist indefinitely, in the effort to eliminate Israel, thereby preventing stability from taking root in the region? Does that one issue prevent Arabs from seeing their own peril from *Al Qaeda*? From Iran? From repression? From lack of economic progress? From looming demographics?

7. What is the significance of 40 million Iranians under 15 years of age? What is the significance of 75% of the Arab World under 25 years of age?

8. What is the significance of the Iranian blog, that made the assertion that the one thing the "Islamic Republic" had proven to all Iranians, in its tenure, was that there is no God? [From *We Are Iran: The Persian Blogs*, edited by Nasrin Alavi.]

If any of my readers have answers to any of these questions, please do add a comment to this chapter. I am a witness in the West for the fact that most Arabs and Muslims live very peaceful and family oriented lives, and are appalled by the behaviors of *Al Qaeda*. But, I am not Muslim and not Arab, so my "witness" is considered suspect. Some feel I have been duped.

Chapter 62
Double Standard?

The August 25, 2006 edition of *The New York Times* carried a story on P. A20, which was troubling, when you consider that the United States is often accused of a double standard. The headline was: "New York Man Charged with Enabling Hezbollah Television Broadcasts." It seems a Mr. Javed Iqbal, whose business is supplying satellite TV packages, was facilitating the broadcast of Al Manar, the Hezbollah television station, in the United States. Mr. Iqbal was required to put up $250,000 in bail, because he is considered a flight risk. He is, therefore, currently in jail.

The problem is that during the early part of the recent conflict between Israel and Hezbollah, CNN's Pipeline program, which is broadcast over the Internet, was carrying Al Manar on one of its four news feeds. I am a personal witness to this. Where is the warrant for the arrest of Wolf Blitzer, and the rest of the CNN crew, who facilitated that news feed?

Unless U.S. Attorney Michael J. Garcia has something else, which was not reported in the article, he either needs to arrest the CNN actors on $250,000 bail, or release Mr. Iqbal. Mr. Garcia, you can't have it both ways, at least not in The United States of America! I would like to know if this is a real example of a double standard!

Chapter 63
We Need to Turn It Around

Debbi and I just spent the afternoon at a matinee of Oliver Stone's new movie, "World Trade Center." Before we went, I regarded it as a kind of "medicine," that I had to take in order to understand the message that is being conveyed to the World through cinema. It had an incredible message of hope!

Mr. Stone avoided all of the easy sensation of typical 9/11 images, and instead spent most of the movie in the faces of two courageous men, who were saved by untold numbers of equally courageous people, in what surely was a manifestation of hell on Earth. There was zero mention of the perpetrators, or their motives. It mainly focused on the situation for people on the ground, especially the first responders, who did not really have any idea of what was going on around them.

I wish I could expect that all cinematic versions of those events would convey similar messages, but I am sorry to say that we seem a long way from that. Nearly five years have passed, since the events of that day, and yet we as a species seem to be accelerating in the wrong direction. If we are to solve the many problems of our very troubled World, we need to be heading in a completely different direction, on innumerable fronts.

Who will join me in trying to reverse the horror?

We need to do this before the *Tsunami of Blood* overwhelms us all!

Before we went into the theatre, Debbi expounded to me one of her incredible moments of enlightened insight. I asked her, "Why don't you say such things when I have a tape recorder available? I'll probably forget what you said by the time we come out of the theatre."

When we came home, we did our best to reconstruct her wisdom. It goes something like this:

1. Christianity, Judaism, and Islam are not irreversibly broken, but they are critically broken.

2. They need to accept and acknowledge that fact, and work to fix themselves. The first step would be starting with not allowing their own religion to be used as a weapon to harm others. Each of these religions is reprehensible in this regard, so there is no need to point fingers and assign blame.

3. It is said that, "Religion is a crutch, but who isn't limping?" Regretfully, these days religion is commonly used as a bludgeon rather than a crutch.

Ernest Becker taught us, in *Denial of Death* and *Escape from Evil,* that it is part of the human condition to assign blame and destroy scapegoats, both literally and figuratively. Humanity will only survive if we rise above these instinctual behaviors, and find a way to peace and prosperity, that is closer to God. We may have received those instincts from God, and perhaps for very good reason, but God also provided us with reason to overcome these base behaviors, when the time is right. Are we of the 21st Century the right humans to use this reason, or are we not? History will tell!

The recent conflict between Israel and Hezbollah was a giant step in the wrong direction. Who has the strength, wisdom and vision to turn and take an equal giant step in the other direction; and then another; and another? There is an old Jewish saying, which is apt: If not us, who? If not now, when? There is a Chinese proverb that says that, "A Journey of 10,000 miles begins with a single step."

I started to take steps in the other direction at the beginning of the events described in this book. At times, I feel as if I am walking in the surf, with a rip tide, which will drag me out to sea. Here is one more step. Who is with me?

Chapter 64
News Flash
August 29, 2006

I just saw a news report, in which Secretary Cheney accuses the President's foes of lack of courage to fight terror (http://www.cnn.com/2006/POLITICS/08/29/rumsfeld.ap/index.html) . I say the President, Cheney, Rice, Wolfowitz et al. lack the intelligence to have policies, which eliminate more terrorists than they create. (As I pointed out in Chapter 57, according to my estimate, the ratio in the wrong direction was 10,000:1 in the recent conflict between Israel and Hezbollah.) Guys, what are you thinking? The World is far worse off, since 9/11, thanks to your ignorant, bull in the china shop methods of dealing with things. This does not mean that I would not have booted the Taliban out of Afghanistan; I would have. But, I wouldn't have bugged out immediately afterward, leaving a country in stress to its own devices. As for Iraq, I am personally happy that Saddam Hussain is now in the prisoner's dock, but the rest of the mess is beyond belief. No wonder we have no credibility in the Muslim World.

Chapter 65
Democracy? Who Are They Kidding?

The President and Ms. Rice have been going around pushing the wonders of Democracy for the past six years, and getting lots of people killed in the process. I wouldn't have expected much more from him; he's a "stick figure," who serves as a front man for the people who are really running our country. But, Condi should know something a little better. She holds a Ph.D. after all, and was teaching at Stanford, which one wouldn't normally expect to suffer fools.

The truth is that we in The United States have a Democracy, which is still unfolding. We can expect it to have profound changes, even in the time that Mr. Bush still has in office. The Supreme Court of the United States interprets the very Constitution of the United States (their only job) approximately 2,000 times per year. Mr. Bush and Ms. Rice, and their Neocon buddies, continue to buckle down on our civil liberties, and sell people a brand of religion, which is seriously flawed. Fortunately, we do have enough of a set of Checks and Balances in our American system, after 230 years. We Voters will ultimately be able to throw the bums out, and regain our rights.

Their vision of a "Jeffersonian Democracy" in the United States really never existed. Our Founding Fathers were slave holders. Thomas Jefferson couldn't have built that nice house down in Charlottesville, "Monticello," now a National Monument, without keeping 150 slaves. There were no power tools in those days; only hard work under the hot sun. The same is true of Mr. Washington's "Mount Vernon." And there's a reason why there are so many black Americans with the names Jefferson and Washington. They are actually descended from these Founding Fathers, in the literal sense. I leave it to my readers to fill in the blanks.

Then there are Women's Rights. Women were no better off than women in the Middle East, only 90 years ago. It was only then that they were given the vote, and much later still before their husbands actually let them exercise that vote. Later today, I will attach to my photo galleries a picture of my Great Great Grandmother, Louisa Doxtater Conover, and her three sisters, along with my Great Great Great Grandfather, which was taken near the turn of the 19th Century. Their attire is not so dissimilar from the abayas of Saudi Arabia. And Joseph Doxtater, their father, wore a full beard, much as the men of the Middle East do today.

As for the Civil Rights movement, it was only in the 1950s that Black Americans truly began to push for their rights. White Americans pushed back, and heinously tried to prevent them from receiving them. In 1957, I missed an entire semester of school, because the Governor of Virginia closed all of the public schools in the State of Virginia (just across the Potomac River from Washington), to prevent the necessity of integrating. Fortunately, due to my father's naval service, we moved to Philadelphia, and I began my 7th grade year five months late, but I was recently told by Mahdi Bray, Executive Director of the Muslim American Society, Freedom Foundation, who lived near me in those days (though we could not have known one another), that in some rural Virginia counties, black children did not get back into school for five years. Ironically, these bad times in America are practically forgotten. In fact, Mr. Bray is the only American I have met in the last 20 years, who even remembered the incidents when I mentioned them. How soon we forget!

When I came to Washington, to begin my Marine Corps service, in the summer of 1968, "Resurrection City" (housing 300,000 demonstrating Black Americans) was erected on the Washington Mall, in front of the Lincoln Memorial. The day I arrived, four Marine Corps Lieutenants, in uniform, were murdered by Black Americans in Georgetown. In those days, a White person took their lives in their hands walking behind The Supreme Court of the United States, because Capitol Hill was controlled by tough Black men, especially at night.

Things have changed dramatically, thanks to the non-violent movement led by The Reverend Dr. Martin Luther King, Jr., in honor of whom we now have a National Holiday, much to the chagrin of many Americans. We still have prejudices in our country, as many Muslim Americans know currently, but relations between Blacks and Whites have improved dramatically. By 1985, Debbi and I lived 10 blocks East of The Supreme Court, in what was deemed a safe neighborhood on Capitol Hill. Even so, over the next 10 years, we were victims of 15 crimes, including being witnesses in a murder trial, and armed robbery. So everything wasn't all that hunky dory on Capitol Hill even then; or even now, for that matter. There are buildings along H Street, NE, which are still boarded up or bricked up since the time of the riots, which followed the murder of Dr. King, in 1968.

So just what is it that Bush and Rice are selling? Have they improved the situation for our nation's poor? Most would say, "No!" They are hypocrites, of the first order. If I were Ms. Rice, I would be embarrassed to attend ceremonies on Martin Luther King Day. It is to her credit that she is the first Black Woman to be appointed Secretary of

State, of course, but what has she done for other Black Americans? I am sure there must be something, but whatever it may be, it has not come to my notice.

So the issue is not Democracy! You can move through all of the motions of Democracy, and still be saddled with the same corrupt society.

Chapter 66

Economics; Human Rights; Right to Pursue Dreams

The real issues for the Muslim World are economic opportunity; education; human rights; and the right and freedom to pursue dreams. These have nothing whatsoever to do with Religion. The unfortunate and very dangerous fact is that the many of the regimes across the Muslim World have disenfranchised their lower classes. These illiterate masses have little to do and are unable to even support themselves and their families decently.

If we look across the Muslim World, from Morocco to Indonesia, we can see the same pattern. Where artificially repressive practices survive, the people are not sufficiently benefited by the natural resources and economic opportunities of their countries. You can see it clearly in the *per capita* Gross Domestic Product of the countries in question. And yet, there is clear evidence that there is nothing inherent in being a Muslim country, which makes the results so pathetic for the lower classes in their populations.

In the United Arab Emirates, which is surely a Muslim country, the enlightened monarchy has improved the living standards of its people. In 2003, they were 5th in the World in *per capita* Gross Domestic Product ("GDP"), only behind very small special cases, like Bermuda, and ahead of the United States. No, they don't have all of the freedoms we enjoy in the United States. The foreign workers, who are the backbone of the work force, will largely, not earn citizenship. But one does not see the artificial repressions of women and Muslims generally, which is the order of the day in Saudi Arabia. While the Kingdom boasts of its wealth in many ways, it is only 75th in *per capita* GDP, a clear report card on the economic performance of the government.

Noam Chomsky, one of the World's leading intellectuals, who is known for his support of the Palestinians and Lebanese (he visited the Israeli border on the Lebanon side, with *Hezbollah*, only two months before the recent conflict), opines in *Manufacturing Consent*, that in every society the top 20% manage things, and the bottom 80% just take orders. The reason they are willing to do so is that their governments and societies generally provide them with many distractions to keep them happy. In the United States, for example, we have over one hundred professional sports teams, whose antics during every season of the year, draw out and resolve the aggressive instincts of most men. Chomsky commented archly that, when he was in high school, he got to wondering why he should care whether the high school football team won or lost. He didn't know anyone on the team. But then he realized that many things in society, from sports teams and SUVs for hunting, for the men, and washing machines, SUVs for the soccer Moms, and shopping malls for the women, not to mention the right to work, are mainly in society to keep this 80% busy, so they don't realize what's really going on in the economy. And then there's television, which absorbs 20-25% of most people's day. As long as most people can support their families, and enjoy these distractions, they are happy. Even the militancy of most of the Black community has evaporated since 1968, primarily because the Black community, too, has been able to enjoy these distractions.

The problem is that in the Muslim World, the governments have not realized the importance of these distractions. The discontent of their populations is a direct result of the repressions, which hold their economies back. Last December, in Alexandria, Egypt, I heard a statistic from a representative of the World Bank, which said that the United States is 2,400 times more creative than Egypt, and that the gap is widening rapidly. The reason is not because Americans are smarter than Egyptians, but rather, because the Egyptian system of government and society does not support and enhance the creativity of their people. Many Egyptians living in the United States contribute to the USA side of the ratio.

The insurgency in Iraq is largely nothing more than this. The young men have nothing to do, because this interminable war, introduced by the United States, has stopped the economy cold. As a result, they listen to radical elements, and become insurgents, thinking somehow that will make the lives of their families better, if not for them, at least for generations to come. I have heard that many Iraqis feel that they were better off under Saddam Hussain. Who could doubt it after the news of 40,000 killings during 2006?

I have pointed out, in the Introduction, that in Saudi Arabia there are approximately 1.5 million young men between the ages of 15 and 23. I saw a statistic yesterday, which said that 70% of the Muslim World is under 25 years old. There is a 22% unemployment rate among Saudis in a country that employs approximately 6 million foreign workers, because the local population is not well enough educated to handle the existing work. According to *The World Almanac and Book of Facts 2006*, school is only required for people 6-11 years of age, and there is only 78.8% literacy. If you take away the oil revenues, which are primarily produced by foreign labor, Saudi Arabia's *per capita* GDP of $14,500 would be far below other developing regions. These statistics speak for themselves. Further, by a long tradition of government handouts, an adequate work ethic is lacking in the lower classes. What are the distractions that are keeping these young men busy? If they are not distracted, and the lower classes cannot support their families, what would we expect them to do with their time in the next ten years? One can only pray so much.

Even India, with its claim to be the engine of growth for the 21st Century, is only kidding itself. Its *per capita* GDP is $3,100, and it has 59.5% literacy. The Chinese, with approximately the same size population and a more repressive regime, has opened up its economy to the point where their trade surplus with the United States, and therefore the health of their economy and the welfare of their people across the country, is at least 20 times higher than India's. China's *per capita* GDP is $5,600, while its literacy rate is 90.9%. Meanwhile, the bureaucrats in Delhi can't figure out how to show the agrarian part of the country how they will benefit from economic progress. I've heard that India expects 8% growth this year, but without the crushing weight of bureaucracy, that number should be 20%. India is the second largest Muslim country, by population, and yet its Muslim minority largely suffers economically, more than the Hindus. How are the young men of Muslim India going to support their families and have hope for the future, unless economic changes are made swiftly? My Indian friends, who believe that the 21st Century will be an Indian Century, have forgotten that unless their prosperity is spread across the country, there could be quite a few more bloody bumps in the road. If I were betting on whose century it will be, I would put my money on China. But then, with its red shifted [referring to the Doppler Effect] creativity and productivity, the United States may yet make it another American Century.

I haven't even begun to talk about human rights, and the right and economic well being required to give people the power to pursue their own dreams. That's why people still aspire to come to the United States and Western Europe in their millions. It is to pursue their dreams without frustration by their leaders. I make no judgment here on the style of government, *per se*, but I do suggest that leaders who fail to see the need for Chomsky style distractions and economic well being for their people fail to do so at their own risk.

It is for these and other reasons that this book is named *Tsunami of Blood.* A tsunami is an energy wave, which is not apparent on the surface and travels at 500 miles per hour. When it reaches shore, the tragedy is realized. In our Modern Age, the energy wave travels at the speed of light, and will overwhelm us, unless we begin to understand our peril.

The United States and Israel lost the media/blogosphere war hands down in July! *Hezbollah*, with its Al-Manar television station and modern sophistication, has proven that radical elements can control the ideology and lives of unsophisticated people, who have no hope for the future. All of us need enlightened leadership, which understands that we are not back in the days of Movietone News. When you commit an atrocious act, much of the World knows it in less than 5 minutes. We are also well beyond the days when governments could control an ignorant population with the sword. If the people have nothing to live for, they don't mind dying, and now instant communications is telling them that they can be heroic in the process.

Unless all of the governments of the "Civilized World" learn to spread their prosperity, even within their own populations, the radicals will have an easy time convincing their growing numbers of followers to take it away from us with guns, and bombs, and box cutters! As I have pointed out, in many Muslim countries, the masses have little else to do but pray and watch television; and now the radicals know how to control the airwaves as well as the mosques.

Chapter 67

The American Dream Is a State of Mind

Place has nothing to do with "The American Dream." That is, the right to aspire to become the best and most successful human being one can become. My first Dutch ancestors in North America were simple farmers, who only wanted the right to farm and live their lives in peace. But, they were unfortunate to live at the beginning of the 17th Century, during the so-called "80 Years War," when Catholic Spain sent troops to Protestant Holland every summer to bring the Dutch into their fold, and make them all Catholic. The Dutch were Blessed with a country, much of which was under sea level. When the fighting got bad enough, the Dutch flooded their country, and the Spanish, realizing the winter would be cold in such a wet dreary place, went home to sunny Spain for the winter.

My ancestor, Wolfert Gerritsen van Couwenhoven (from whom I am descended after 15 generations), had the opportunity to take his wife and three sons to populate the Dutch Colony of New Amsterdam in 1625. His family was among the first 200 settlers of what is today New York City. He served under an indenture, for the first six years, so, in effect, he was contractually bound to his employer, the Dutch West India Company, much as foreign workers are bound in much of the Middle East today. His wife, "Little Nell," was a hard worker, in those days, and earned a lot of money in the fur trade, which was not subject to the indenture. In 1630, Wolfert and his son returned to Amsterdam, and bought their freedom from their indenture. When they returned to New Amsterdam, they built their first freehold farm, which appears on the first map of Manhattan Island, the so-called "Vingboom Map," which was created in 1639, and is available in copies at The Library of Congress. A few years later, Wolfert's second son was killed by Native Americans on Long Island, so he decided to lead a group of farmers north. In "Wolfert Gerritsen van Couwenhoven and the Founding of New York," which was published in *The Journal of Long Island History*, Wolfert is credited with taking part in the founding of four American cities: Manhattan; Brooklyn; Albany; and Rensselaer.

What's the point? There was hardly complete freedom in North America at that time, but there was enough freedom to follow one's dream. They worked hard. Wolfert and Nell suffered the loss of a son. But they lived "The American Dream" 150 years before the founding of The United States of America, escaping religious persecution and impoverishment by acquisitive landlords in the process. Along with the founders of "The Plymouth Colony," they found a place to practice their actual beliefs in peace, without anyone bringing their morality into question. What would have happened if "Little Nell" hadn't had the freedom to work and trap, and earn money to buy the freedom from the indenture? Whisper who dares!

Today there are new frontiers to conquer! They are frontiers of the Mind. When Humanity conquers those frontiers, celebrating The Glory of God, our Diversity, our children will live in Peace everywhere!

Many societies in the Middle East make it extremely difficult for their women to work. By so doing, they impoverish many of their citizens, by taking advantage of only half of their available brain power. Is there any wonder that their performance is so poor on *per capita* GDP? What are they thinking?

Chapter 68

The "Butcher of Qana" on Capitol Hill

An Arab acquaintance, living in Saudi Arabia, brought the following story to my attention: "'Butcher of Qana' Finds No Safe Haven on Capitol Hill," which was published on the "Electronic Lebanon" web site.

This story illustrates what makes me very proud of The United States of America. Click through and note the ability of a dissident group to assemble, and pointedly and successfully get its message across (non-violently). Perhaps this marks the beginning of the end of domination by the Israel Lobby of American foreign policy in the region. One can only hope so! I say so because without all points of view, alternatives and consequences being brought to the attention of and discussed with and by our leaders, we can never hope that the best decisions will be made. These points of view often come up from minorities, who have a unique perspective. They get motivated to this kind of concerted non-violent action because they are in an "injured" constituency. The result is that our legislators, executive officers, and judges have the opportunity to see a fuller picture of an issue, before they make decisions. In the recent conflict between Israel and Hezbollah, I understand there was one vote in Congress, which was unanimously in favor of Israel. This means that even the six Arab American Members of Congress voted in favor of the resolution (or they may have avoided the floor that day or abstained, so as to avoid offending anyone). I always am suspicious when a vote is unanimous, because it suggests that other points of view have not been heard widely.

I know that many of my Arab friends have been hurt by the behavior of the Bush Administration in the recent conflict. They were incensed by the callousness of our President and his minders. Me too! The result of that arrogance is to give The United States a black eye within the Muslim community, not to mention a serious decline in prestige generally. As I mentioned earlier, I believe the Administration's behavior allowed militant gangster organizations to change minds in their favor by a factor of 10,000 for every 1 member of Hezbollah killed, and I believe my estimate is conservative (though I hate having that tag applied to me in today's political environment). The math is quite simple and compelling. If there are approximately 100 million young Muslim men between the ages of 15 and 24, and if only 10% of them were turned toward militancy because of the behavior of the President's flunkies, then that would mean 100 thousand new militants. If we give them the benefit of the doubt (which we definitely should not, except for the purposes of this illustration) and said that all of the deaths in Lebanon (about 1,000) were Hezbollah fighters, then the President would have created 10,000 new enemies for every one killed. That does not seem like the calculus for success in any war of which I am aware. Dumb! Dumb! Dumb!

Who is it that's defending the United States? Is it the Bush Administration, with this kind of wacko calculus; or might we be better off defended by leaders who are better at math? I take issue with the assertion that those who do not agree with the President lack courage. Mr. President, you will not win friends and influence people that way. Your majority in the last election was too slim to be so cavalier with your rhetoric.

As I often say, the way our system works is sometimes messy. We allow people to confront their opponents, often noisily. But the system has served us well over generations. I am heartened to see Muslim groups entering the fray. It means that the flaws of The United States, which are too often reflected in the behavior of the Bush Administration, are finally being addressed. I wish I could wave a magic wand, and make it all happen at once. Alas, it will take time to change minds, and when you have to get through such thick skulls, it's more difficult by an order of magnitude. But, *Inshallah*, this demonstration tells me that we are on the road to peace, albeit at the beginning of the road.

Still, there is much work to be done! My acquaintance writing to me from Saudi Arabia was the first I knew about this demonstration, so the demonstrators have not broken through to mainstream consciousness. My Arab friends tell me that this is because the mainstream press is dominated by the other point of view. Perhaps so! I've not looked at the numbers to know whether this is 100% true. If it is true, though, it's time for a change, or "Big Brother" will soon be knocking at our doors.

Finally, let me draw everyone's attention to a very good web site, which does credibly present the news from a Palestinian and Arab perspective. The site is "Electronic Lebanon." It seems to me that it is incumbent upon all of us to understand issues from all points of view, before making decisions and forming opinions, which have such a major impact on how the World will develop in the 21st Century. "The Enlightenment" of the 17th and 18th Centuries taught us that having more information can improve lives over time. This is one more example of that. I know the changes will not be as rapid as the webmasters and bloggers might hope, but from my point of view, they're on the right track.

Chapter 69
On Separation of Church and State

Never in my wildest dreams did I imagine that an office holder in the United States of America, sworn to uphold The Constitution of the United States, would call the separation of Church and State, embodied in The First Amendment, "a lie." I would never so imagine, because so many of our countrymen came to our country expressly to escape religious persecution, including mine (See Chapter 67 of *Tsunami of Blood*).

This is what Rep. Katherine Harris, the woman who made sure that Our Fearless Leader became President, in 2000, said to a religious magazine recently.

Our Founding Fathers knew from bitter memory and experience that when religion is mandated by the state, it stifles everything else. Many of their families, like mine, came to The United States to escape religious persecution. They therefore embodied these 45 Sacred and God Given words in the 1st Amendment of The Constitution of the United States:

"Congress shall make no law respecting an establishment of religion, or prohibiting the free exercise thereof; or abridging the freedom of speech, or of the press; or the right of the people peaceably to assemble, and to petition the Government for a redress of grievances."

Chapter 70
"The Rapture" Comes, but Life Goes On

I believe in God!

If not a "good Christian" and Buddhist, I still follow these traditions.

I could accept the Five Pillars of Islam entirely, if I were born in a Muslim culture, but I was not, so I accept most of them, but not all of them. For example, I would not give *zakat* to a Muslim organization, as I'm behind on my tithes in Christianity. I do accept that Islam supports the spiritual needs of 1.3 billion people.

Fantasyland abounds in our World. Like messianic charlatans of all time, too many of today's religious leaders have perverted their cultural and religious traditions to support insidious aims. Like the fairy tale of "The King's New Clothes," they have persuaded tens of millions of their followers to believe things that are poppycock, telling them that God has "told them" such things.

I believe that God speaks to all of us, every day. Each of us has the choice to believe what God is telling us directly, or follow the ravings of someone who says that God speaks to them only. Unfortunately, our World is a mess today because the mind control games abound in the World, and many less clear thinkers accept a plausible fiction.

They bend an especially effective and time worn methodology to their purposes, to gain dominance over our minds. That is the concept of group psychology. One need only refer to *Triumph of the Will,* by Leni Riefenstahl (http://www.leni-riefenstahl.de/eng/bio.html) , chronicling the Reich Party Congress of 1934 in Nuremberg, to see how effective this technique is. One particular scene, which is embedded in my psyche for all time, shows 10,000 Nazi soldiers all shouting their allegiance to Adolph Hitler, while dramatically executing the Nazi salute. It is chilling indeed.

In the psychological context, we all have "anchors," which are programmed into our psyches. When someone uses a word or a phrase, or refers to an event, or whatever, it immediately makes us think of something else. This is precisely why we are moved by poetry, or writing, for that matter. In my case, the "anchor" of the Nuremberg rally, usually pops into my mind in religious contexts, these days. In one case, about 10 years ago, when I was visiting Singapore, a Chinese friend took me to an English language "born again" Christian church service. There were about 5,000 people in a single auditorium. Since I was a brand new visitor, with no lead up to this experience, I was able to hold my psyche aside and dispassionately observe what was happening. Everyone else in that auditorium got into a kind of trance, and would have accepted anything those American preachers put into their minds. There were various techniques used, but they all amounted to the same thing. In one particular part of the service, the minister had everyone waving their hands back and forth over their head, much like "the wave" at a professional sporting event. I had to do this too, in order to be polite to my host, and as I did it I could consciously feel my psyche being pulled into the group trance. It was a spooky experience!

Debbi and I went to see a comedian one time, and one of his tricks was to say that he could make everyone in the room beat time to the same rhythm, without doing anything. He asked each member of the audience to take out a quarter (an American coin), and begin beating it on the table in front of us, at any tempo we chose. Within 20-30 seconds, everyone was beating in exactly the same rhythm and tempo. It sounded exactly like an army marching across a concrete courtyard. The Nuremberg rally immediately came to mind! If you have a lot of people in a room, try it sometime. It's foolproof! [I presume you may need 50-100 people, but I may be wrong. I only saw it done this one time.]

Last spring, while I was visiting the Middle East, a Muslim friend told me that according to *The Koran*, he would get more "benefit" from God, if he prayed along with other people, rather than alone, in his five times per day prayers. He told me that there is actually a 27:3 ratio of the "benefit." What he said was that he would get "27 points" if he prayed in a group, but only "3 points" if he prayed alone. He was not clear on who was awarding the points, but since Muslims have a direct relationship with God, I presumed he meant God. This is only hearsay, as I have not seen the actual passages in *The Koran*. Again, I thought of Nuremberg!

This is not to say that any of these three activities is intrinsically wrong in any way. Rather, it is an observation that all of us can easily be dragged into "group think" if we are not very careful. I am certain I have succumbed on many an occasion; as when I participated in parades in the U.S. Marine Corps [and everyone knows all Marines think alike—just kidding].

This book is an example of an act of individuality, but as the Japanese say, "A protruding nail gets hammered down." So it is not surprising that I have already had many attempts from friends to warn me away from writing it [and, I infer, resume in the "group think" model]. Most recently, Debbi's cousin did this by asking me whether I was OK under the Patriot Act. I told her I hadn't read it, because I was afraid it would make me too depressed.

It is a stark reality that we are stomachs fitted with teeth, who consume fields of other creatures of God, flocks of animals and birds, and schools of fish in our brief tenure on the Earth, our Planet, while leaving huge quantities of waste in our wakes. This was the attention getting assertion in Ernest Becker's *Denial of Death*, for which he won the Pulitzer Prize in 1974, and *Escape from Evil*. That, notwithstanding, I am told by my social psychologist friends that he was a devoutly religious man.

Becker's point was that the stark reality is too much for all of us to cope with directly, so we use the invention of culture as a kind of avoidant coping. As my friend Sheldon Solomon tells it, upon hearing of 9/11, many people said to themselves, "That was just awful, now I'm going to go out and buy a chain saw and a lemon." He was being facetious, to make the point.

There are a few psychological concepts, which are common to all humans. We all feel guilt. It is a natural tendency within us to want to assign blame, as a way to assuage our guilt. And, it is always handy to assign that blame with a scapegoat. Let's see how this can be misused.

Many of my Saudi friends feel guilt [by association], because 15 of the hijackers on the 9/11 planes were Saudi. In the first year after the incident, I had many strangers come to me, when I was in Saudi Arabia, and compulsively apologize for the incident, and assure me that neither they nor their religion had anything to do with the horrible attack. But that didn't eliminate all of the subconscious guilt they were feeling.

More recently I have seen an example of how group think can be bent in a negative way. This came from the various "conspiracy theories" surrounding 9/11. It is alleged that a Finnish military expert had calculated how the collapse of The World Trade Center towers was a demolition job, rather than the result of the airplane crashes. Upon my reading, however, it seemed to me that he was showing how preposterous such a proposition actually is. He was calculating the need for the placement of 24,000 "cutting charges," taking 30 men 4 months to complete, for example, or a small nuclear weapon. Someone outside of the conspiracy would have noticed!

Nonetheless, this hypothesis that the collapse of the buildings was a planned demolition operation is being re-circulated as a proof that the guilt for the actual event was in the Bush administration, which is being blamed as the perpetrator (read "scapegoat"). The subconscious mind can cause us to say and do all kinds of things that we should be aware of and avoid.

Recently, the fundamentalist Christians were running around saying the conflict between Israel and Hezbollah was evidence that the "end of days" was near, and that "The

Rapture" would scoop them up into heaven, leaving the rest of us poor sinners to burn to death in agony. What I want to know is, if they thought God was going to scoop them up into heaven, did any of them stop paying their mortgages? Probably not!

I believe that we are the manifestation of God's intent. By "we," I mean all human beings. God did not expect to have one religion dominate another. If he did, why isn't there a majority religion on the Planet today? The Glory of God is our Diversity, and it is that, which will be the salvation of our species. Ultimately we will understand that good and bad things come out of all cultures, all religions, and all ethnic groups. We will all adopt the best from everywhere, like Starbuck's, and we will disavow counterproductive ideas, like slavery. When we all accept that notion, our children will live in peace everywhere.

Chapter 71

Should We Fear Iran's Nuclear Developments?

We had a visitor in Annapolis on Sunday, September 3, 2006! She's the U.S.S. Annapolis! She's one of the reasons why we have nothing to fear from an Iranian nuclear weapon. Remember the scene in "Crocodile Dundee" when Crocodile is being mugged, and he says, "Now that's a knife." You get my drift ..... They would not use it on Israel either. Jerusalem is one of the three holiest sites in Islam. MAD worked for us before; why not now? Except, in this case, the "m" would have to be lower case ..... (if you need it at all). [For the Navy men in the group, yes, I do know she's not a boomer, but she has 12 Tomahawk missile tubes, and they can carry ...... Whisper who dares!]

One question is, "Why is Iran spending money on nuclear research rather than on basic economic development?" Last time I checked, Iran had the 99th per capita GDP in the World, at $7,700. Good work Islamic Republic!

Chapter 72

The Power and The Glory

The news I posted earlier, about Mahmoud Ahmadinejad, the "President" of Iran, demanding that liberal and secular professors be eliminated from Iranian universities, just made me want to chortle with laughter. How stupid! That's a certain way to make sure that his people stay in ignorance! He must not be afraid of triple digits, because that's just where his 99th on the *per capita* GDP standings is headed. Somehow, though, I think his citizens might have something to say about that.

"The Power," referenced in the title to this chapter, relates to "The Power" of the people. In the same sense that the people could sweep the Islamic Republic into power, at a time of ignorance, they can just as quickly sweep it out of power. Shirin Ebadi, in her valedictory work, *Iran Awakening*, said that she was initially in favor of the revolution. That lasted exactly one month, until the Islamic Republic demoted her from judge to clerk. She's spent the quarter century since then working against the horrors of the "Islamic [I use the term loosely, here, since I don't think there's anything Islamic about it—it's all about power, who's on top, and who's living well] Republic." I think there are a lot of people still living [many have been murdered, by Ebadi's testimony], who hate the direction their country has gone, and want a change.

Since 1991, Iran has increased its population by 40 million, to 70 million people. That means a wave of young people, who will not be restrained by the *abaya* and the *hejab*. While some of their mothers may have supported the revolution, history has given them a long sad lesson in tyranny and poor economic performance for their country and their families. Where is their hope for the future? These young people will not be held back!

Why am I so confidant? Because of this very blogging medium, on which you are reading this book. I know that there is a virulent Blogosphere within Iran, and that it reads plenty of information from the West. This was not the case for the fathers and mothers of those bloggers. This is a group that knows that many many of their Muslim brothers and sisters live a much freer and more comfortable life, within the tenets of Islam. They live in countries, whose standard of living has not been held back by charlatans. So why should they be deprived? So that Mr. Ahmadinejad can get his kicks tweaking the Western press? That may have been fun the first few times, but when his administration has done NOTHING for the people, and each of its actions is aimed at draining the coffers of the country, his own people will call him on it. Why waste money on nuclear weapons you can never use, for the reasons I mentioned earlier, when you can advance the standard of living of your people? Is there really a good reason for this? If anyone can defend this policy, please comment to this post, because I'd really like to understand the rationale. The United States need do absolutely nothing.

And the GREAT thing is that Mr. Ahmadinejad cannot shut down the Blogosphere within Iran. He would cause an immediate insurrection, not to mention causing his country to be cut off from all of the wonderful new developments in the World in science, technology, human rights, etc. At the very minimum, his scientific establishment, regardless of how pious, would insist on having access to the Internet of the outside World. His problem is that once he lets even one link into the country, the system can be easily spoofed, and the information can get through. Yes, he can clamp down on it, and make it very difficult for a time, but this would surely cause his *per capita* GDP to sink like a stone, and would immediately cause dissent among his own supporters.

So, when Mr. Ahmadinejad does something stupid, like cutting down on academic freedom, he is on the road to his own demise. We in the United States need do nothing, because the People of Iran will not allow this inauspicious behavior to continue. This is "The Power" to which I refer.

As for "The Glory," you'll recall that in Chapter 6, I explained that Diversity is The Glory of God, and it is the engine, which gives The United States of America its unique power and economic strength. What I now see going on is that "The Glory of Diversity—The Glory of God" is now being spread throughout the World, not only within The United States, by the power of the Internet and the Blogosphere. It is the latter, however, which has juiced up this phenomenon. The Internet was moving in that direction, at a glacial pace, but the Blogosphere has speeded up the process exponentially.

What do I mean? I mean that every time a good idea comes up in the Blogosphere, it will be adopted by many instantaneously, around the World, much as there are four Starbuck's coffee shops in one of the hospitals I visit in Saudi Arabia (that's in one building). At the same time, bad ideas will be crushed by public opinion, as I believe Mr. Bush's handling of the Israel v. Hezbollah conflict has crushed whatever image he may have had or hoped for in the World, and demonstrated that diplomacy will no longer be exclusively handled by stuffy old men with hide bound ideas of the future. Unless the Bush Administration gets a handle on its media game plan, it can expect to go down in history as the worst presidency in history, bar none. The new video, cell phone, Blogosphere technologies are just going to eat up politicians who haven't figured this out!

This means that the phenomenon of "The Glory," which I mentioned in Chapter 6 as the "secret sauce" of the success of The United States of America, is now being spread around the World, and is unstoppable, even in a repressive country like Iran. It is a messy process, of course, but it is a never ending process, which will always enhance the lives of human beings on the Planet. I am very optimistic about this phenomenon.

So, my message to Mr. Ahmadinejad is, "You go, boy!" A few more shots in the foot like this, and you won't have any toes. How are you ever going to run in a political race, or any other kind of race, once you have no toes? As they say in India, "He's clever by half." A threat? What kind of baloney have you been eating?

Chapter 73

Overwhelmed with Wombs

Recently, there is a theory going around the Internet, that Islam will overcome the West, because Muslim countries are reproducing at significantly higher rates than Westerners of Caucasian race. Oriana Fallaci, the much praised journalist, who exposed the truth about warfare from Vietnam to Panama, joined this chorus in her recent "trilogy," which has sold millions of copies in Europe, and is now popular in the United States. Her theory is an alarmist screed, which denies that we have within our power the antidote to any such risk.

Ten thousand years from now, the races of all human beings will have merged dramatically. By this, I mean skin color and racial features. The color will be darker than the white supremacists of today would like, and lighter than the darkest peoples of today. This process is on, and it is beyond the control of any artificial culture to stop. Boys will be boys; girls will be girls. Ms. Fallaci sounds racist in her screed; or at the very least alarmist about the "march of Islam."

The antidote is in the fact that all peoples, when out from under the repression of venal theologians and politicians, seek the same basic rights and freedoms, as they go about their lives, trying to make life better for their children. These are embodied in the 45 Sacred words found in the 1st Amendment of The Constitution of the United States:

"Congress shall make no law respecting an establishment of religion, or prohibiting the free exercise thereof; or abridging the freedom of speech, or of the press; or the right of the people peaceably to assemble, and to petition the Government for a redress of grievances."

The hurly burly of human development, sometimes with bloodshed, will never stop until every human being shares these five Freedoms. There will be pushes and shoves. The ignorant fundamentalists of American Christians would love to cut back on the Freedom of Religion, denying our basic value of separation of Church and State, much as the *Mutawas* of Saudi Arabia keep a tight grip on the behaviors of Saudis within the borders of their country. And yet, these efforts are surely destined to fail. Mankind will not be repressed, and will advance only so fast as the repression is lifted. This fact has been widely known since "The Enlightenment" of the 17th and 18th Centuries, but has been hidden outside the West by leaders, who have kept their peoples in ignorance, in order to control the wealth of their countries. But, with the Blogosphere, their nefarious games are "caught out." The truths of their repressions will be known far and wide, and they cannot hide behind security walls, and murderous repressions.

The process is a long one, and sometimes bloody, but it will never be stopped, regardless of race, color, or creed. So yes, the World of the future will have a common race. Our progeny will worship in religions, which are further developments and improvements on the religions we follow today. But all of the World's people will ultimately enjoy the Rights and Freedoms embodied in the 1st Amendment. These days I travel in modern countries, which still do not see the inevitability of this truth. Many do not enjoy the Rights and Freedoms we Americans enjoy. Indeed, these Rights and Freedoms are still being expanded, even in the United States. But the process for expanding and enhancing these Rights and Freedoms is on—2,000 cases a year before The Supreme Court of the United States alone—and, when I travel, the movement is palpable, everywhere I turn.

So we have nothing to fear from the wombs of Islam! Those wombs will produce more human beings, who will seek the same things that all human beings have sought since the beginning of time. As human beings populated the World, their races developed differently. But when the World's humans have no other place to go, they will populate the spaces of the mind with Peace and Freedom. There is no other choice. Ms. Fallaci may have had to live with a World that is somewhat different than the World of her childhood, but so will we all! [Ms. Fallaci died just after this piece was written, so she will not have to face a World she found distasteful.]

Chapter 74

In Memoriam

September 8, 2006

While the beat goes on in Iraq, with 180 people per day killed by their fellow Muslims, I want to express my sorrow too for the 37 people (mostly Muslims) killed by a bomb in Malegaon, India on September 8, 2006. What a senseless carnage! What does it get anyone?

Chapter 75

What It Takes to Win the War on Terror

No one can doubt that President Bush has failed to win the "War on Terror." Indeed, many, including this writer, argue that the Bush Administration policies have done nothing but make matters much worse! In Chapter 58, I explained that the recent Israel/Hezbollah conflict, in which the Administration's leaden hand was laid bare for all to see, created more than 10,000 new enemies for every member of Hezbollah killed. Indeed, I believe that to be an exceedingly conservative estimate. That's not a very good formula for winning a war of any kind!

How is it that Germany and Japan, our two worst enemies only 61 years ago, are now among our strongest allies, with among the strongest economies of the World, and have been in that status for more than 40 years? The answer is the huge economic push that was given to these countries by the Marshal Plan, immediately following World War II. Compare that to the Bush Administration. In their massive reorganization of the federal government, they put the U.S. Agency for International Development under the Department of State, so that its budget could no longer be easily monitored from outside the government, and then eviscerated major programs, sending the money to the Pentagon instead, so as to reduce the apparent costs of the war in Iraq.

It doesn't take much to understand what it takes to be successful. In the September 5, 2006 edition of *The New York Times*, P. A21, John Tierney reported on Estonia's remarkable economic boom, in "New Europe's Boomtown." Coming from the repressed Soviet style of economic performance in under 20 years, Estonia is now the envy of modernizing Europe. Most notably, it ranked #1 on *The State of the World Liberty Index*. Former Prime Minister Mart Laar simply cut away all of the impediments to Freedom, and Estonians responded with phenomenal economic performance. He credited his results to just having read Nobel Prize winner Milton Friedman's *Free to Choose*, which argues for open markets, and open (including foreign) competition in everything. Friedman pointed out that when government regulation steps in to try to adjust an economic situation, the results are always horrific for that country's people. One example I recall, from my own reading of *Free to Choose*, was that the Japanese government began to try to "buy" the American market by giving $1,000 subsidies on the purchase of each Japanese automobile, thereby allowing prices to be lower. The result was a gift of $1,000 from the people of Japan to every buyer of a Japanese car in the United States—a subsidy to Americans! One need only review the history of Japan's economic performance over the last 20 years to see how ineffective the policy was for the people of Japan.

What does this have to do with the "War on Terror?" I ask you, where do we think the social problems are, which make citizens susceptible to being recruited by *Al Qaeda* and its progeny. The Middle East, right? If you examine the statistics in the *The State of the World Liberty Index*, you very quickly realize that the region which performed the poorest of all regions in the World was the Middle East. Furthermore, if you compare Freedom to GDP (which translates to economic well being of population), you immediately see a strong statistical correlation between Freedom and Prosperity (as measured by *per capita* GDP), and a reverse correlation to violence. The worse off people are financially, the more likely they are to be susceptible to *Al Qaeda* recruiters.

Here are the *Freedom Index* rankings for some of the countries of the region, in rank order, followed by their 2005 GDP rank:

54.	Israel	28
68.	Bahrain	35*
72.	Kuwait	44*
95.	UAE	23*
99.	Jordan	103
103.	Oman	41*
105.	Lebanon	90
110.	Morocco	109
112.	Qatar	11*
121.	Pakistan	128
122.	Saudi Arabia	46*
125.	Egypt	112
144.	Yemen	175
147.	Iran	74*
149.	Syria	118
158.	Libya	58*

*Countries where GDP numbers are skewed by huge revenues from petrochemicals. Since much of the petrochemical work is done by ex-patriot laborers, what does this list tell you about the real economic plight of most of the citizens of these countries?

So, why is it that the President is not encouraging reductions in repressions in these countries? Why is Mr. Bush not putting more and more money into U.S. AID, and other relief agencies? He and his cronies have no vision, that's why! And they don't seem to have any economists, who can analyze a reasonably simple economic report and draw some conclusions from it, which would lead to effective programs. Let's buy more guns! That's all they know how to say. The only problem is, every time they "plant" a terrorist, 10,000 new ones emerge in his place. How are we going to win the "War on Terror" that way?

Yes, the "War on Terror" will be won, but it won't be won by the Republicans. They don't understand economics, and the importance of Freedom. All they know how to do is start wars, so that their cronies in the defense industry can make more millions. They thought a finger of purple ink would solve all of the problems of the Middle East. The problem was that they were dipping the wrong finger! That's what the elections in Egypt, Palestine and Lebanon have told us, not to mention Iraq.

Chapter 76
A Time for Cynicism

The very idea that the United States has not been able to find Osama bin Laden ("OBL") is laughable. It so happens that I served as an Intelligence Officer, during part of my time in the U.S. Marine Corps. Even with technologies we were using in Vietnam, 35 years ago, OBL should have been easily findable. Is there anyone out there that still believes the misdirection coming out of the Bush Administration that OBL is hiding in the remote mountains of Pakistan and Afghanistan? This is not possible. Even the least experienced tester of satellite imagery, which is in the public domain on the Internet, knows that you would be able to recognize any sort of regular human activity on the ground, so long as you had a satellite pointed at it. I haven't personally checked to see whether there is a public domain satellite pointed at that mountainous region, but is there anyone who can read this that doesn't think that the U.S. military has at least one satellite covering all of the questionable regions of Afghanistan, Pakistan and Iraq? If there is one of my readers, who can identify a web site where we can all look at a public domain satellite pointed at these regions, please let us all know in my comments section to this post. Gosh, if the CIA can't find OBL, maybe one of us can!

But seriously, he's not out there. He would have been spotted long ago, by methods which cannot be mentioned here. Here in the Middle East, where I am currently traveling, there is urban legend that OBL suffers from renal failure, meaning he needs dialysis on a regular basis. Three or four years ago, I was in a taxi in Dubai, when the driver told a colleague and I that he once had OBL as a fare. He got into the cab, looking very bad, and said he had to hurry for his dialysis appointment. Now, I'm not an expert on such things, but I'm fairly confident that OBL is not receiving dialysis in the mountains.

On the same ride, my colleague and I were going to visit the famous *Burj Al Arab* Hotel, the Seven Star hotel, which looks like a sail, in Dubai. I have attempted to go to the *Burj* five different times, but only succeeded in getting in three. There is very serious security around that hotel, and you actually have to pay to enter the lobby. The first time, we were told that we could not enter because American General Myers, then the Chairman of the Joint Chiefs of Staff, was having a private party there. Maybe so; fair enough. The second time we went to have tea there, and look around. We had to pay US$80 to pass the guard post. That was the occasion on which we noticed a large construction project, just outside the gate, approximately 300 acres in size. Around this particular site was a twelve foot tall fence, which had the following written in ten foot tall letters every 20-30 meters, all the way around: "Bin Laden Construction." Ever since then, my colleague and I have **joked** to one another that OBL is actually resident in the Penthouse of the Burj, in the style of our famous Aviator, Howard Hughes. Still, we have never seen any evidence to rule out our particular hypothesis.

It seems to me that it is quite possible, and I have NO information which truly suggests this pure conjecture, that OBL's location is well known to our various intelligence services, and they are simply keeping him staked out, because the communications and comings and goings there would provide MUCH more intelligence value than shutting that source down, and throwing the guy into Gitmo for five years, until one of President Bush's kangaroo courts can screw up his prosecution so badly that the Supreme Court of the United States will have to order him released. Of course, I don't think I'd want to be released in that situation, if I were OBL, since there are just a few other countries, which have legitimate beefs against the guy.

This is where the cynic in me says that if my conjecture is true, and the Bush Administration really does know where OBL is, then it stands to reason that an equally cynical election gambit would be to "magically" find him in the week or two before this November's election in the USA, thereby proving what a wonderful job the Republicans have done in protecting us from the bad guys. Is my conjecture true? Whisper who dares!

By the way, have you noticed where Nick Robertson, Anderson Cooper, and Peter Bergen are this week? They're out in the mountains of Afghanistan (before the snow flies, of course), interviewing the odd street peddler about whether they've seen OBL. And, if they had seen him, would they turn him in? That's a pretty high powered and expensive hot dog maneuver to get ratings; CNN sending its consultants, senior foreign correspondents and anchors (note the weight of the word) out to find OBL, when Uncle Sugar can't! You mean, we can't find something more important to everyone than Anderson Cooper standing in front of an artillery piece, which, yes, is firing registration rounds out into the sage brush, so that they can hit the enemy, if they ever return to fire a rocket from that exact same spot that they fired one once before. Yikes! A new low in hot dog journalism! BUT, wouldn't they have been the heroes if the Veep had suddenly announced that we found him out there, right under the noses of these characters. Are we being played much, or what?

Chapter 77

The Importance of Unbiased Media

As I did my statistical research for "Chapter 75: What It Takes to Win the 'War on Terror'," I ran into another statistical index, which caught my eye. This was the 2005 World Press Freedom Index. When I checked my trusty Google desktop query, it turned out that the Index is published by an organization called *Reporters sans Frontieres*, so I clicked the link and waited.

Regretfully, I got a nasty message back saying "Access to the requested URL is not allowed!" I was traveling in Saudi Arabia at the time. This rather surprised me, since I am traveling in the country, which is the home of *Arab News*, which I know to be one of the most outspoken and unbiased newspapers in the World. I rarely see them pull a punch. So why would this country of sun and sand restrict access to this particular site? Whisper who dares!

Well, never mind! The silly censors are wasting their time, because I simply popped down a couple of lines on the Google™ links and low and behold, I got the answer I was looking for, http://www.worldpress.org/Americas/2166.cfm right here! Those of you who are actually in Saudi Arabia can see just where you stand, which is a true irony, considering the high quality of unbiased reporting from the writers of the fine newspaper I just mentioned. The United States did quite poorly on this Index, ranking 44th, particularly thanks to the imprisonment of Judith Miller.

In turn, this site led me to a powerful article, which expresses my feelings about what has happened to the American media so succinctly, that I urge you to read it now: "Can a Biased Media Prevent the Next World War?"

I will quote one short paragraph, for the benefit of those of you who need the short version: "At a time when media around the world, especially in least likely places such as the Middle East, are gradually reaching new heights in promoting unprecedented political openness, the quality of news coverage, programming, and the overall credibility of the American mainstream media is ironically on a declining trend as more and more media organizations are abandoning objective standards of journalistic ethos and becoming the 'facilitators of venomous discourse' and the 'purveyors of misinformation and propaganda.'"

What a sad state of affairs! Meanwhile, one must go to Yemen, a place that most Americans would equate with total lawlessness, to read the real truth about what the Bush Administration's policies are doing to The United States: "Al-Qaeda, Muslims are Infidels in Bush's 'Freedom Agenda'"

I pray that those journalists, who continue to commit themselves to get the true story out, may survive and prosper, and that all Americans will recommit themselves to the values of The First Amendment of the United States of America!

Chapter 78

Muslims Elected George W. Bush

The Muslim World has been fuming about the behaviors of the Bush Administration for quite some time now, but let the record reflect that it was the Muslims themselves, who put the man in office.

The rest of us, quarrelsome Americans, are pretty evenly divided between the red states and the blue states. This means that any sizeable minority can swing American elections at their will, if they are all of a common mind. Muslim Americans account for approximately 1 million members of the American electorate, which is sizeable enough to make a difference. In our evenly balanced electoral environment, minority status doesn't mean downtrodden, and therefore not worth the trouble to vote; it means **powerful**, because a swing of Muslim votes can change the results dramatically.

Remember all those "chads" and lawsuits around the time of the 2000 election. None of that would have been necessary if the Muslim community had voted against President Bush. But they didn't. They voted for him. The espoused reason was that Al Gore had Joe Lieberman as his running mate. As the story goes, the Muslim Americans reasoned that since Mr. Lieberman is a member of the Jewish community, he would willy nilly side with Israel on every decision. What they failed to understand is that the Jewish Community is in the pockets of all national politicians in The United States. Therefore, support of Israel, *per se*, is not a very good litmus test for how a leader will face the World.

During the Israel/Hezbollah conflict, there was a vote in The Congress of the United States in support of Israel. The vote was unanimous in favor of its support for Israel. This means that the six Arab American Congressmen failed to vote against the measure. They might not have voted for it, but by abstaining or absenting themselves, their behavior amounted to the same thing, because it showed there was no dissent. Why would they do that? Perhaps they think a vote against the Jewish community might spoil their chances for re-election. Is that true? Whisper who dares!

I have no similar anecdote to cover the results in 2004. I just reason that even if most voting Muslims voted against Mr. Bush, there were likely 20-30% who did back the President, for various reasons. 10% of the Muslim vote is at least 100,000 votes. That could have made the difference in the razor thin victory the President achieved in many states.

Therefore, it is important that all of the World's Muslims talk to their Muslim American friends and relatives, who have the right to vote, and urge them to get to the polls on November 7th, and vote for a Congress and Senate, which will put a speed bump in the way of the juggernaut, which is the Bush Administration's neocon agenda with no checks and balances.

Chapter 79

Response to a Conservative

A conservative friend recently forwarded me a screed, which suggests that "all's fair in love and war." He is particularly upset with Senator John McCain, for bringing up reality in the context of the President trying to push through his kangaroo court system for detainees in Gitmo. He questions whether The United States should abide by Article III of the Geneva Convention (which we, largely, probably wrote in the first place). Here is my response:

If we are not willing to follow the rule of law, we are no better than our enemies. We have a system, within our country, regarding how matters of this sort are handled. It is often a messy process, but it is the best one the World has devised to date. It seems to me that John McCain can better speak to these issues than anyone. The President should listen!

As for whether the detainees at Gitmo, or anywhere else for that matter, are covered by Article III of the Geneva Convention, that is a matter which will be decided within the context of our messy process. The angst of Mr. Sowell seems to be that the issue is coming up at an inconvenient time in our election cycle.

If we are going to win the "war on terror," we are going to need to understand that this war will be won, in large part, in the court of international public opinion. The Bush Administration is currently losing that aspect of the war hands down. My math is very simple. There are approximately 100 million Muslim young men in the World between 15 and 23. If only 10% of them were further radicalized by the Administration's behavior vis-a-vis the Israeli/Hezbollah conflict recenlty, that means Mr. Bush has created approximately 10,000 new enemies for every member of Hezbollah killed. That is not a very good way to win any war, but particularly not this one. The impact of what the USA did was felt far beyond Lebanon. By the same token, since Mr. Bush seems to be winding up for a battle with Iran, the same issues will be in play. The demographics do not support the behaviors of the Administration.

As for nuclear weapons in the hands of Iran, I ask: Could they ever use them? Signing an order to use such a weapon, for an Iranian, would be signing one's own death warrant. The visit of the USS Annapolis, to my own town, reminded me of this undeniable fact. There are two other reasons, though. Jerusalem is the 3rd holiest place in the Muslim World, and anyone destroying it would not be regarded with favor in the Muslim World. An attack on Israel, would bring radioactive fallout to Iran, since it's down wind. Not to mention the Israeli nuclear response, which would likely be quicker than an American nuclear response. Just what are we worried about?

I would commend to your correspondents two books, which give one the expectation that Iran will solve its own problem of government, much as the Soviet Union collapsed, if we just let it. These are: *Iran Awakening*, by Shirin Ebadi, the 2003 winner of the Nobel Prize for Peace, and *We Are Iran,* about blogging in Iran. In the latter, one of the young bloggers mentioned that the one thing the Islamic Republic had proven to all Iranians was that there is no God. The only thing that can stop this process in Iran, where there are currently 30 million young people under 15, is the knuckle headed policies of the Bush Administration.

It is very clear to me that any attack on Iran will be contrary to our best interests in "winning" the "war on terror." The Sunnis disrespect the Shia, right up until the time when the USA attacks the Shias. KSA fears the development of nuclear weapons in Iran, right up until the time the USA attacks Iran.

The "war on terror" will only be won through Islam, and by working with moderate leaders in the Arab World. Boots and tanks will not do the trick. The demographics make it so.

We have a more important war going on, and that is the war against the principles of the United States of America--the principles, which made us a Great Country. Mr. Sowell's article is representative of this insidious direction, which some of our leaders have taken.

I know that many of the readers of this are conservative, and will be angry with my position. That's the way our system works. Good ideas come up, and they are adopted by everyone in the World (ie Starbucks--there are 4 Starbucks cafes in one building where I work in Saudi Arabia). Bad ideas come up, and they get pounded down. Going to war with Iran, is a REALLY bad idea! Abrogating the provisions of the Geneva Convention, in the perception of the rest of the World, is a REALLY bad idea! If we are going to have peace, we are going to have to win it; and that means winning the PR war. We can no longer rely on our army beating their army; that we can do. As Iraq proves, though, there is a lot more to it than success with force of arms. The battle will not be between the USA and Iran (as it was between the Allies and Germany in WWII). Those days are gone! The battle will be won on cell phones and blogs, and it is already global and quite dangerous to us if we do not understand where the battlefield really is.

God Bless the United States of America, and our Sacred Freedom to express our views, and in the messy process of debate, find the correct balance, before it's too late!

If you want to understand thoroughly why our current policies are wrong headed, please read Ernest Becker's Pulitzer Prize winning book *Denial of Death* and its companion volume *Escape from Evil.* Though written in 1974, they exactly predict what the Bush Administration is doing, and the inevitable consequences of these behaviors.

Chapter 80
To God Direct!

Perhaps some of my Muslim friends can help me here. Over the years, many of you have been telling me that the unique and special thing about Islam is that every Muslim can have a direct connection with God—no middle man, like the Pope! I think that's just great, and it comports with my own views, which explains why I am quite comfortable among Muslims. I'm actually also very comfortable among my Catholic friends, whose affiliation with the Pope is tenuous at best.

As I understand it, the reason there are no grave markers in Saudi Arabia, even for a King, is because such a marker would be creating a monument to a mere mortal, which would be a dilution of this direct relationship with God. The destruction of graven images in the Old Testament of the Christian Bible comes to mind. God is God!

My friends, who know why the rest of this chapter seems to be in code, will understand why I am going to write it that way, and those of you who don't know why, will just have to follow along. Some things just can't be explained. Whisper who dares!

During my recent trip to a sunny place, a certain anomaly on this principle came to my attention once again. In that place there are people who have taken it upon themselves to adjudicate the behaviors of their fellow citizens, in the name of God. We won't mention their name here, either in English or in Arabic. For the purposes of this chapter, let's call them, "The Saints."

Now in this place, there was recently a cause *celebre*, because The Saints had long ago decided that the fairer gender could not be employed as sales clerks. This got to be just a tad embarrassing in the context of selling under things to that particular gender, since its members do not appreciate having to buy their unmentionables from foreign members of the opposite gender. The matter was taken up for review by The Saints, and low and behold, The Saints reconfirmed their previous ruling, in the name of God!

Now, I'm a pretty liberal kind of guy, but if anyone insisted that the lady of my house would be required to buy her unmentionables from a member of my gender, I would not take that particularly well. I would get up and do something about it. But, the members of my gender, in that place, inexplicably, have let this ruling stand.

Now, here's what I need some help with: If it's true that Muslims have a direct line to God, then why do The Saints have any standing at all? If a prospective responder to this question would be reticent, for fear of what The Saints might think or do, then please feel free to write to me privately at skip@wordsmatter.tv. I really want to know how and why this is justified.

The Team, under which I was brought up, had Saints like this right up until 1834. One of my favorite stories about them appears in Daniel Boorstin's book, *The Discoverers*. Boorstin recounts the story that Galileo had committed the unSaintly act of writing that the Sun does not revolve around the Earth. He was brought up on charges for a certain (unmentionable here) crime. He was an old man, so he finally was forced to swear to a confession of his unSaintly behavior. Fortunately for us, for the amusement it brings us now, even in his day there were court reporters, who wrote down every word. Galileo came forward, knelt down before the Saintly judge, put his hand on the Bible, and swore before Almighty God that the Sun does revolve around the Earth. His penalty for his unSaintly behavior was that he could never again work in that science in which he was so instrumental. He was confined to house arrest for the last four years of his life. During that time, he invented "two new sciences—one concerned with mechanics and the other with the strength of materials." Since my Team's Saints had made his books not acceptable in polite company, his last book had to be smuggled out of Italy, and was translated and published in Holland (from whence my ancestors came). This last book, according to Boorstin, "laid the foundation on which Huygens and Newton could develop the science of dynamics and, eventually, the theory of universal gravitation." (Pp. 325-26, paperback edition.)

So, you see, I think Galileo, too, had a direct relation with God. He knew that God would not take his oath before my Team's Saints seriously, because God knows the Truth of the matter. So Galileo, four years from his death, sickened by the treatment of his incarceration by the Saints, speaking for the record, made monkeys of them for all time.

Does this story remind you of anyone you know today? It does me! I read it today! (Wink, wink, to them's knows.)

Chapter 81

On Monarchies and Nehru Jackets

What is the difference between a monarchy and socialism? They both have central planning, but in a monarchy, the leaders and their families do not have to keep up the pretense of equality with their people.

The fundamental flaw with both systems is central planning. It is fundamental and long accepted in the world of economics, that central planning cannot work. We saw it cause the Soviet Union to collapse. We see that in countries, which continue to try to centrally plan their economies and development, the *per capita* GDP is pathetic.

I had the privilege of studying economics under two highly respected economists, Dean Bill Meckling of The William E. Simon Graduate School of Business Administration at The University of Rochester, and Professor Mike Jensen (then at The Simon School, and now Professor Emeritus from Harvard Business School). The *Journal of Financial Economics*, which Jensen founded, has consistently been rated in the top 5 in its field, for over a decade. Here are two stories they told about how central planning fails:

1. In the 1970s, when you drove in the Soviet Union, none of the cars had windshield wipers. Whenever it began to rain, all of the cars would stop beside the road. The drivers would get out and put their windshield wipers on their cars and drive off. The reason for this was that central planning had not predicted the correct number of windshield wiper replacements needed—a shortfall, in this case—which meant that when the first pair of wipers failed, it was common for drivers to steal the wipers from a newer car. The only way to prevent such pilferage was to keep the windshield wipers in your car, except when you were actually using them.

2. Again in the 1970s, Meckling and Jensen observed a plate glass factory, where they were making huge plate glass windows. At the end of the production line, the pieces of glass were being broken into a large metal hamper, and the broken

> glass taken back to a melting oven, where the glass could be molded into new plate glass once again. This was caused by overproduction. The central planners had not estimated properly again, and made too much glass. In order to maintain the skills of the factory workers, the government was keeping the production line operating, but not shipping the glass, because it was not needed in the field.

In a properly functioning economy, proper requirements are determined by an addition of all of the requirements from the field, applying statistical deviation models, to get the production within reasonable limits. This works, because a gas station owner can better estimate how many windshield wipers of what type he will need in a year. He places his monthly orders accordingly. The same would be true of architects, whose buildings are consumers of plate glass. When their inputs are not taken into account, the accuracy of estimating decreases drastically. This is why central planning is an inefficient way to organize an economy. The individual always knows better than the state what his needs will be, in all things, for the coming year.

You can also identify an economic system, which is not functioning properly, by the amount of black market activities, which exist. It is easy to see that Afghanistan is dysfunctional because the main product of the country is illicit in every country of the World. If the markets were functioning properly, growing poppies would not be necessary to survive.

Monarchies and socialist countries are supposed to provide for the welfare of their people. When the size of the population increases exponentially, though, the orders of magnitude for ordering, and keeping everything in balance, get thrown out of whack. If you order the right number of windshield wipers, you might send improper stocks to different regions, thereby undermining your genius of guessing right on the overall volume. It is individuals, who can properly predict their needs better than any economist or statistician, sitting in an ivory tower.

The result of these failures of the centralized approach will always be discontent within the population. This is why successful monarchies, the ones we can expect to still be sitting 25 years from now, have all given up the reins of day-to-day economic organization to secular governments. Such constitutional monarchs achieve two functions: they avoid being blamed when things go bad; and they have a handy scapegoat if such is the case. They can embrace success, but make failure an orphan, for which they cannot be blamed.

Recently, a friend from a sunny place commented that it is an embarrassment that an apparently "rich" country, can only produce a few thousand new jobs each year. When I first took my business to Pakistan, one of the government officials there asked how his ministry could help. My answer was simple, "Just get out of the way." That didn't happen in Pakistan, but it did in India, after 40 years of failed socialism. As a result, my company created 5,200 new jobs in India, and the industry we pioneered created 15,000 new jobs. In Pakistan, 100 new jobs were created, but none remain today. Was all of that because of the "helpfulness" of the ministry planners? Whisper who dares!

The solution for Saudi Arabia is very simple. Spend one week studying the Uniform Commercial Code (that's good enough for a start), and then adopt it as the law of the land. Then get out of the way, and let any of your citizens build any kind of business they want with anyone. There can be limits, of course, for public health or safety reasons, among others.

In the summer of 1981 or 82, the People's Republic of China had about 450,000 private businesses—mostly street vendors. The Chinese decided to open private registrations to anyone. Within 1 month they had over 12 million applications for new businesses, so they shut down the process, because the central planners were uncomfortable that they would not be able to control the process. The story demonstrates that within the human condition is a desire to make something happen. If you give your people the chance, they will make things happen far better than the central planners. China's trade surplus with the United States is twenty times that of India, its apparent rival. Why? It is because, in India, they overcame socialism, but they failed to overcome the bureaucracy, which weighs down their economy. The entrepreneurs have to carry all of those bureaucrats on their backs! There still is bureaucracy in China, of course, but one imagines it is quite a bit less burdensome in the places that count.

Recently, I read an advertising supplement from *The Washington* Post, about Saudi Arabia and all of the nice new infrastructure the government is going to build over the next few years, in a place where no city exists today. Most of the country's investment is going into that, or a sunset burdened industry, which represents more than 50% of the country's GDP. Meanwhile, a monarchy, which borders the sunny place, pretty much got "out of the way," and let people build businesses as they saw fit—even foreign people. The result, in 2003, was that the sunny place's *per capita* GDP was 75th in the World, while the bordering country's *per capita GDP* was 4th.

I saw an example of this type of infrastructure building, based on central planning, which proves Meckling and Jensen's point. There is a sunny place, which built a nice new hospital grounds, intended to be the largest tertiary care hospital in its part of the World. The facility cost $661 million, and was completed in 1995. Trouble is, it wasn't opened until 2003, because no one had properly predicted the operating costs of such a facility, and even today, after throwing away lots of obsolete equipment, which was brand new in 1995, the facility is only ½ operational. Meanwhile, in the neighboring country, a brand new medical city is being built, by allowing entrepreneurs from the World's leading healthcare organizations to build projects according to their own plans. Each project is much smaller than the one in the sunny place, but these are the bricks upon which a great facility and employment enhancing industry will be operational. The project in the bordering country started 10 years later, and will finish several years before the centrally planned operation.

Of course, populations are no longer ignorant. They can see the economic results of the policies of their respective governments. This is why monarchies should retain their perquisites, but hand over the development of their countries to well incented and hungry professionals, who can keep the people busy building capacity and infrastructure. Failure to do so in a timely manner seems a recipe for disaster.

As King John of England acknowledged, in 1215, it's better to be a constitutional monarch than no monarch at all! As Meckling and Jensen pointed out in my economics class, those many years ago, it's better to have an economy guided by the "invisible hand" of free enterprise, than central planning, where the devil is in the details!

Chapter 82

I Rest My Case

Tariq A. Al-Maeena's story in today's *Arab News,* "Something to Chew Over," exactly proves the point made in Chapter 81, that central planning does not work. Can anyone in the World imagine anything more important than water? Human life is not possible without it! And yet, in the Kingdom of Saudi Arabia, with its reputation for riches in liquid, albeit the undrinkable kind, but certainly with ample funds to acquire all of the water supplies it might ever need, the "Ministry" is unable to deliver water efficiently, to the places it is needed. According to Mr. Al-Maeena, they maintain 6,000 tank trucks, just to be able to move water to places of crisis, where water supplies are short. These shortages are symptoms of the inefficiencies in a centralized planning system.

The last time I heard a story like Mr. Al-Maeena's, the year was 1972 or 1973, and the venue was Vail, Colorado, home of "mountain spring water." In that summer, the water level in the reservoir had dropped down below the intakes of Vail's water treatment plant, so the government was obliged to hire "water buffalos" (tank trucks, like the ones mentioned in the story) to "truck" water into the small community of construction laborers who people Vail in the summer, of whom my brother, Sam, was one.

The problem was and is, in that clime and place, that the streams and rivers of Colorado are infested with *giardia,* a nasty little one-celled parasite, which gets into your bowel, and gradually, over years, works its way up into your liver, destroying it, and your life in the process. Water treatment plants "purify" the water supply of *giardia,* but when you bypass the water treatment, mayhem follows. In Sam's case, he became gradually less well over many years. He was referred, finally, to Dr. Thomas E. Starzl, "The Father of Transplantation."

The only way Vail's contamination was known outside the community was because of Dr. Starzl, who was seeing many liver patients coming from the Vail area in the years following the water treatment plant incident. By investigation, he finally realized what had happened. According to family lore, every human living in Vail that summer is either dead (and has been for many years), or has had a liver transplant.

Sam was steadily treated by Dr. Starzl, and his team, for many years. At some point he was told that eventually, in perhaps 10 years, he would need a liver transplant. When Dr. Starzl moved his transplant research to Pittsburgh, Sam followed him, and, in 1988, underwent three liver transplants. He died on August 18, 1988, from complications of the surgery. He was 39 years old.

This is all by way of saying that I have an up close and personal experience with the problems of water shortages. And it is so easy to fix!

All the government has to do is let private businesses create water supply businesses wherever they want. Of course, the quality of what they produce, import, and bottle must be regulated, that is an appropriate role of government, but Saudi Arabia would solve its water shortage problem very quickly, without doing anything centrally, except write the regulations, a matter than can be handled quickly and easily, because there are many successful models throughout the World.

One wonders, then, if inefficiencies occur in the most basic commodity, water, what other inefficiencies exist in Saudi Arabia's centralized planning system? There must be many! Whisper who dares!

Chapter 83

Where Are the Moderate Muslims?

In answer to the armchair critics in the West, who say, "Where are the moderate Muslims?" I say they are everywhere! Just because we don't see them frequently in the West, does not mean no action. There are **<u>many</u>** millions of courageous Muslims, who are working to stop injustice in their societies, improve education, seek out and eliminate corruption in their governments, moderate religious aberrations, and resolve the problems of our World. It is time for CNN, MSNBC, BBC, and the rest of the mainstream media to start highlighting their work! They are the ones who will carry the future of Islam with them! It is they who will be our friends and neighbors, and contribute to our economies of the future!

It is they who are the keys to peace in Iraq, Palestine, Israel, Lebanon, and Iran.

Chapter 84

Imperialist Power

Many of my Arab friends have claimed to me for some time that The United States is an "imperialist power," that is out to control the World. I have denied this on more occasions than I wish to remember, citing our withdrawals from Germany and Japan after World War II, and our unilateral cessation of hostilities in Iraq, at the end of Gulf War I, not to mention the fact that, after defending the Kingdom of Saudi Arabia with the entire United States Marine Corps Fleet Marine Force and half of the U.S. Army on its soil, we withdrew, when we had a potential occupying force already in place, immediately after the conclusion of Gulf War I. These are not the actions of a country seeking world domination.

I was wrong!

I do think my previous view does represent the understanding and belief of a very large percentage of my fellow citizens. Most of us would just as soon raise our families in peace, like everyone else in the World, and leave others alone. Furthermore, dissent will become cacophonous, if any Administration keeps deploying troops with the objective of domination through an occupying force.

Nonetheless, on reading Noam Chomsky's new offering, *Imperial Ambitions*, I am persuaded that imperialism is one legitimate way to look through the prism of our complex set of World events, to see what is real. Indeed, the Bush Administration has made such a view quite credible, albeit unachievable in reality, which is plain for everyone to see.

The truth is that there are forces at work, which are far beyond the ability of any army to dominate. It is the American economy, not its military, which dominates the World. We have a greater than $200 billion annual "trade deficit" with China. Actually, there is no such thing. Americans receive hundreds of billions of dollars worth of goods and services from China in return for electrons (we don't even bother with the little green pieces of paper anymore). The Chinese consider this a fair trade. They then must "spend" these electrons, which have value only in The United States of America (and oil producing countries, which accept dollar denominated electrons for oil), so they use them to buy American government bonds, thereby supporting the Bush Administration's spending habits of a drunken sailor.

Meanwhile, the oil producing countries trade oil, which they cannot eat or drink, for the same un-green electrons, which they cannot eat or drink, meaning that they or their surrogates, too, have to invest them back into the USA. Isn't it incestuous!?

There is nothing insidious about these facts. This is the way economics works, when it is working properly. When Bush and his buddies want to "own" the oil fields, that helps their private interests, because one presumes they think they can create a monopoly in a commodity, which even OPEC was unable to monopolize. Their ownership is meaningless for the rest of us, though, since they have to sell on the World oil market, which finds its pricing no matter what they do, short of forcing the rest of us into wars, which do cause instability and higher prices. This is why oil men should not control armies!

BUT, that does not mean that America's actions will not look like military imperialism over the next few years. They will! If the Muslim World does not get a handle on its youth, as I have said since the Introduction, it is likely that one or more "friendly" governments will fall to home grown insurrections. If these occur in oil producing countries, they will jeopardize the World's oil supply, which is a vital national interest of the United States, and which will, in turn, engender a military response from the United States, which will, in its turn, look like imperialism. Whether it is, or not, depends upon where you sit. But the reality is that the American people will not support military intervention unless their lifestyles are put in jeopardy. And, the American people will not support a long term foreign occupation, as I expect the November 7, 2006 elections to confirm.

In an irony of our World, as I wrote the last paragraph, my e-mail received an alert: "OPEC Ready to Cut Oil Supply." To those of my friends, who shake in their boots about such a headline, not to worry! Cartels don't work, because their members cheat. This was confirmed by the 1973 actions of OPEC, which did nothing but cut the revenues of countries, which stuck with the embargo. Meanwhile, Americans were slightly inconvenienced by lines, for 3-4 weeks, as I recollect from my own experiences at the time. In this current story, the Saudis are reported to be voluntarily accepting a disproportionate share of the necessary decrease in revenue, but I am sure they will stick to that only so long as it seems in their best interests to do so—namely, they think Mr. Bush's adventurism after November 7, 2006, Election Day, will cause oil prices to rise sharply again, thereby giving them a bigger return for Saudi Arabia's limited resource, and by reducing the output now, they can keep the prices relatively high until Mr. Bush's bludgeon kicks in once again, thereby making future price increases seem less arbitrary and onerous.

Regretfully, I fear my Arab friends are in denial about the depth of the problems with their youth in their own countries. I am not talking here about the progeny of my friends, who tend to be from privileged groups, but rather the poor, whose plight has been largely ignored (with a few notable exceptions, of which my friends will certainly remind me). Since the oil fields in these countries tend to employ the poor of India, Bangladesh, Indonesia, and other disadvantaged countries outside the Arab World, there is little doubt that policies supporting the use of ex-patriots in these hot, dirty, and thankless jobs, in this economic sector, are artificially and broadly depressing the conditions of the Arab poor.

Chomsky observes that when the structure of power and domination in a country goes out of whack, eventually the people recognize the problem and commit to changing the situation. He claims that every [political?] change in history has been so motivated. Regretfully, the comfortable intelligentsia of the Arab World is not yet at this point of "recognition," which can mean that the recognition will only come after bloodshed. As Chomsky pointed out, murderers like Adolph Hitler and Hideki Tojo are able to gain strength because of apathy and equanimity within their societies. Does Dr. Zawahri aspire as they did? Whisper who dares!

The inevitable march of human progress, short of nuclear annihilation, will ultimately cause all of the economies of the Earth to be interdependent. At the macro level, they already are. Because The United States proved the most effective model for building a vibrant and interconnected economy, it will seem to some that The United States is intentionally dominating other parts of the World. This will NOT be done with the military, however, as we have seen. Other parts of the World will begin to seem more and more like The United States in their behaviors and values, as India and China already have in the past decade. BUT, this will not be because of some intentional policy from the top, and certainly not from wrong-headed Administrations, such as the one presided over by Mr. Bush. It will be because, in every contract (short of those entered into at "gunpoint"), both sides gain something they want. Cumulatively, that means that the United States receives more than $200 billion more goods from China in a year than it ships out to China, meaning that China is holding in return a large pile of un-green electrically charged air. They like it that way! If they didn't, they would stop. But, to stop would mean stopping the entire economy of "The People's Republic of China." This they cannot do. So, it can be said that The United States already does dominate China, but it is not imperialism in the sense that Chomsky and my friends criticize. But, seen through the prism in a certain way, yes, it can be called imperialism. It is imperialism that the peoples of the World pray for, so that they, too, can have a lifestyle worth defending, as much as most American do.

I am not apologetic for the lifestyle my fellow Americans and I enjoy. We stand on the shoulders of our forefathers and mothers, who suffered in many of the same ways most people of the World still do, so that their progeny could have better lives. Their sweat and blood has paid dividends, because we enjoy the most effective system of government in the World, and have done since 1776. It is a terribly flawed system in many ways, but it is better than all the rest. We improve our system year by year, through our legislatures, courts, and checks and balances. The problem with most governments is they have not accepted improvement and change as readily, so they have been left behind. We can reasonably say, "The American form of government is the worst in the World, except for all the rest."

My point of all of this is that I am seeing things change in the World, which are causing the types of improvements that gave The United States its dominant position. Many of these changes are facilitated by innovations, which came from improvements in technologies and communications facilitated by the American system. Most of these changes will improve the lives of people everywhere. Because The United States has a 230 year head start, many of these innovations will make it appear that imperialism is on the march. BUT, it will only be because the people of the World have decided that the innovations Americans have adopted are really the best for them too. The Bush experiment has done one thing emphatically, and that is to prove that old style imperialism has the same future as the Dodo bird, which flies backward in ever decreasing circles until it flies up its own anus with a low "Whoooooop!"

[N.B. The last word in this chapter is to be read in a rising falsetto!]

Chapter 85

Bush as Neville Chamberlain?

If a new war with North Korea or Iran is sold to us soon, it is very likely that pundits will say that President Bush does not want to appear weak, like British Prime Minister Neville Chamberlain, who on September 29, 1938 became the poster boy for appeasement, by signing the "Munich Agreement," which effectively ceded the Sudetenland to Germany. He thought that by so doing he had averted a war. Of course, he had not, and many since have argued that Britain should have gone to war against Germany at that time, rather than eleven months later, on September 1, 1939, when Germany invaded Poland.

The argument will be made that Iran's belligerence now is analogous to Germany's in 1938. Fortunately, the realities don't really add up to a sufficient analogy. Germany had spent the time since Hitler repudiated the Treaty of Versailles, in March 1935, building up an impressive military machine, ready to conquer all of Western Europe. It will be argued that now that North Korea has "the bomb," it will certainly sell it to Iran, which means that Iran is effectively a "member of the club" from now. This, in turn, means that both North Korea and Iran's military power is now effectively as dangerous as Adolph Hitler's was in 1938. This argument is valid to a degree, but the conclusions, which war mongering Neocons will claim flow from it, are flawed.

I think President Kim Jong Il woke up on October 9, 2006, with a headache he had not anticipated. He has overspent his nation's budget for years, starving his population in the process, in order to become a nuclear nation. His belief is that he now has a "product" he can sell to the bad boys of the World. His problem is that he cannot use his nuclear weapon, without killing himself and destroying his country in the process, and no major country can possibly let him become the "local nuke pusher." He might get away with selling one or two weapons to someone, arguably Iran, but as soon as this is known, I presume rational heads in the United States government, regardless of the party in power, will feel the undeniable need to change the regime. Such behavior cannot be tolerated in today's dangerous World.

As for Iran, Ollie North observed that North Korea will sell its fledgling product to Iran, thereby making Iran a nuclear nation immediately, instead of 5-10 years from now, based on its own development. I will assume this is true, but I will also argue, as I did in Chapter 71, that Mr. Ahmadinejad will find nuclear weapons as useless to him as they are to President Kim. What, pray tell, would he do with them, that wouldn't be self destructive in the process? Even if we fast forward 25 years, to a time when Iran holds hundreds of nuclear weapons, the same calculus applies:

1. Signing an order to use a nuclear weapon amounts to a death sentence for the Iranian signer, and the end of the supporting regime, probably "by return mail";

2. Radioactive fallout from the most likely target, Israel, not to mention retaliatory strikes from Israel, and American nuclear submarines, would soon rain down on the population of Iran, considering prevailing weather patterns and treaty arrangements, thereby obliterating the Persian culture; and

3. He would have gained the condemnation of fellow Muslims, for destroying the third most holy site in Islam, namely the Dome of the Rock in Jerusalem.

President Kim's strategic situation also suffers from points 1 and 2 above, with America's allies appropriately revised.

Presidents Kim and Ahmadinejad both have a problem now. While it was fun tweaking the big boys with the threat of developing and/or acquiring nuclear weapons, that threat is now gone. Meanwhile, both have impoverished their people to have sufficient funds for this fool's errand. The excitement of the ability to insult the West, and make us fear them, kept their people quiet during the fun times. But the game is over now. We will see whether their people continue to tolerate such abject failure to provide for their needs. The party was great, but the hangover might not be to their liking.

You see, no President of the United States in the 21st Century is anything like Neville Chamberlain. Chamberlain faced the prospect of a long and gruesome war, with fighting power being in relative balance. There is nothing like that today, at least not in the nuclear context. Continued adventurism, to include the use of nuclear weapons, would be a short circuit to the stone age for the initiating country, and perhaps for all of humanity. The United States and the Soviet Union realized this long ago, and the money wasted by the Soviets in building up power they could never use meant that the regime finally did change, without a shot ever being fired. The Russian people are still suffering the consequences of letting the "Cold War" go on as long as it did. Presidents Kim and Ahmadinejad may all too soon, for them, realize that their support is made of shifting sands.

Chapter 86

Iraqi Death Report, True or False?

The October 11, 2006 edition of *The New York Times*, carried an article entitled, "Iraqi Dead May Total 600,000, Study Says". The Bush Administration immediately contradicted the numbers, suggesting the number may be as low as 25,000. The latter number is hogwash, of course.

What genuinely bothers me about the study from researchers at the Johns Hopkins Bloomberg School of Public Health, aside from the fact that it is based on an extrapolation is the accompanying graphic, which seems to suggest that the area to the southeast of Baghdad had a relatively smaller casualty rate, not to mention the fact that the period March '03 to April '04 had relatively the fewest deaths.

The foregoing results cannot be accurate, in my view, and it would be great if some researcher who is closer to the issue would confirm my surmise, which is as follows:

Prior to the American invasion, the Iraqi Army was said to be something approaching 500,000, with 100,000 attributed to the "Republican Guard" alone. Where did they go? There isn't enough of an insurgency to account for all of these men. My hypothesis is that they were largely obliterated in the zone between Baghdad and a point 60 miles southeast of the city, in the two weeks immediately preceding the fall of Baghdad.

You will recall that during the early part of the invasion, the various former general talking heads on network television were showing an "order of battle," which said that the "Republican Guard" was aligned in this 60-mile zone southeast of Baghdad. I presume that much more of the Iraqi Army than that was in that region. The American forces raced up the road to a point 60 miles from Baghdad in relatively little time, perhaps 10 days at most. They then essentially stopped for two weeks, ostensibly for re-supply.

My hypothesis says that the real reason they stopped was so that most living things in that region could be obliterated by airpower. Knowing the effectiveness of American bombing capabilities in a "no holds barred" air assault of this sort, I can imagine that most scorpions would have a hard time staying alive—I recall a story before Gulf War I, which described an American bomb, which would suck all of the oxygen out of a one square kilometer area, killing everything that moved. I, therefore, believe that the vast majority of the Iraqi Army was destroyed at that time. If not, where did they go? The press has been surprisingly un-inquisitive on the point of the whereabouts of the Iraqi Army. It surely was not that measly column of scared young boys, walking down the road at the "end of the hostilities."

Furthermore, near any major city of 5 million people, the population density gets greater and greater the closer you get to the city limits. For this reason, I surmise that there were also a huge number of civilians, who failed to leave the area in a timely manner. If my hypothesis is correct, this would belie the graphic from the Johns Hopkins study.

At this point in time, I can't prove it, but I think the numbers contained in the Johns Hopkins study are closer to the truth, for the foregoing reasons. I would estimate that there were 2-300,000 deaths in that "kill zone," during that two week period alone. Is my hypothesis correct? Whisper who dares!

If my hypothesis is not correct, what happened to the Iraqi Army, leaving aside the scared privates high tailing it down the road at the end?

Chapter 87

Muhammad Yunus, Beacon for Peace

On October 13, 2006, I learned Muhammad Yunus, had won The Nobel Peace Prize! Hooray! He has done so much for Bangladesh and the World, that I cannot imagine any more deserving recipient. The model of his Grameen Bank had already been copied in 44 countries 10 years ago, and includes at least 10 banks in the United States. If you live in the developing World, I urge you to learn how his model works, and implement it in your own country. Within 15 years, Muhammad Yunus went from loaning $27 to 42 people, to being the largest bank in Bangladesh. I have a couple of personal reminiscences of Muhammad Yunus, which I will share here.

My favorite story dates back to about 1996, when the developing World was struggling with cell phones. The Indian Telecommunications Minister came to Washington, and gave a speech at the U.S. Chamber of Commerce, at which he said that by the estimate of his ministry, the Government of India would be able to make certain that there was at least one telephone in each village in India (300,000 villages didn't have a phone at that time), by the year 2006. As I recall, that speech was in about December.

The following February, I visited Muhammad Yunus in Dhaka. He was in the process of creating "Grameen Phone," a new venture to assure that every village in Bangladesh had a telephone. His bank had 1,000 branches in Bangladesh, and he simply found an entrepreneur in every village, who would be the telephone entrepreneur. He gave a cell phone to each one of these individuals, and said to them, "You charge 4 taka per minute; you pay 2 taka per minute" (about US$0.10 per minute for the user; US$0.05 per minute for Grameen Phone). Within two months, every village in Bangladesh had a telephone!

The Indian Telecom Minister's view is an example of the hidebound thinking that makes it impossible for central planning to work efficiently. Muhammad Yunus's thinking is an example of the future!

Another favorite story is Muhammad Yunus's approach to automating his bank. By 1996, he had 1,000 branches, 400 of which were men on bicycles, who would reach every village of Bangladesh at least once per week. Grameen Bank is a membership organization, meaning that to be a member, one must save at least 1 taka per week (about US$0.025 per week). This became a bit of a problem in bookkeeping, because, by 1996 Grameen Bank had 2 million members, and how were they to keep all of the books for 2 million 1 taka transactions per week?

An American software company came in and bid to set up the system for US$1 million. This would involve 2 million entries per week. Who was going to do all of that data entry? And who would pay for that? Muhammad Yunus's internal team solved the problem for 5% of the proposed American cost. They said, "Since 95% of the deposits are made successfully every week, let's simply assume that all deposits were made on a timely basis. Then, all we have to do is make entries for those deposits not made." This strategy saved 95% of the data entry, and US$950,000, because the Grameen team accomplished the task internally in a couple of months.

If we are going to have peace in the World, developing countries are going to have to be able to advance the standards of living of their people very quickly. Muhammad Yunus has been showing us how to do it since 1976! I can think of no one more deserving of The Nobel Peace Prize! Congratulations!

Chapter 88
Death of My Father

An unfortunate thing happened on my way to writing a book about my first year of producing "Words Matter." Israel attacked Hezbollah on July 12, 2006, only one month into the project. On that day, "two roads diverged," as Robert Frost had it, and I took the most trodden, down which Bill O'Reilly and his motley group of Neocons, who have done nothing more than falsely polarize the country, making God fearing Christians think that somehow God would want us to kill our fellow man; would want us to lose our compassion for our fellow man, who were not wired as most of us were, and therefore will not reproduce; and would want us to gather in great groups in front on giant television screens and watch hypocritical leaders tell us why their behavior is more "Christian" and God fearing than Muslims, who worship the same God.

Three decades ago, I was commenting on David Attenborough's *Gandhi* movie to a Japanese friend, saying that I really liked Gandhi's vision that God and spirituality amount to Truth and Love. She was a Catholic, and she told me that Christianity amounted to nothing more than this. I was taken aback, because I had been a practicing Christian, at various levels, for 25 years, and I had never heard that. On reflection, though, I have made my own study of The Bible, and I believe she was correct.

Gandhi said, "For a time, tyrants can seem very powerful, but in the end they always fail. Only truth and love will prevail." Looking at the Neocons foaming at the mouth; and the evangelicals holding big-screen rock concerts of mass euphoria in their churches every Sunday, it's hard to remember that. But, in the end, it now appears that some of the evangelicals have come to realize that their interests and those of the Neocons diverge. Amazingly, all of the promises of the Neocons to make The United States a "religious and God fearing" country, have failed to materialize—I guess, because God didn't want it that way. God wanted us to recognize that we have strength in our Diversity, and that a condition of permanent war is not in the best interests of anyone, except people who choose to tear the very fabric of who are as Americans for their personal and private gain.

But I digress, yet again. My friends from the Terror Management Theory School of psychology, following Ernest Becker's lead, had pointed out to me last fall that all human beings want, at their most fundamental level, to have their lives count for something. In my case, a "reminder of death" in the form of the actual death of my father, firmly set me on the path of telling what I have learned about life and venal politicians and theologians, probably for the rest of my life. I am honored that so many people, now in 108 countries, think it is worth their time to read my thoughts here.

I returned from my December 2005 trip to the Middle East energized. I had positive reinforcement on my "Words Matter" project from Lubna Hussain, a respected columnist, and from my friend, Mohammed Teleb. Their interviews told me that my instinct was right; that the mainstream media had the Muslim World all wrong. And, even if I were the only non-Muslim to say so, I should keep saying so as loudly as I could.

Two days later, on December 17, 2006, I was celebrating the Christmas holidays with friends when I had a call from my sister saying that our father had collapsed on the stairs, and been taken to a hospital. Debbi and I gathered our belongings and our collies together, and headed north.

My father, Donald T. Conover, was suffering from the ravages of 60 years of smoking. He had lived his life honorably, as a naval officer and then a college administrator, but for the previous 8 years, he had been tethered to an oxygen machine. Every time I visited him, in those 8 years, I said goodbye, as if it would be the last time, knowing how frail he was becoming. By the time he died, he weighed 112 pounds and had less than 10% body fat.

We were very fortunate, because today's medical technologies mean that in many cases it takes about 3 weeks to actually die. Debbi and I had returned from the trip in which we got to spend 2 days together in Alexandria, Egypt, and then another 5 days in Venice. This was especially meaningful to Dad, because he had visited both in his Navy years. In 1947, his ship, the U.S.S. Stormes (DD 780), was parked in front of the Danieli Hotel in Venice for 3 weeks, only a stones throw from the Doge's Palace. Debbi and I had known this during our trip, so we had brought him back a poster of the fascinating stairway at the Danieli, for a Christmas present. When we went into Dad's hospital room, we affixed the poster to his wall.

Over the next two weeks, I was able to privately share with Dad our photographs of our two visits. These were moments of special closeness between us, and we both appreciated the opportunity. In the end, be-tubed and sedated, he told me, "I don't know how to die." I told him he should leave that matter to God, and he seemed relieved that it was a final task he need not undertake. Early in this process, he had asked me when my next trip to the Middle East was planned, and I told him January 17, 2006. He had taken the knowledge, as if he understood that he had to go by then. Finally, on January 11, 2006, he died in his sleep, while the family was eating Sushi, his requested final meal, at our ancestral farm.

One of the last things I told him was, "I feel you in me every day." He had responded, with a meaningful man-to-man look, "I know."

I barely have a recollection of the January 17th trip. We had agreed that we would take a month to prepare a proper memorial service for Dad, and we were glad we did. Finally we did, on February 18, 2006. The Navy provided full military honors. One week later, his third great grandson was born to my eldest daughter.

Life goes on! We all want to raise our families in peace. Let's do that! We all want to leave our "mark" on the great ledger of humanity. My father did it in many ways, but I will always feel that what I write here, and do with my other work, are a testament to his humanity; and--with a nod to Sheldon, Jeff, Tom, and Neil--to my own.

Chapter 89
Dean Dianne Lynch

The birth of Nicholas, my third grandson, meant that I would have to return to Upstate New York very shortly. Having just buried my father, I knew it was important to help my mother move on with life, so I promised to take her to see Nicholas very soon after he was born. At the same time, I had, for months, been trying to interview Dean Dianne Lynch for "Words Matter." I had spoken with Dean Lynch during the Christmas season, but the combination of our busy schedules made it impossible to meet. Finally, on March 2, 2006, mother and I set out to meet Nicholas for the first time in Rochester, by way of Ithaca. It was not exactly "on the way," and typical of the region, there was a blizzard.

Dr. Dianne Lynch is Dean of the Roy H. Park School of Communications at Ithaca College. I had long wanted to interview a journalism educator, to provide an educator's perspective to how journalistic responsibility has been taught, and add credence to my view that the "Muslim Story" was being badly handled by the mainstream press. Dean Lynch graciously agreed to the timing for this interview.

The "Muhammad Cartoon Controversy" was still in the headlines. In September 2005, a Danish newspaper published twelve cartoons, which featured satirical images of the Prophet Muhammad (PBUH). In Islam, the base assumption is the worshiper has a direct relationship with God. Therefore, images of anyone are frowned upon, because they could become idolatry. Images of the Prophet are expressly forbidden for everyone. Most of us in the Judeo-Christian World would have no reason to know this, and I feel confident that the Danish editor did not know it prior to publication.

As the controversy swirled, it engendered a series of protests. This was just two months after the London bombings, which were the origin of my project, so tensions were still very high around the World. The mainstream media began reporting on these protests in a rather inflammatory way. At first, very few noticed that it was happening, but by December, Muslim leaders were calling for protests in the form of boycotts of Danish products and more demonstrations. The protests caused hundreds of millions of dollars of losses for Danish firms, which in turn made it an ever expanding story. The new protests, which reached a crescendo in January and February 2006 were top news around the World.

My criticism of the stories was that they were enflaming the news. Instead of showing a demonstration of 300 people from a distance, at the Danish Embassy in Jakarta, for example, the media chose to show extreme close-ups of extremely angry and violent looking demonstrators. A demonstration of 300 people is not a particularly large event, when you consider that we're used to demonstrations of up to a million people in Washington. But, when you put the camera in the demonstrators face, and don't show the larger context of life going on normally, people get the idea that perhaps they too should riot violently. Protests in Nigeria, in the few days after the Jakarta demonstration, killed at least 20 people. Overall, there were about 150 deaths caused by the riots, which arose from the Danish cartoons.

It begs the question whether the riots were incited by *Al Qaeda* or some other group. The fact is that the media kept stirring the pot by reporting in a more and more inflammatory manner, until the whole World was paying attention to something of relatively little import. If *Al Qaeda*, or some other group, did incite the riots, then it seems to me fair to say that the media played right into the hands of terrorists, making their effort easier by orders of magnitude. This was the context in which Dean Lynch's interview was conducted.

The burning question was the breadth of the idea of our Freedom of the Press, in the context of publishing the Muhammad Cartoons. In the course of the development of the story, several editors, including student editors in university newspapers, had reprinted the cartoons, simply to push back and demonstrate that they had Freedom of the Press. Unfortunately, these actions simply enflamed the news further. Dean Lynch and I both believe that the Freedom of the Press is very near absolute, but there are certainly bounds. You cannot shout "Fire!" in a crowded theatre, unless there actually is a fire. You can't say something untrue about another person, either orally or in writing. This is not a crime, but the Tort of Defamation, a civil wrong, which can subject you to money damages. Of course, the Prophet Muhammad (PBUH) is dead, so the law of Defamation would not apply.

But there still is a boundary, beyond which a journalist cannot go. Here is how it came out in my interview with Dean Lynch.

"SKIP: Would you accept the statement that now that we know what the reaction is about the cartoons, that it would be unethical for a journalist to continue to publish?

DEAN LYNCH: Absolutely!

SKIP: And you would agree that that would, in effect, be incitement to riot?

DEAN LYNCH: I agree that it would be irresponsible. Whether it meets the threshold of incitement to riot, I do not know. Read your community. I think one of the responsibilities a newspaper has is to understand its culture and its community. There are situations in which I would say, "Yes, it is incitement to riot."

Major excerpts of our one-hour interview (video, audio, and transcripts) can be found at http://www.wordsmatter.tv.

Chapter 90

SAMAR FATANY

With respect to my many Saudi friends, I must here state my own perception about their society, *vis-à-vis* women. Over four years of visiting the Kingdom of Saudi Arabia, I had come to believe that it was a country of misogynists, or at the very least, a country which has manifested men's subliminal fear of the power of women, by making its women virtual prisoners. Each time I visit the Kingdom, I am struck by the fact that society is nearly devoid of "the feminine principle." Yes, one does see black shrouds floating around the streets and ubiquitous shopping malls, but there is little reason to associate that black shroud with femininity.

While I normally don't notice this immediately, upon arrival, I always feel it viscerally when I return to a place that allows its women in society. Normally, I arrive in Dubai from Riyadh, and even though I am 60 years old, I have a physical and emotional response to the first woman I see. I say to myself, "Whoa! That's a woman!" It is as if I was on a planet with only one gender.

Separation of women from society is not a tenet of Islam, as is evidenced by all of the other Muslim countries I have visited, so it seems to be a particular fetish of the Saudis. I have never understood how Saudi men could tolerate such a condition. Of course, for a married man this is less of an issue, but for post-pubescent pre-marital men and women, I imagine that this must be a burden of some magnitude. Further, it impoverishes the Saudi economy, because it essentially takes half of the population out of the productivity of the society, thereby causing Saudi Arabia to subsidize other developing countries to the tune of the salaries of approximately six million foreign workers. The Saudi women I know are intelligent, diligent, sophisticated, and hard working, but the "Saudi system" largely ignores this asset, to its detriment.

I say all of this to give you a sense of my perceptions, as of May 15, 2006, and to set the context for what happened next in my narrative. I happened to be in Riyadh again on May 15th, when I opened my *Arab News* to Samar Fatany's article, "Women Hold the Key to Prosperity or Failure." What a pleasant surprise! My heart was in my throat as I read Samar's piece, and realized what a risk (in my perception) she must be taking by publishing such opinions. Naturally, I immediately wanted to interview Samar for "Words Matter," because her words and opinions would clearly demonstrate that very significant change is "in the works" in Saudi Arabia, albeit behind closed doors. But, how would I meet her with only a few days left in my May visit to the Kingdom? And, if I made contact, how could I persuade her to "go on the record" on American television.

Remembering "six degrees of separation," I decided that if I called enough of my friends in the Kingdom, someone would have an idea of how to meet Samar. At the time, I knew nothing about her whatsoever, except her name. *Arab News* blocks the "guts" of its own newspaper online, inside the Kingdom, so I couldn't even read any of her earlier columns, though I knew they existed in great volume, from the titles and four-line excerpts that *Arab News* does allow. It turned out I was right! The very first friend I called said, "Yes, I know her. She's the one I have wanted you to meet! I will get her cell phone number for you, and call her with an introduction first." Within an hour, Samar and I were on the telephone, arranging to meet for our interview five days hence.

It turns out that Samar Fatany is a highly respected English language radio commentator in Saudi Arabia. She had interviewed my doctor friend several times on her program, regarding health issues. She writes frequent op-ed pieces for *Arab News*, and is famous for her positions promoting women's rights in the Kingdom. Many excerpts from our 90 minute interview can be viewed at www.wordsmatter.tv, where it is currently featured. She and her friends have been very active in attempting to dispel the misperceptions about Islam, which are found in The United States and Europe. Samar is just one of the many courageous columnists, reporters, editors and staff of *Arab News*, which is known for effecting progressive change in the Kingdom.

My interview with Samar, on May 20, 2006, opened, for me, another level of understanding about the needs of Saudi Arabia, the Middle East in general, and its people. It reconfirmed for me the peril we all face in not fully understanding the demographic pressure, which the entire Muslim World faces. The conflict between Israel and Hezbollah, which began 7 weeks after my interview with Samar, and one month after I began writing *Tsunami of Blood,* proves the validity of my title, and represents the "tip of an iceberg" of problems we all face in the next quarter century. Let us pray that our politicians start doing their jobs, instead of misdirecting the attention of the American people with inconsequential issues like what consenting adults do behind the closed doors of their bedroom.

There are approximately 100 million young Muslim men, between 15 and 23. If only 10% of them were radicalized by the behavior of the Bush Administration and Israel over the summer of 2006, we have a serious problem, which needs to be addressed before it gets totally out of control. The mess in Iraq is bad enough! But, if we do not understand our greater peril, we may find ourselves burying our grandchildren. At this point in time, there is very little evidence that our leaders around the globe have realized the magnitude of the problem, and addressed it in any way. In this condemnation of politicians, I include Republicans and Democrats, Arabs, Jews, Persians and Europeans, not to mention most other political leaders around the World. Regretfully, I expect to be writing on this topic for the rest of my life.

Chapter 91

Moralists at Sea in a Sea of Immorality

For a group of people dependent upon religion for their political life, the Bush Administration has shown itself singularly inept at recognizing the importance of religion to the solution in Iraq. As I wrote in Chapter 4, and have maintained throughout this project, only through Islam will the answers for the Middle East be found. On October 20, 2006, on a flight to Chicago and reading through *The Washington Post*, I was astounded that in all of the commentary, debate, and gnashing of teeth about the situation in Iraq, not one person—political, military, theologian or journalist—mentioned religion as anything like a possible cure.

Meanwhile, on October 19-20, 2006, in Makkah, the Organization of the Islamic Conference ("OIC"), convened a meeting of Islamic scholars from Iraq and elsewhere, to try to fashion a consensus about finding an end to the violence. Praise be to God! Never mind that no one in the Bush Administration seems to have even noticed! Never mind that no one in the western "mainstream media" has seemed to notice! Never mind that this may be the most important development in the whole bloody mess! Never mind that the Bush Administration is adrift, and claims to be willing to accept valid ideas from any source! Never mind that these are all so-called "God fearing" men and women, who supposedly rely on God for the answers.

The truth is that the Bush Administration only gives lip service to God. If that were wrong, why wouldn't they seek the answer through theologians of faith and religion in the Middle East, whose very lives hang in the balance? Do they not understand that the God of Abraham is also the God of Jesus and Muhammad (PBUH)? Do they not understand that "God works in mysterious ways," and those ways are always through the actions of human beings? Do they not understand that if some Muslims are misusing their religion, then it is other Muslims who are going to have to change that situation? What credibility can Christians and Jews possibly have in delineating what Islam is, and how it may be used?

Where are the moderate Muslims? That is a question that I often hear voiced in the American press. In Chapter 83, I pointed out that they abound. They met in Makkah October 20, 2006, in an attempt to solve their own problems without guns, and bombs, and nuclear arms races. They were doing God's work! Perhaps if the rest of the World had noticed, the murderers in their own country would have noticed too.

Where are God's faithful in the western world? I'm afraid they have not heard the Word of God, so they have abdicated their responsibilities to do God's work, and left our policies for the Middle East to war mongers, who want to destroy the very fabric of The United States of America with their fear mongering ways; the better to control us!

With apologies to my friends and relatives, who have followed an evangelical path, I have to say, "You have missed the point of the teachings of Jesus Christ." I was once told by a person very close to me that when I die I will go to Hell. That assertion hurt me very deeply. That is the type of religious militancy, which has led our most faithful Christians to support murder and mayhem in the Middle East. Wouldn't the better comment have been, "I am concerned for your immortal soul, and I would like to work with you over the rest of your life to help you find a place in Heaven?"

That is the type of misguided religious militancy, which has caused Christian evangelicals to blindly support the Bush Administration, which has brought Hell on Earth. This is an Administration that does not believe in finding answers through religion—and by this, I do not mean interminable power prayers and ravings in stadium size churches. I mean faithful people, who can turn off the Neocon harangue long enough to actually hear the Word of God, and then get out there and make a difference, not with a gun, but with an olive branch. The Muslims put all of you to shame, because they are in Makkah today, setting aside their differences, in the spirit of trying to find pragmatic solutions through religion. Iraq is not a sectarian fight, and these people know it! I pray that God will speak to them clearly!

Iraq is a multi-faceted feud—brother against brother, tribe against tribe, region against region; a series of old fashioned vendettas! How do you end a feud? It only ends when the society in which it is taking place decides it will end and its people will live in peace. I suggest that most Iraqis must be ready for this solution, given the number of deaths they have seen in the past 30 years. The question is, how do men and women of good will make the point and make it stick? This must be done through the intercession of religious leaders, both in the Middle East and the West, who know that murder is not the answer, nor the teaching of God. Only if all of the theologians, of whatever faith, embrace the Word of God, and listen to God's teaching, will peace be found.

Ever since 9/11, evangelical Christians have been part of the problem. Their hateful pronouncements against Islam, from the pulpit, contradicting the lesson of Acts 19, have done nothing but enrage young Muslims and empower the mob, making us more vulnerable in the process. The Bush Administration, which they supported, has destroyed the reputation of The United States, and made us far less safe according to its own intelligence agencies. It is time to accentuate the commonalities within humanity across the World, rather than our differences. It's time to bring the Word of God to the peace process. Religion is not the only answer, but it is certainly an important part of the answer. It's time for all Christian leaders to become part of the solution, as Muslim theologians are doing today. That's the Christian thing to do!

Chapter 92

Withdrawal from Iraq Costs and Benefits

In order to make rational decisions regarding the future, we must take ourselves out of the temptation of placing blame for the current state of affairs in Iraq. There can be no doubt that in the fullness of time, the Bush Administration will be blamed by historians for many mistakes since the events of 9/11, and the timing of the invasion of Iraq will be one of them. The eventual need for such an invasion is a matter academics will debate *ad infinitum* and *ad nauseum* from the safety of their ivory towers. None of this will help any of us solve today's problems, however.

For the sake of discussion, let us assume that the debate is only about whether or not the United States should withdraw its forces from Iraq immediately. Many of my Arab friends are suggesting that, if we withdraw as quickly as possible, things will quiet down in Iraq, and all will be well. Unfortunately, it is the premise of *Tsunami of Blood* that this is wishful thinking. Let us consider the issue from several perspectives.

FOR IRAQ:

Regretfully, it seems to me that there is little hope to staunch the violence in Iraq, unless the Iraqis themselves, uniting their combined wills across their Islamic faith, make it so. How do you end a feud? It will end when the community itself decides that there will be no more killing. Last week, at Makkah, leading clerics representing all Iraqi Muslims met and agreed that the killing should stop. So far, no evidence has come to my attention that suggests that this agreement has had any impact on the fighting.

From where I sit, it appears to me that U.S. military action has been limited to self-defense and limited patrolling. It is entirely inappropriate to compare Iraq to Vietnam. At the height of the Vietnam War, there were more than 500 American military personnel per week being killed. That is roughly 20 times as bad as current American losses in Iraq. That fact reflected the intensity of the pursuit of the conflict on both sides. If the

US was pursuing its military options most aggressively, this is the type of casualty rate we would be seeing. It remains to be seen, of course, whether the passing of the American elections on November 7, 2006, will result in more or less aggressive actions on the part of the American military, but for reasons of American opinion, the Bush Administration will keep American casualties low until then. My guess is that, after the elections, the Bush people will want to become more aggressive, in the fool's errand of saving their reputations for posterity.

In terms of the death toll, it now appears to me that there is little help for the Iraqi people, in either case. Let's consider the costs and benefits of an American withdrawal for the people of Iraq:

Benefits:

1. Any perceived American withdrawal would give the Iraqi people the pyrrhic victory of having pushed the "infidels" out of a Muslim land. There would be a brief period of euphoria, but based on the events of 2006, it seems clear that the tribal warfare and vendettas will continue, until they burn themselves out or the Iraqi people themselves find a way to end them.

2. Individual militias and "strong men," would have a clear shot to take control of the country, with the ability to import weapons more freely. Which group comes out on top would be like a game of wheel of fortune, but it is clear that no one can predict the outcome today.

3. Any other country with visions of regional hegemony would be left with a clear field, meaning Iran would be able to influence future events with greater impunity. For the Iraqis, they may be exchanging Americans for Persians—not infidels, perhaps, but traditional enemies.

4. The attraction of Iraq as a tourist destination and training ground for *Al Qaeda* may gradually dissolve, and many of the foreign (Muslims) may see fit to begin to go home.

Costs:

1. It seems to me that the killing will continue in Iraq, in approximately the same proportions, until the Iraqi people themselves decide to end it. A few steps have been taken in this regard, and we can all pray that Iraqis generally will demand peace, but I see little evidence that this idea is gaining traction, at the moment. Time will tell.

2. While an American withdrawal would continue to provide all Arabs with a handy

scapegoat for the mess, the "fig leaf" of denial of culpability would gradually disintegrate. In a year or two, it would be very difficult to continue to claim that all of the ongoing problems were created in Washington. The harsh glare of reality would penetrate more and more.

3. Without unity and a degree of solidarity, the political vacuum would invite strong neighbors, and neighbors once removed (like China), to increase their influence in the region, thereby keeping the Iraqis weak. It seems to me that Iraq's only hope is unity. A balkanized country will gradually be divided up by the vultures. Who can doubt that an American withdrawal would invite Iran to take control in the Shiite areas? Facing such a reality, the Saudis would have to take control in Sunni regions, so as to avoid the Iranian army on its own border.

FOR THE UNITED STATES:

Whether we like it or not, the United States government, regardless of the political flavor of its Administration, is in a position of making decisions for the future of many countries. There is very little that can be done to change this fact, without giving up our own national security, which neither major party can countenance. The resentment, which is heard around the World, is an expected result of this reality. There seem few eventualities, which are going to change this fact in the short term, unless the fabric of humanity crashes down around us. With this fact comes both power and responsibility. I believe most Americans can and do accept this responsibility, whether consciously or unconsciously, with compassion, based on our own troubled history. Regretfully, behaviors of others can cause Americans to react without compassion, if they feel their own security and standard of living are threatened.

Let us consider the benefits and costs to the United States of withdrawal from Iraq:

Benefits:

1. The broad cadre of Americans, who now see the Iraq war as wrong in the image of a 21st Century Vietnam, would be briefly vindicated. These people have not considered the consequences to the broader Middle East, nor to a future played out over the next 5 years.

2. There may be a brief dip in the number of American casualties.

3. Difficult domestic political issues would finally take the attention of our politicians, for a period of time, which could give us a chance to solve some of our domestic problems.

Costs:

1. *Al Qaeda* would be emboldened, and greatly strengthened. Their evil ideas would gain credibility everywhere. Iraq would be their new training base, which they could exploit with relative impunity, protected by the wrong kind of militia.

2. American allies and trading partners in Saudi Arabia, Egypt, Jordan, the GCC, would be put at immediate risk. Returning foreign fighters from Iraq would spread their hateful doctrine with impunity among the 100 million frustrated and impressionable young men of the Muslim World (57 countries), fomenting revolution, and Iraq style guerilla conflicts across the region. The "party line" of *Al Qaeda* and extremists, who have hijacked Islam, is that these regimes do not represent true Islam. Many Muslims have come to believe them, or they cynically recognize this position as one that can gain power, and use it among ignorant populations.

3. Iran, and its calculating President, Mahmoud Ahmadinejad, would be emboldened to expand its hegemony in the Shiite World. Without finding some accommodation with the West, Iran would have to do this in order to raise the standard of living of its own people.

4. North Korea's President, Kim Jong-Il, would be further emboldened to improve the standard of living of his people by selling black market arms and nuclear weapons to the highest bidder. At some point, this is a scenario no American President can accept.

5. I have never doubted that, sooner or later, *Al Qaeda* will attack the United States again, with probably horrific consequences. The question is whether they will be set completely free to attack across the Muslim World, as well as the United States and Western Europe. It does not seem in anyone's interest to allow them to metastasize in this way, since everyone's way of life, from Riyadh to Los Angeles, will be put in jeopardy.

FOR *AL QAEDA*:

Benefits:

1. *Al Qaeda* will trumpet this great victory against the "infidels" across the World, thereby enhancing their recruiting of children for their evil purposes.

2. *Al Qaeda* would be able to relieve its focus on Iraq, and aim at other targets across the World more quickly. *Al Qaeda*'s enemy is time, because the indoctrination of young people wears out with time, and with the press of human nature. The suicide bombing strategy can work for a time, but when its results provide little

gain, its allure will be fleeting, even to ignorant children. Ultimately, the word gets back to all Muslim families that these people are manipulating their faith for their personal gain. The Will of God is manifest through the affairs of men. Repeated losses is God's way of "speaking." Unfortunately, in the short run, withdrawal of the United States can also appear to be God's Will in the other direction.

Costs:

1. The opportunity to expand operations, also provides the danger of revealing methods of communication with leaders. The West is not so clueless in intelligence as it was after 9/11. *Al Qaeda's* leadership will be at greater risk.

2. Such a pyrrhic victory would create an expectation of action from the World's crazies. The longer action is postponed after such a "victory," the less influential *Al Qaeda* will become. But the very effort to create action will, in its turn, reveal the contours of their whereabouts, strategies and tactics, causing significant losses among their leadership. Ultimately, they cannot prevail.

3. *Al Qaeda* has a problem, now. When they attack, they also reveal flaws in their organizations, which allow us to destroy them. As history has now shown, they can withstand an attack far less than the United States. While 9/11 was horrific, it ultimately did little to change the way most of us live. But, the destruction of *Al Qaeda's* Afghan infrastructure, did cost them much more heavily, relatively speaking.

FOR IRAN:

Benefits:

1. Opens the field for Iran to gain further hegemony over regional Shiite populations.

2. Eliminates "threat" of an American force on Iran's western border.

3. President Ahmadinejad and the "Islamic Republic" gain stature in the international community, because he will be seen as one of the primary individuals manipulating the "all powerful" United States out of the region.

4. Gains further prestige for pushing the "infidels" out of the Iraq, from behind the scenes. Makes up for its losses of ground in Lebanon, thanks to the destruction of Hezbollah infrastructure.

5. Gains better land access to Syria, through an even friendlier Iraq.

6. Gains strategic leverage over Kurds.

Costs:

1. Loses "fig leaf" of Shiite controlled Iraqi government to hide its actions.

2. Puts Sunni Arab nations in greater fear of Iran's intentions, thereby engendering a Middle East arms race at the minimum, and a nuclear arms race at the worst.

3. Arms race requires further financial investment, thereby further impoverishing Iranian people, and causing aberrational behaviors, which will not be acceptable to the international community.

4. Gradually loses scapegoat of American power in the Middle East.

FOR MODERATE ARAB GOVERNMENTS IN THE MIDDLE EAST:

Benefits:

1. Ignorant populations would be briefly distracted with the euphoria of "victory" against the infidels, taking the pressure off of domestic issues in the short run.

2. Western trading partners would become more dependent upon their negotiating whims.

Costs:

1. *Al Qaeda* would be "gunning" for them.

2. Persians would be "gunning" for them.

3. They might be pushed into a nuclear arms race in the Middle East, since the United States would be proven an unreliable defender, thereby further degrading the standards of living of their people at large, because of the cost of such useless activities.

4. The euphoria would eventually wear off, and then serious domestic troubles would have to be faced fully.

5. Much of their intelligentsia would, if threatened with Iraq style murderous behavior, "abandon ship," leaving the devil to take the hind most.

We have problems aplenty across our troubled World. Let us understand our peril, and stop thinking that there is some easy solution, which can somehow prevent all bloodshed in the near future. Regretfully, there will be many more deaths before peace is found. The question is whether American politicians, and their diplomatic counterparts, have the intestinal fortitude to make the decisions, which will reduce the number of deaths of all peoples to the minimum.

The campaign debate of 2006, where Democrats demand withdrawal from Iraq on some sort of timetable, is only rhetoric playing to America's lamentably ignorant electorate. What the Democrats really think will only emerge once they recover some of the power, which they abandoned through their own incompetence of leadership and organization in recent years.

There are no easy answers. There are only the illusions of easy answers in the writing of flaccid analysts, who do not themselves face the facts of how the World is organized today. Do not suggest to me that it is not God's Will! God has made it so!

Conclusion

"Saudi Arabia is like a frozen chicken in your freezer on the day you lose power. It's already dead, and it's frozen in time. At first, you hope the power will return, to refreeze the chicken. As time goes on, you get more and more worried. You get to the point where you try to blow on the chicken to prevent the inevitable defrosting, but, in the end, you cannot prevent the smell."

—Anonymous

In the five months it has taken to write *Tsunami of Blood*, many things have happened, but all have served to confirm my fundamental premise: The population demographic of the Muslim World is a time bomb, set to destroy moderate regimes in the Middle East, America's allies, and western civilization as a whole. The order of magnitude of the problem is far beyond what we are seeing in Iraq, and in the conflict between Israel and Hezbollah, in the summer of 2006. The demographic is a cohort of approximately 100 million frustrated young men between the ages of 15 and 23, living across the Muslim World, who have little education, frustrated ambitions, and few to guide them to a better life. We'll call this cohort "the demographic."

Soon, the hostilities in Iraq will simmer down. This can happen because Iraqi politicians have finally seen that they must compromise among themselves; because clerics who signed the Makkah protocol last week, calling for a cessation of killing between Shiites and Sunnis, have succeeded in persuading the feuding parties to "take a breath," and find a way to national reconciliation; or because a majority of the belligerents within Iraq are dead or completely war weary. Or, the killing in Iraq will end from a combination of these factors and others, which is the likeliest scenario.

Once the gangs of marauding murderers have been leashed, the 12-30,000 foreign fighters in Iraq will begin to have visions of going home. The same porous borders, which allowed them to enter, will facilitate their return to their homelands. These individuals will have the social manners of "junkyard dogs," who hate the West, to be sure, but hate the regimes in their own home countries nearly as much.

When the "junkyard dog" fighters mix with the disgruntled demographic, anything can happen. I was told on December 13, 2006, that I should not worry about this eventuality. If you were in a position of power, what would you do given this ethical dilemma?

Fortune magazine speculated on April 11, 2006, that any one of six horrific scenarios could occur, from an American attack on Iran to the fall of the Saudi royal family. An econometric study placed the price of a barrel of oil, in the latter case, at $262, approximately four times the highest ever experienced. Politicians in the United States will be unable to staunch the anti-Muslim feeling in the United States caused by a price increase to $10 to $15 per gallon of gas in the United States. Further major military involvements in other countries of the Middle East, with great loss of life, will become inevitable, because the American population at large will insist on maintaining its standard of living, in the face of all of the evidence that we should cut back.

In my view, many of these consequences are inevitable. This is the origin of the name *Tsunami of Blood.* A tsunami is an energy wave, which travel across a body of water at up to 500 miles per hour. It is practically imperceptible until it reaches a shoreline, at which time it rises up and engulfs everyone and everything in its path. 9/11, the Riyadh bombings of 2003, the London bombings of July 2005, and the conflict between Israel and Hezbollah, are small examples of what can happen when such a wave of dissatisfaction about how our World has developed hits a distant shore. President Bush has said emphatically that he believes we can expect further strikes within the United States, and I believe him without reservation. Some plots will be foiled, before they can cause thousands of deaths, but some will have their effect.

What can be done to reduce the inevitable bloodshed?

1. We must first recognize that the peril, as described throughout *Tsunami of Blood,* is a real one. Iraq, with all of its horrors, is only a small example of what can happen across the Muslim World, with its collateral damage in the United States.

2. We must recognize that all of the solutions to the myriad problems of the Middle East cannot be achieved with military action. In a World Muslim population of approximately 1.3 billion people, most are moderate, who see the shortcomings of traditional cultures, as they have developed across the millennia, and want to modernize them as much as we do. It is only through working with the World's moderate Muslims that solutions can be found.

3. We must be eternally vigilant to our great peril, in not understanding the forces which govern our World. We must not allow our politicians to manipulate us with mindless slogans and hateful rhetoric.

4. We must demand that our politicians fully analyze all of the risks our nation faces, and implement policies, which ameliorate those risks. No administration will prevent the *Tsunami of Blood* from hitting our shores—the problems are too big and intransigent. But politicians, who understand its contours, and provide enlightened leadership, will reduce its effects.

5. Leaders, who try to distract our attention with inconsequential matters, like how consenting adults behave behind the doors of their own bedrooms, do us no favors, and are derelict in their duty to protect our nation. When we see endless debates over whether the words "under God" should be said in our Pledge of Allegiance, we should immediately be on notice that the speakers are ignoring their first obligation to provide us with national security. Above all else, the reason for a federal form of national government is national defense. Otherwise, we could as easily operate as a balkanized set of 50 independent sovereign states, which we are but for the tasks we have transferred to our central government because of economies of scale. If the Congress is not paying close attention to national defense as a first priority, its members are not doing their jobs, plain and simple.

As I have said from the beginning of this project, we must not withdraw from Iraq willy nilly. I agree with President Bush entirely on that matter. Unfortunately, he has failed to explain to the American people why we must "stay the course." I will say it simply here. We live in a dangerous World. The World has set itself up based on economic, political, military, and religious considerations, which were valid in their time, but which have been overwhelmed by the technologies and events of the twentieth century. Much of our thinking as human beings has not had sufficient time to adjust to the new realities. These failures to adjust reflect themselves differently in different cultures, but they are most apparent today in the aberrational behaviors we see across the World. There is no one group, which is at fault. We are all experiencing these aberrations, though in different ways, and in different degrees of intensity. Only if the leaders of all countries of the World understand this phenomenon, will we find our way to peace for future generations. The "forces of evil" are those venal politicians, who seek to exploit these aberrations for their personal gain, leaving solutions for future generations.

None of the major religious groups, be they Buddhist, Hindu, Muslim, Jew or Christian, will ever dominate all of the others, without bringing the entire fabric of humanity down around them in the process. This is obvious! Indeed, it was God who created them all in the first place! We must therefore find ways to live together on our fragile planet. This is God's will! The sooner we all realize this, the sooner we will find the solutions to problems, which will be manifested in a *Tsunami of Blood.*

Acknowledgements

Tsunami of Blood was made possible by the ideas and encouragement of my wife, Debbi, and our many friends and colleagues. Debbi once referred to me as her "kaleidoscope," and I have taken pleasure in the description. She has always been supportive, no matter what colors and shapes she sees through the lens of our long and successful marriage.

My partners and colleagues, who allowed me to take up the cause of Arabs and Muslims, while still pursuing our combined endeavors, were always supportive. For reasons they know, I will not mention them here, but they know who they are!

[Three people from _____] were the first to encourage me on the path of becoming a "media mogul." They gave me the guidance I needed to produce credible television interviews and other productions far from home, and accepted the need for the material I have provided them.

Special thanks to Dr. Philip R. Harris, co-author and co-editor of *Managing Cultural Differences*, now in its 7th edition, for taking the time to write the Foreword to *Tsunami of Blood*, and for his ongoing encouragement.

I am most grateful for the intellectual stimulation provided by Professor Sheldon Solomon of Skidmore College, one of the principal investigators of *Terror Management Theory*, for both encouraging the project and enduring my first interview attempt, which failed because of inadequate equipment. Since then, Sheldon has provided further guidance on many occasions, and led me to Dr. Jeff Greenberg of the University of Arizona, Dr. Neil Elgee of the Ernest Becker Foundation, Dr. E. James Lieberman, a retired psychiatrist, and Greg Bennick and Patrick Shen, who co-wrote and co-produced the award winning documentary *Flight from Death: The Quest for Immortality*, which has proven to be an early guide to what is troubling our World today.

Many thanks, too, to the many professionals, educators, business executives, and thoughtful citizens of the Planet, who have agreed to be interviewed for my developing projects, including, in the general order in which they were interviewed:

Professor Sheldon Solomon, Professor of Psychology at Skidmore College
Professor Jeff Greenberg, Professor of Psychology at The University of Arizona
Dr. Philip R. Harris, author of *Managing Cultural Differences*
Mr. Teymour Adham, of Sahara Adventure Company, Alexandria, Egypt
Ms. Lubna Hussain, Columnist for *Arab News*, in Riyadh, Saudi Arabia
Mr. Mohammed Teleb, a professional engineer living in Doha, Qatar
Mr. Abdellatif Omar, a computer engineer and entrepreneur in Riyadh, Saudi Arabia
Ms. Carolyn McCool, formerly Director of UniFem in Afghanistan
Mr. Randy Allen, an immigration attorney in San Francisco, California
Dr. Dianne Lynch, Dean, The Roy H. Park School of Communications at Ithaca College
Ms. Carole Chouinard, Producer, The Tavis Smiley Show on NPR
Mr. Ray Greene, The Philosopher of the Woods and my lifelong friend.
Ms. Samar Fatany, Columnist for *Arab News*, in Jeddah, Saudi Arabia.
Dr. Neil Elgee, Director of the Ernest Becker Foundation
Mr. Greg Bennick, co-writer and co-producer of *Flight from Death: The Quest for Immortality.*

I am also grateful to the following leaders, who have allowed me to videotape their talks and lectures, for the benefit of helping the World's people understand the various issues we all face:

Ambassador Chas. W. Freeman, former U.S. Ambassador to Saudi Arabia
Ambassador Ned Walker, former U.S. Ambassador to Israel
Mr. Robert Lacy, author of *The Kingdom*, a definitive history of Saudi Arabia.

Finally, many thanks to Mrs. Jocie Salveson, of The Lockwood Agency of Visalia, California, who took responsibility for developing the cover art and page layout for *Tsunami of Blood.*

Finally, I want to acknowledge the role of my daughters, their husbands, and our grandchildren, who provided a major part of the impetus to get many of these ideas, particularly those relating to what it means to be an American, down on the printed page. Diversity is the Glory of God, and America is the proof of its efficacy!

I am grateful to many others, who know who they are, but are omitted here for reasons they know but you need not.

Bibliography

Tsunami of Blood is intended as a personal commentary, rather than a scholarly journal or book. As such, it is heavily dependent upon the 1st person experiences and observations of the author over a lifetime. For this reason, no attempt is made to provide an exhaustive scholarly bibliography.

To the extent that this work was inspired by anything, you should refer to three particular works:

The Denial of Death, Ernest Becker, 1974. Winner of the Pulitzer Prize.

Escape from Evil, Ernest Becker, 1974.

"*Flight from Death: The Quest for Immortality,*" documentary by Patrick Shen and Greg Bennick, 2004. Winner of numerous film festival first prizes.

All of these works are available online from book merchants.

Other works of interest have been mentioned in the text and included in the index.

The author has been partially informed by current newspaper articles, a sampling of which are contained in the section entitled "What Skip Read Today" in the online version of this book at http://www.tsunamiofblood.com.

Index

Symbols

1984 48, 175
9/11 17, 20, 36, 39, 55, 75, 85, 87, 88, 91, 105, 114, 153, 155, 163, 165, 201, 203, 221, 280, 283, 287, 292

A

Abu Yousef 65, 66, 71
Adham Compound Hotel 69, 71
Afghanistan 11
Agence France 91
Ahmadinejad 91, 92, 93, 121, 165, 189, 190, 191, 192, 197, 225, 226, 227, 262, 286, 287
A'isha, Barakah 16
Al Arabia 24, 25
Al Capone 81, 147
Aldous Huxley 48
Alexandria 65, 66, 69, 71, 77, 78, 82, 91, 210, 268
Al Jazeera 20, 24, 25, 58, 71, 99, 100, 101, 182, 196
Alkhobar 83
Allah 36, 51, 140, 146, 147
Alma 61, 62
Al Maliki 158
Al Manar 142, 164, 199
Al Qaeda 11, 12, 32, 50, 84, 104, 141, 145, 146, 163, 190, 197, 198, 234, 240, 272, 284, 286, 287, 288
American Dream 62, 213, 214
Anderson Cooper 238
Annapolis 223
Apostle Paul 44
Arab News 83, 84, 91, 93, 100, 143, 149, 163, 239, 253, 276
Arthur F. Burns 176
Ayman al Zawahri 145

B

Bahrain 15, 26, 234
BBC 20, 58, 71, 83, 91, 99, 100, 255
Becker. *See* Ernest Becker
Bill Meckling 249

Bill O'Reilly 157, 161, 164, 167, 168, 267
Billy Pilgrim 31
Brave New World 48
Buddhism 29, 72
Buddhist 29, 30, 122, 219, 293
Burj Al Arab Hotel 237
Bush Administration 74, 87, 100, 104, 113, 149, 153, 155, 168, 171, 182, 189, 191, 193, 215, 226, 233, 237, 238, 240, 241, 242, 243, 244, 245, 257, 258, 263, 276, 279, 280, 281, 283, 284
Butcher of Qana 215

C

Camp David Accords 176
Canada 15, 16, 69, 71, 77, 140
Carter 175
central planning 249, 250, 251, 252, 253, 265
Charles Clarke 26
Chick & Ruth's Deli 131
China 14, 15, 24, 211, 251, 257, 259, 285
Christian 44, 45, 50, 57, 58, 59, 78, 120, 134, 139, 155, 219, 220, 247, 267, 271, 280, 281, 293
Christiane Amanpour 195
Civilization 147, 165, 177, 179, 180, 182, 185, 187
CNN 9, 16, 17, 20, 23, 24, 25, 26, 57, 58, 71, 83, 91, 92, 93, 97, 99, 100, 101, 106, 111, 122, 133, 134, 135, 136, 141, 163, 195, 196, 197, 199, 238, 255
Condoleeza Rice 161, 189
Congress 44, 68, 74, 86, 88, 131, 158, 159, 213, 215, 217, 219, 229, 241, 242, 293
Conover Doctrine 180, 181
Constitution of the United States 113, 205, 217
Council on American-Islamic Relations
CAIR 181, 193
Crusades 96

D

Daniel Boorstin 87, 248
Danish cartoons 59, 272
Debbi 17, 29, 30, 43, 49, 50, 65, 66, 201, 206, 220, 268
Democracy 103, 114, 158, 205, 207
Denial of Death 49, 202, 221, 245
Deuteronomy 45
Dianne Lynch 59, 271
Diversity 15, 41, 42, 99, 179, 214, 222, 226, 267
Doha 19, 109, 119
Donald T. Conover 268
Dr. Thomas E. Starzl 253
Dubai 25, 65, 154, 237, 275

E

Ed Koch 171
Egypt 11, 65, 66, 69, 70, 71, 72, 77, 79, 81, 82, 119, 120, 127, 141, 164, 176, 210, 234, 235, 268, 286
Ernest Becker 35, 49, 116, 122, 129, 141, 202, 221, 245, 268
Escape from Evil 49, 95, 116, 122, 129, 141, 202, 221, 245

F

feud 32, 33, 122, 133, 139, 140, 280, 283
First Amendment 26, 217, 240
Five Pillars 219

Flight from Death 29, 30, 35, 49, 54, 55
Fouad Siniora 16
Founding Fathers 41, 47, 68, 99, 205, 217
Fox News 9, 111, 157, 161, 163, 164, 167, 168, 171, 172, 173, 175, 176
Freakonomics, A Rogue Economist Explores the Hidden Side of Everything 137
Freedom of the Press 58, 99, 272
Free to Choose 233

G

Galileo 87, 248
Gatwick 25
GDP 15, 190, 209, 210, 211, 214, 223, 225, 226, 234, 249, 251
George Orwell 48, 175
Germany 91, 104, 114, 168, 177, 233, 244, 257, 261
Gitmo 89, 238, 243
God 13, 15, 16, 36, 42, 44, 45, 59, 75, 77, 87, 88, 95, 114, 116, 117, 120, 131, 134, 152, 179, 180, 185, 186, 190, 192, 193, 198, 202, 214, 217, 219, 220, 221, 222, 226, 244, 245, 247, 248, 267, 268, 271, 279, 280, 281, 287, 289, 293
Governor Romney 47, 48, 61
Grameen Bank 265, 266
Grameen Phone 265
Greg Bennick 35, 50
Gross Domestic Product. *See* GDP
Guantanimo Naval Base 89. *See* Gitmo
Gulf War 128, 257, 264

H

Haida 139, 140
HAMAS 188
Hamas 115, 116, 122, 153, 177
Hamdan 74, 75, 113
Hamdan v. Rumsfeld 74, 113
Hannity. *See* Sean Hannity
Hatfields and McCoys 32, 33
Henry Kissinger 14
Heritage Foundation 47
Hezbollah 16, 17, 115, 122, 123, 125, 127, 128, 134, 136, 141, 142, 143, 145, 146, 147, 153, 154, 155, 164, 165, 171, 172, 177, 187, 188, 189, 190, 191, 192, 193, 195, 197, 199, 202, 203, 209, 211, 215, 216, 221, 226, 233, 241, 243, 267, 276, 287, 291, 292
Hideki Tojo 259
Hindu 293
Hitler 32, 100, 127, 177, 219, 259, 261
Holy Land 96, 188

I

India 15, 25, 26, 39, 96, 211, 213, 227, 231, 250, 251, 259, 265
In the Wake of 9/11 53, 95, 116
Iran 32, 91, 104, 128, 143, 152, 153, 159, 163, 164, 165, 171, 172, 176, 185, 190, 192, 198, 223, 225, 226, 227, 234, 243, 244, 255, 261, 262, 284, 285, 286, 287, 288, 292
Iraq 11, 12, 18, 24, 31, 32, 33, 43, 57, 59, 61, 70, 103, 127, 128, 129, 133, 134, 136, 139, 140, 146, 151, 153, 158, 164, 165, 172, 176, 185, 193, 196, 203, 210, 231, 233, 235, 237, 244, 255, 257, 276, 279, 280, 283, 284, 285, 286, 287, 288, 289, 291, 292, 293
Islam 13, 14, 16, 20, 25, 26, 31, 32, 33, 44, 50, 57, 58, 59, 60, 62, 72, 78, 91, 116, 125, 126, 133, 134, 135, 139, 140, 145, 147, 195, 196, 197, 202, 219, 223, 226, 229, 230, 244, 247, 255, 262, 271, 275, 276, 279, 280, 286

Israel 14, 16, 17, 78, 91, 115, 116, 120, 121, 122, 128, 141, 142, 143, 145, 147, 149, 154, 158, 163, 164, 165, 171, 172, 176, 177, 181, 185, 187, 188, 189, 190, 195, 197, 198, 199, 202, 203, 211, 215, 221, 223, 226, 233, 234, 241, 244, 255, 262, 267, 276, 291, 292

J

James Howard Kunstler 151
Japan 10, 14, 53, 73, 85, 104, 162, 169, 233, 234, 257
Javed Iqbal 199
Jeddah 19, 83, 84
Jeffrey Greenberg 35, 49, 53
Jerusalem 78, 105, 106, 223, 244, 262
Jimmy Carter 175
Jim Webb 157
Johnny Cochran 114
John Paul Stevens 74
Johns Hopkins Bloomberg School of Public Health 263
Jordan 11, 120, 127, 234, 288
Joseph Goebbels 176
Joseph Sisko 14
Justice 44, 45, 74, 75

K

Kalmbach 23, 57, 84, 195
Kalmbach Distinguished Alumnus Lecture 23, 84
Katherine Harris 217
Katrina 165
Khaled Almaeena 149
Kim Jong Il 261
King Abdullah 33, 91, 92, 143
Kurt Vonnegut 31
Kuwait 15, 26, 127, 128, 234

L

Leadership Shame of the Week 181
Lebanon 12, 16, 17, 26, 115, 116, 121, 123, 136, 142, 143, 146, 147, 154, 158, 163, 165, 171, 176, 177, 181, 185, 188, 193, 195, 209, 215, 216, 234, 235, 243, 255, 287
Leni Riefenstahl 219
London 12, 19, 20, 21, 23, 24, 26, 43, 83, 84, 119, 125, 181, 271, 292
Lt. Col. Rich Higgins, USMC 123
Lubna Hussain 83, 84, 93, 95, 100, 101, 103, 268
Luten Station 21

M

MAD 223
Madame Curie 16
Madelleine Albright 16
Makkah 19, 33, 91, 92, 279, 280, 283, 291
Makkah Declaration 33, 91
Managing Cultural Differences 53
Manufacturing Consent 104, 209
Margaret Atwood 50
Marine 17, 27, 67, 206, 220, 237, 257
Mart Laar 233
Media 24, 97, 157, 168, 170, 175, 179, 239
Media Shame of the Week 157, 168

Michaela 61, 62
Michael J. Garcia 199
Middle East 17, 19, 20, 24, 25, 33, 36, 70, 78, 79, 81, 82, 85, 103, 104, 116, 121, 128, 129, 143, 147, 149, 151, 153, 154, 158, 159, 161, 165, 168, 171, 172, 185, 189, 193, 196, 198, 205, 213, 214, 220, 234, 235, 237, 239, 268, 276, 279, 280, 285, 288, 291, 292
Mike Jensen 249
Milton Friedman 233
Mitt Romney 47
Mohammed 43, 70, 71, 109, 119, 120, 268
Mohammed Abbas 70, 71
Mosque 126
Ms. Kawther 133
Muhammad 265, 266, 271, 272, 279
Muhammad Yunus 265, 266
Mumbai 111, 114, 133
Munich Agreement 261
Muslim 11, 15, 20, 23, 24, 25, 26, 32, 33, 39, 47, 48, 50, 51, 54, 57, 58, 59, 62, 63, 66, 71, 72, 77, 78, 81, 82, 83, 89, 91, 92, 93, 100, 104, 116, 120, 122, 125, 134, 135, 139, 140, 141, 147, 149, 157, 158, 163, 164, 165, 167, 168, 169, 170, 171, 176, 181, 185, 187, 189, 193, 195, 196, 197, 198, 203, 206, 209, 210, 211, 212, 215, 216, 219, 220, 225, 229, 241, 242, 243, 244, 247, 258, 268, 271, 275, 276, 281, 284, 286, 291, 292, 293
Muslim Brotherhood 77, 81
Mutawa 152

N

Nasibah bint Ka'b 16
Nasrallah 147
Nasrin Alavi 152, 198
Nazi 32, 114, 219
Neocon 171, 175, 205, 280
Neville Chamberlain 127, 261, 262
Nick Robertson 238
Nicolae Ceausescu 137
Nihad Awad 181, 193
Noam Chomsky 104, 137, 209, 257
North Korea 153, 172, 261, 262, 286

O

O.J. Simpson 114
OIC Summit 91, 92, 93
O'Reilly. *See* Bill O'Reilly
Oliver North 157, 164, 167, 168
Oliver Stone 177, 201
Ollie. *See* Oliver North
Oman 15, 20, 26, 234
One Percent Doctrine 101, 182
Oriana Fallaci 229
Osama bin Laden 11, 23

P

Pakistan 24, 26, 57, 146, 234, 237, 250
Palestine 14, 17, 72, 105, 115, 116, 154, 172, 185, 189, 235, 255
Patrick Shen 35, 50
Paul Volcker 175
Peter Ferrara 86, 88

Phil. *See* Philip Harris
Philip R. Harris 53
President George W. Bush 18, 43, 47, 55, 57, 68, 74, 75, 85, 86, 88, 89, 91, 92, 113, 114, 116, 121, 145, 151, 153, 157, 163, 165, 175, 181, 182, 189, 190, 193, 215, 216, 217, 225, 233, 234, 238, 241, 242, 243, 261, 262, 286, 287, 292, 293
Press Manipulator of the Year 92
Prophet 58, 59, 134, 136, 271, 272

Q

Qatar 15, 19, 26, 109, 119, 127, 182, 234

R

Rapture 222
Red Brigade 83
Reporters sans Frontieres 239
Republican Guard 263
Resurrection City 206
Rice. *See* Condoleeza Rice
Rich Higgins 123, 157
Riyadh 23, 41, 83, 137, 275, 286
Robin Wright 164
Ruth Benedict 53

S

Saddam Hussain 85, 127, 128, 203, 210
Samar Fatany 278
Saudi Arabia 11, 12, 15, 19, 20, 26, 33, 39, 41, 83, 84, 91, 95, 101, 120, 127, 128, 137, 141, 143, 152, 161, 164, 206, 209, 210, 215, 216, 221, 226, 230, 234, 244, 247, 253, 254, 257, 258, 275, 276, 286
  Royal Family 12
Sean Hannity 164, 167
Security Council 18, 172
Sharm al-Sheik 119, 120
Sheldon Solomon 35, 49, 53, 95, 116, 157, 221
Shia 32, 59, 133, 134, 139, 244
Simon Graduate School 57, 84, 249
Slaughterhouse-Five 31
Spanish-American War 58
St. Catherine's Monastery 119
Stephen R. Covey 153
Steven D. Levitt 137
suicide bomber 21, 49, 51
Sunni 32, 59, 133, 134, 139, 285, 288
Supreme Court 67, 74, 88, 99, 113, 131, 205, 206, 230, 238
Susan B. Anthony 16
Syria 11, 128, 143, 153, 159, 165, 171, 172, 176, 185, 190, 234, 287

T

Tariq A. Al-Maeena 253
Telephone Game 117
Terror Management Theory 35, 36, 50, 54, 115, 116, 122, 157, 268
Teymour Adham 70, 71, 77
The Bible 45, 87, 247, 248, 267
The Chrysanthemum and the Sword 53
The 7 Habits of Highly Effective People 153
The Denial of Death 116, 122, 129

The Discoverers 87, 248
The Handmaid's Tale 51
the Hatfields and the McCoys 60
The King's New Clothes 219
The Long Emergency 151
The New York Times 127, 233, 263
Theodore Roosevelt 152
The State of the World Liberty Index 233, 234
The Twentieth Terrorist 163
Thomas Jefferson 205
Tiananmen Square 69
Treaty of Versailles 261
Tsunami of Blood 11, 12, 13, 39, 85, 99, 104, 137, 141, 149, 163, 164, 171, 193, 196, 201, 211, 217, 276, 283, 291, 292, 293

U

U.S.S. Annapolis 223
U.S.S. Maine 58
United Nations
UN 18, 123, 172
United States 11, 13, 14, 15, 16, 17, 18, 21, 27, 29, 32, 33, 39, 40, 41, 42, 47, 48, 50, 58, 61, 62, 63, 67, 68, 69, 70, 71, 74, 75, 76, 77, 78, 81, 86, 87, 99, 101, 103, 104, 113, 114, 121, 122, 123, 127, 128, 129, 131, 135, 137, 141, 147, 149, 151, 152, 153, 155, 157, 158, 163, 164, 165, 171, 172, 176, 177, 181, 182, 186, 189, 191, 193, 199, 205, 206, 209, 210, 211, 214, 215, 216, 217, 226, 227, 229, 230, 234, 238, 239, 240, 241, 243, 244, 245, 251, 257, 258, 259, 260, 261, 262, 265, 267, 276, 280, 281, 283, 285, 286, 287, 288, 292

V

Vancouver Museum 139
vendetta 133, 139
Vice President Cheney 182
Vietnam War 106, 283

W

Wall Street Journal 26
Washington 12, 17, 44, 105, 107, 125, 155, 164, 181, 193, 205, 206, 251, 265, 272, 279, 285
Washington Post 12, 44, 125, 164, 181, 193, 251, 279
White House 50, 153, 154, 155
William Randolph Hearst 58
Wolfert Gerritsen Van Couwenhoven 40, 213
Women 33, 205, 276
Words Matter 12, 15, 18, 25, 29, 35, 49, 84, 100, 111, 116, 126, 135, 267, 268, 271, 276
World Trade Center 96, 177, 201, 221
World War II 53, 73, 100, 104, 116, 172, 177, 233, 257
www.wordsmatter.tv 9, 12, 25, 36, 50, 57, 83, 84, 275, 276

About the Author

Skip Conover is an international business executive, with more than three decades of living and working overseas. He has built successful businesses in Japan, the Republic of Korea, India, Pakistan, and Saudi Arabia, in addition to his home base in the United States. In July 2005, he formed Words Matter, LLC as a vehicle for addressing the many problems he sees coming in the Middle East, thanks to the myopic behaviors of too many politicians.

In addition to writing *Tsunami of Blood*, Mr. Conover produces a weekly television program, *Words Matter*, and has launched the Words Matter Radio Network (http://www.wordsmatterradio.net), as a further means for individual citizens to enhance the debate about major political issues. You can hear the author's reading of this book at the "On Demand" stream.

Mr. Conover is a graduate of Hamilton College (B.A. 1968). He has been an attorney since 1975, receiving a J.D. from The State University of New York in 1974. He also holds an M.B.A. from The William E. Simon Graduate School of Business Administration at The University of Rochester, and was honored as a Distinguished Alumnus in 2005.

Skip also served in the US Marine Corps where he was awarded the Bronze Star Medal with Combat "V" for Vietnam Service. Mr. Conover retired, after 20 years in the Fleet Marine Force Reserve, as a Lieutenant Colonel, in 1991.

Skip's insights continue in his blog at **www.tsunamiofblood.com**.
And vistit his websites: **http://www.wordsmatterradio.net**
http://www.wordsmatter.tv.

www.ingramcontent.com/pod-product-compliance
Lightning Source LLC
Chambersburg PA
CBHW020813300326
41914CB00075B/1729/J
9780615139784